Behind Jagged Edges

of

Silhouette Trees

Behind Jagged Edges

of

Silhouette Trees

A Novel

Stacy E. Rogers

Behind Jagged Edges of Silhouette Trees

Copyright 2024 by Stacy Elena Rogers

All rights reserved.

ISBN 9798218457549 (Paperback)

Printed in the United States of America

Stacy E. Rogers Publishing, LLC

www.stacyelenarogers.com

For those who sought safety through silence,
and those who dared to speak up…

this is for you.

A'isha

"*Education*? What education!? You will not just take off and travel the world like some crazy person!" her father screamed; his words soaked in a thick Arabic accent. "You will stay here in Morocco, marry Samir, and raise a farm and family like every good Muslim woman is expected to do! Inshallah!"

"But Baba, that is not the life I want for myself! That is not who I am."

"Then who are you? Tell me! In the name of Allah, who do you think you are? What kind of girl is living under my roof!" he hollered, approaching her with his hand raised above his head, ready to strike. A'isha stood in a corner of her bedroom, glaring at her father.

"What is going on in *here*?" her mother asked in a hushed tone, afraid the village might hear a commotion in her household, yet again. She pushed open the door to the bedroom A'isha shared with her younger sister, Basha. A space confined by clay walls of ginger tint and a small window that welcomes a splash of midday sun filtered through chicken wire mesh.

"Nabeel! Nabeel! Please don't!" Aaminah yelled, grabbing her husband's arm.

He yanked his arm away. "I will no longer accept her disrespect for our home! She refuses to clean or learn how to cook. She cannot even prepare a simple tagine dinner like Basha." He glanced at her feet. "She doesn't even remove her shoes at the door! All she wants to do is play dinifri with Tayseer's sons or talk with that girl—what's her name? Saira!" His saliva splattered on A'isha's face; the pungent smell of mint tea and nicotine on his breath made her nauseous. "You are fifteen years old!" he yelled. "*You*, A'isha, should be in the kitchen with your mother, learning to cook dijaj and harira for your future husband and children."

"I don't want a future husband! I don't want children! I want to study at the jamiya in Fez. I want to leave these boring mountains. There is a world bigger than Morocco, Baba, and I want to see it."

Nabeel glared at his oldest daughter, clenching his teeth. He inhaled deeply, expanding his barrel chest and exposing with each breath a tuft of gray hair at the rim of his collar. He thundered out of her bedroom, leaving his wife and daughter in the wake of his rage. Locking her eyes onto the tattered green tapestry at the foot of A'isha's bed, doing what she could to avoid the plea in her daughter's eyes, Aaminah followed her husband and quietly closed the door.

A'isha yanked off her hijab, threw it onto the floor, and stomped on it with her rubber-soled sandals, leaving imprints of dirt from the roads of Ouirgane, the rural Amazigh village she called home. A village of huts built with hand-molded bricks of straw and honey-colored clay that hang onto slopes of unpaved roads tucked into the bosom of the High Atlas Mountains. A village defined and contained by a patchwork of fertile soil, apricot in hue, which is farmed and fed by a mild, seasonal rain. Freckled with juniper bushes, almond trees, and bountiful sprays of wild mint and thyme, the blend of aromas mingles with the thinness of air and is intoxicating to the rare European who appears in search of a thrill.

In these mountains, the traditions of the Imazighen ancestors are honored by generations of families who live communally, sharing livestock, harvest, and milk, following Allah's command. They mount mules to carry generous portions of produce to the nomadic tribes who reside on a plateau, living on the fringe of existence, huddled in tents of cowhide and burlap, nestled in humility and resting in hope. The Imazighen of Ouirgane live with the absence of electricity and plumbing, unburdened by amenities, and life unfolds in rhythmic ease to the gurgle and soft flow of the Oued Nfis, a freshwater river sustained by the snowcaps of the High Atlas Mountains. The river quenches the villagers' thirst and assists in their routine of life. It is where the women, clothed in colorful kaftans and hijabs, walk with palm-woven baskets upon their heads and babies wrapped onto their backs. They gather at its banks to wash clothes, bathe their children, and sip sweet mint tea as they watch the sun move across the sky, sharing laughter, storytelling, mythmaking, and gossip.

A'isha plopped on her bed and stared at the ceiling, then jumped up, grabbed the World Book encyclopedia off her dresser, flipped through the pages, slammed the book shut, and plopped back on her bed. *I'll study in America!...Or should I go to India?* Tapping her fingers impatiently on the wooden stool that separated her bed from Basha's, she glanced up at the lamp given to them by Amir, her father's close friend and business partner, in celebration of Eid al-Fitr.

When A'isha was an infant, Amir and Nabeel scraped together as many dirhams as they could borrow and save and bought a small storefront between the butcher and barbershop in the heart of the village. They quickly became known as the best seamstress and cobbler in the High Atlas Mountains, although competition was sparse. The Imazighen from the villages of Asni and Anraz would bring their sandals, slippers, and saddles to Nabeel for repair; and the merchants of Marrakesh would drive an hour's journey into the red hills of Ouirgane to buy the colorful abayas carefully sewn and beaded by Amir, then return to the massive medina of Marrakesh to sell them for a profit.

A'isha loved Amir. To him she would turn, seeking the compassion her father lacked. Amir had a way of making A'isha feel understood and accepted. Often, he would stand behind Nabeel, nodding at A'isha, encouraging her to tell her father she wanted to go outside to shoot marbles with the boys rather than play in a dollhouse with her sister. And whenever she proudly declared, "I'm going to travel the world!" and her father would laugh and wave her away, Amir would toss a glare at Nabeel, then turn to A'isha and say, "With Allah's guidance, you can do anything you want with your life." Desperately, she wanted to believe Amir, but her father's actions always spoke louder and would chase her away from their kitchen table, wrestling with frustration and doubt.

A'isha smiled as she thought of Amir, but her face quickly fell into a frown as she glanced at the worn copy of the Qur'an next to the lamp. Her aunt gave it to her to mark her first completion of Ramadan when she was twelve.

"Thank you for giving this to A'isha!" her mother had exclaimed as she hugged the Qur'an and planted a kiss on each cheek of her sister-in-law's heavily powdered face.

"Just be sure she reads it," A'isha's aunt replied as she folded her arms, sternly looking at her niece. "It will help her grow up and understand the life of a Muslim woman. It was helpful to me, and it will be helpful to her. Inshallah!"

"Of course, she will read it, won't you, A'isha?" her mother had replied as she flipped through the Qur'an and hurried toward her daughters' bedroom, carefully placing the gift on the stool where it remained, read only by Basha.

A'isha shook her head rapidly as if to shake away the memory of that night. Everyone had discussed her future and never asked if she had hopes and dreams. She felt invisible.

Rolling her eyes, she turned her attention to the Mu'addin. *Hmm, call for prayer. It must be noon.* She turned onto her side, curled into a fetal position, and envisioned her father placing his white silk taqiyah upon his head, then unfurling his sajadah at the foot of his bed, facing it eastward, toward Mecca. And she imagined her mother sitting solemnly at the kitchen table, chin resting in the palm of her hand, sipping freshly brewed mint tea, her brow creased with concern.

"Allahu Akbar, Allahu Akbar." A'isha listened to the adhan, amplified from the mosque's minaret, and frowned at the thought of her father. *By now, Baba is in salah, kneeling on his shins and knees, bowing in submission and humility. His forehead is touching the sajadah, and he is whispering the adhan to himself,* "Allahu Akbar, Allahu Akbar." Allah is the Greatest, Allah is the Greatest.

A tear trickled onto her pillow. *If Allah is the Greatest, then maybe He will understand my problem and help me. Allah, please tell me what I should do. Should I take Saira's advice? Should I tell my mother? Do you even listen to someone like me, Allah?*

Tsewang

Yawning, Tsewang brushed dust off the hem of his scarlet kasaya. He adjusted its drape over his shoulder, tightened the sash, and inhaled, deeply, the cool air of dawn. He stood barefoot on the splintering, red-painted steps of Pali Sholing, a monastery perched high upon a bluff in the Himalayan Mountains in the Kingdom of Bhutan. He gazed at the lush valley below, thinking about his mother.

Pali Sholing became Tsewang's home eight years ago. His mother commissioned him to the State two months shy of his seventh birthday, claiming she could no longer care for him, the fourth of her six children and the younger of her two sons. He was removed from his home by an official who impatiently pried his thin arms away from his mother's thigh, placed his hand over the child's mouth to muffle his screams, and shoved him, along with his small burlap sack, into a rusting black Toyota.

Without removing his sunglasses, the official had peered at Tsewang from the rearview mirror, disgusted by the frail boy whose silken black hair hung just above his swollen eyes. He was slumped at the window, looking toward the sky. He had listened to Tsewang whimper and whisper, "Mother, why? Mother, why?"

as he was driven away from his village, and away from his beloved dog, Nugai. It was a gray day in October, a time when the sun struggles to shine, the winds unleash a low, hostile howl, and an icy chill warns that the harshness of winter is near. The official had not uttered a word to the child as he drove through the forested slopes of Bhutan. Tsewang had wondered where he was being taken, and he wondered why. He searched his mind for a vision of his father and found a vague memory of him.

His father, addicted to betel nut, the euphoric stimulant that grows abundantly in the mountains of Bhutan, often disappeared into the forest for days at a time, seeking to escape the version of a man he was expected to be, leaving Tsewang's mother to care for their children with empty hands and a broken heart. When Tsewang was five years old and able to count, forty-two days passed before he was willing to accept his father's absence and cease awaiting his return.

"Do you think a snow leopard ate him?" he would often ask his siblings.

"No, Tsewang," his oldest sister, Takuma, would say. "Father is in the forest looking for betel nuts. Finding betel nuts is more important to him than we are. It is truth."

As Tsewang sat in the black Toyota, he watched the forest flash by with a speed that spoke to the official's determination and resolve. He felt the distance from his family grow and he thought about the previous night. He recalled its darkness, pierced by a sliver of moonlight that stretched toward him through the slats of cedarwood that defined his family's one-room abode. And with all his might he tried to embrace, for one last time, the warmth and safety he felt as he lay next to his five siblings on a bed of bamboo reeds covered in yak skin and sheep's wool. As the official swept the car around a sharp bend, Tsewang thought about the betel nuts, he thought about the snow leopard, and he thought about his father. His absence troubled Tsewang more deeply than he ever allowed anyone to know, and although he adored his sister and wanted to believe her words, he often asked himself this one question: *Did Father leave because of me?*

✳✳✳

"There you are! I was looking all over for you. You left your alms bowl in the bathroom. Here, I washed it for you."

"Ah, thank you, Tadashi. Now, have you seen my sandals? I know I left them right here on this step."

"What has gotten into you lately, Tsewang?" Tadashi asked, sifting through the pile of sandals. "You have been so very absentminded—more than ever. Here they are. These are yours, yes? They are the only pair that appears to have been chewed by a wild dog."

"Yes, those are mine. Thank you, again, my friend."

"Place them behind the bush so that you may find them upon our return," Tadashi panted. "I mean really, Tsewang, what is the matter?"

"Let us walk or we will be late for pindapata."

"Well, my friend, we would not be able to join the procession without your bowl. I mean, what would you collect your alms with? Your hands?"

They walked away from the monastery, playfully bumping shoulders. The strength of Tadashi's stocky, rotund physique caused Tsewang's tall and lanky frame to stumble. They muffled their laughter as they hurried toward the monks who were walking in a single formation, barefoot and cloaked in burgundy robes. Each holding an alms bowl in their right hand, humility bowing their shaven heads. The elderly and the young lined the roads of Paro, offering the monks of Sholing a dash of buckwheat and freshly picked figs. The chimes of Buddhist temples echoed across the valley, and a solemn chant revealed the spirit of a people shrouded in the scent of jasmine and veiled in the mist of early morning fog.

Tadashi had entered the monastery one month after Tsewang. Before his arrival, he had watched his mother light incense and pray to Buddha daily, asking that He remove this child, her youngest of three, from the destitution that defined her life. She asked that this child be spared the hunger that stole sleep from her two older children, causing them to cry tears she could no longer wash away. Sending him to live in a monastery would mean this child could be saved, but it would also bring honor to the family and make her proud.

She begged her older brother, Doijin, who joined a monastery in the city of Thimphu at the age of twelve, to request his guru's help in enrolling Tadashi at Pali Sholing. She chose this monastery for her son because she wanted him to remain in the village of Paro so he could be close to home. After weeks of awaiting a reply, just days after Tadashi's family celebrated the eighth year of his birth, Doijin returned with good news: the Rinpoche, their spiritual leader, had welcomed the child to Pali

Sholing. His mother explained that this good fortune was a sign of his karma and that he would only upset Buddha and Mahakala, the Deity of Protection, if he refused to leave. The sparrows sang, cranes took flight, and the sun glistened across the Himalayas the day Tadashi arrived at the monastery with his mother, uncle, and older brother.

Like Tsewang, Tadashi had vague memories of his father. For he, too, had abandoned his family for reasons that remained unspoken. But whenever thoughts of his father arose and filled his mouth with an acrid taste of bile, he would rub his mala beads and thank the loving Buddha for blessing him with his uncle, Doijin.

"You're right, Tadashi," Tsewang sighed as they approached the monastery, their alms bowls filled with the morning's offerings. "I have been more forgetful lately. I don't know what's wrong with me." He plopped onto the stairs and dusted the soles of his feet before slipping them into his sandals. "I can't seem to remember anything. I awaken in the middle of the night. I can't sleep, thinking about this and that, and then I'm so sleepy all day."

Tadashi stared at his friend, listening closely, softly chewing a fig. He searched Tsewang's face, looking for the spark in his eyes, seeking the optimism, the energy, the zest for life he once possessed.

"I want to go down to the river," Tsewang said, dismissing himself from his thoughts.

"Let us leave our bowls in the kitchen. It will be to the delight of the others."

Tadashi slipped his feet into his sandals, glanced down at his bowl, and frowned. He placed two figs in his mouth and reluctantly climbed the stairs. They brought their bowls into the kitchen, placed them on the counter, and, as they exited the massive red doors, Tadashi paused, raised his hand, and anxiously whispered, "Wait one moment!" He lifted his kasaya to his knees, ran back to the kitchen, grabbed a handful of figs, and stuffed two into his mouth for good measure.

Standing on the pebbled pathway, Tsewang looked up at his friend. His lips tightened as he watched Tadashi descend the stairs, chewing in delight. "Did you leave any for the novices, or did your greed take over again?"

"I'm not being greedy," Tadashi mumbled. "And no, I didn't leave any for them. I've told you before"—he gulped— "we're not obligated to share our alms with them. They collect their own."

In silence, they walked along the dirt road that bordered the gushing waters of the Paro Chhu River, a tributary of melted snow from the glaciers of neighboring Tibet.

"Tadashi," Tsewang said, gazing at the river.

"Yes, Tsewang?" he replied, savoring the sweetness of his final fig.

"We have been here for eight years. I have not seen my family since I arrived. They haven't even bothered to visit me."

"Are you forgetting we're not allowed visitors? Not even a letter. My family lives right here in Paro, and I've not seen them either."

"I know," Tsewang huffed. "But I wonder what my mother looks like now. I wonder if her hair has turned gray like my grandmother's hair used to be. I wonder if she is well."

Tadashi laughed and puffed out his cherubic cheeks. "Or maybe she is fat and bald like Buddha."

"When will you ever be serious about anything, Tadashi? Really! You think everything's funny. Why is that?"

"Because in everything, there *is* something funny. That is if you allow yourself to see it."

"You think so, eh? Do you think there's something funny in the way we live? With the rats and cold oats and the fleas? You think it's funny that we sleep on the floor?"

"On mats," Tadashi interjected.

"On mats on the floor! What difference does it make?"

"Well, weren't we sleeping on the floor when we lived with our families? And weren't we hungry in our mothers' homes, too? At least in this place, we are sure to have a morning meal before puja."

"Yes," Tsewang replied, "but at least we were with our mothers and our sisters and brothers. At least I had my dog, Nugai." He blinked away tears. "And at least, we didn't have to put up with…"

"With what?" Tadashi asked, turning in the opposite direction, away from Tsewang and the river. He gazed at the rolling hills of Paro Valley, its slopes and meadows freckled with honeysuckle bushes and magnolia trees. On a bluff high above the gushing river, he watched a solitary woman with two long braids of black hair sitting on a stool, nestled in an array of wildflowers, plum blossoms, and white clematis, near a cozy hut made with timber and stone. She was squeezing the udders of a mooing cow and filling a bucket with milk, as her lips moved softly to words of a song Tadashi could not hear.

"Tell me, Tsewang. I am waiting, put up with what?"

"When we were younger, Tadashi, did they not come into your room at night?" Tsewang turned to look at his friend. "While everyone pretended to be asleep. Did they ever?"

"Who, Tsewang? Who do you speak of?" Tadashi asked, gazing at the woman.

"Why do you pretend to not know what I am saying? Have we not played this charade long enough? This game of pretense we have been forced to play since I was seven and you, eight."

Tadashi gazed at the woman.

Tsewang grabbed his arm, causing the drape of his kasaya to slip off his shoulder. He forced Tadashi to look at him. They faced each other, standing inches apart. Neither spoke as they stared into each other's eyes, mouths slightly opened, feeling on their faces the warmth of each breath, unable to find the words that would reveal their thoughts.

"I…I…Oh, Tsewang! Why do you insist on making life so difficult for yourself?"

"Me? Are you blaming *me* because I choose to be truthful? Because I choose to name the nameless? We have been taught that to become a monk, we must practice Satya—that we must live in truthfulness. Such hypocrisy! It is not I who makes life difficult. If you want to blame someone, blame Buddha. He is the one who professed the importance of Satya, not I."

"Sometimes, my friend," Tadashi replied, adjusting his robe, "the nameless should remain as such—nameless." He gently placed his hand on Tsewang's shoulder. "And by doing so, we can surely honor Satya, we can live in truthfulness. And when we honor Satya, we honor yet another important virtue: acceptance, the path of non-resistance."

Tadashi released Tsewang's shoulder and returned his attention to the woman up above. He watched her walk with the bucket of milk in one hand and a rope in the other, leading her cow across the meadow, toward the hut.

"Tsewang," Tadashi said softly, gazing at the woman, "you must remember that the root of all suffering is our resistance to what is. When you begin to simply accept what is, you will no longer suffer."

Tsewang blew air through puckered lips, frustrated by the tension he held for Tadashi, weighed with the sadness he held for himself, and exhausted by the fear he held for the boys in the monastery who are forced to sustain the charade of not naming the nameless.

"Now, we must return to the monastery," Tadashi said. "It is nearly time for our midday meditation, and we must not be late. Let us go."

A'isha

"A'isha! There you are. Saira has been looking for you. Did you not hear her calling your name?"

"No, Basha, how could I hear her or anything else with the Mu'addin blaring out the Zuhr?" A'isha crinkled her nose and mocked him with a whine, "Alaaaahuuuu Aaakbaaar Alaaaahuuu Aaakbaar."

"A'isha, quiet! You will trouble Baba if he hears you."

"I don't care. I'm tired of living my life to please him—him *and* Allah. I want to leave these mountains. There is nothing here for me," she said, throwing herself onto her bed, and tossing her arms above her head.

"Nothing?" Basha replied coyly, easing onto her own bed. "What about Saira? You wouldn't want to leave her, would you?"

A'isha propped herself on her elbows and looked keenly at her sister. She often wished they were closer, that she could talk to her sister the way she could talk to her best friend, Saira. She loved her sister but envied her beauty; she always felt ugly in her presence. She envied the gleam in her mother's eye whenever she looked at Basha, and often wondered, *where is that gleam when Mother looks at me?* She envied the pride her father held in his voice whenever he spoke to the neighbors about the baghrir or couscous Basha prepared the night before, and would wonder, *where is Baba's pride when he speaks of me?*

"I wouldn't want to leave any of you," A'isha said, returning her attention to Basha, "but I have dreams that will take me far away from here."

"Like where?"

"I don't know…maybe to the university in Fez, or even to other countries. Basha, don't you want to leave Ouirgane one day?"

"No, I want to stay here and become a good Muslim woman and raise a family with my husband like Baba and Ommi want us to."

"I guess that's why they love you more than they love me. You're willing to follow their commands, and I cannot."

"It is not their command. It is the command of Allah. And they don't love me more than you, A'isha, you just give them trouble. If you do as they say, you will not have problems with Baba. You cause it for yourself by being stubborn. You should just…"

A'isha studied Basha as she spoke. *She is much prettier than me. Her nose is narrower than my bubble nose, and her hair and skin are softer than mine. And although she is short and chubby and I am tall and skinny, she is more feminine than me. She likes to play with dolls, and I like to play dinifri with the boys. She likes to cook, and I like to run and jump and climb. She likes to stay close to home, and I like to run across the valley and walk in the forest. We are so different. It is no surprise we are not close.*

"…and then you would have no problems," Basha said, brushing lint off her navy-blue abaya. She looked up at A'isha. "Are you even listening to me?"

"Basha, you can blame me all you want, but if Baba and Ommi would just listen to me and accept me for who I am, then maybe we wouldn't argue like we do."

"Well, I didn't come in here to talk about your problems. I came to tell you that Saira is looking for you. She said her mother is sending her to gather mint and she wants you to help her." She picked up her sister's hijab from the floor, brushed off the dust, and handed it to her.

"Uggh!" A'isha huffed. "I'll find Saira. I know where she is." She tossed the soiled hijab into her laundry basket, ran her fingers through her hair, and covered her head with another one from her dresser drawer.

"But before you go looking for that girl," her mother said, entering their bedroom, "you must go to your grandmother's home. I want you to bring her a plate of the pastilla Basha made for us last night."

"Yes, Ommi."

"Basha, you stay here with me," Aaminah added, tying an apron around her slender frame. "The goat needs to be fed and the chicken coop needs to be cleaned."

"But I cleaned it just yesterday. Can't I go with A'isha to visit Jida? I have not seen her since Laylat al-Qadr."

"No, you will stay here with me and do as I say."

"Yes, Ommi," she frowned.

The sisters looked at each other as their mother straightened the tattered mat between their beds with her toes, then walked away.

"The goat needs to be fed," A'isha whined, mimicking her mother. She rolled her eyes and stuck out her tongue.

Basha muffled her laughter with her hand. "Stop, A'isha. She's going to hear you."

"Who cares?" A'isha growled, kicking the rug under her bed. "Let me take your *delicious* food to Jida before Mother begs Allah to strike me dead. I'll see you later."

A'isha walked along the dirt copper road, balancing the basket of food upon her head. The cool air soothed her skin and drew her attention toward the rugged mountains. *It's September. Winter will be here in two months. I wonder if it snows in Fez. I wonder if the students at the jamiya wear a uniform.*

She placed the basket of food onto the ground and kneeled to tighten the straps on her sandals. She snapped her head up at the sound of laughter and noticed two girls approaching. One of them was carrying a basket of lime upon her head, while the other was holding a rope, leading a donkey flanked with two sacks of walnuts.

"As-salamu alaikum," A'isha called out, smiling wide-eyed. She grabbed the basket off the ground and hurried toward the girls.

"Wa-alaikum salaam," the girls replied.

"My name is A'isha! What's your name? I walk this path at least once a week and I never see anyone on it."

"I'm Meena," the younger girl replied. She placed the basket on the ground and sprung up, tugging on her lavender abaya, tight against her large bosom and pudgy arms. "And this is my sister. We are from Asni, but she lives in Ifrane where she attends university."

"Salaam. My name is Nadesh," the older girl said, placing her hand over her heart with a slight bow. She stood tall and thin with caramel skin, and her eyes revealed a wisdom that contradicted her shy smile.

A'isha was speechless. *Maybe Allah does listen to girls like me! Surely, it is a gift from Him that I would meet such a pretty girl on this road…and one who is not a mountain goat like me, but a girl who attends a university!*

"Where are you going?" asked Meena.

"To my jida's house."

"Oh, so you're from this village?" Nadesh asked.

"Yes. I have lived here all my life. But why are *you* here?"

"We're visiting my aunt," Nadesh replied.

"It's amazing that you have family here and we have never met," A'isha said. "What is your aunt's name?"

"Her name is Hira. Do you know her?"

"No, I don't think so, but my jida may. This village is small, and everyone knows each other. Not because it's small, but because everybody's nosy."

The sisters giggled. "Our brother usually brings Aunt Hira to our home," Nadesh said, "but he is in Rabat, training for the military. So, we came to her instead. Ouirgane is a pretty village."

"Yes, pretty boring," A'isha huffed. "So, which university do you attend? I want to go to the jamiya in Fez."

"What do you wish to study?" asked Nadesh.

"I'm not sure, but what I do know is I want to travel the world. I want to experience different cultures, but my father wants me to stay here in Ouirgane and," she deepened her voice, mimicking him, "'raise a family and farm like a good Muslim woman!'"

"You're funny!" Meena chuckled.

"Anyway, that's the life *he* wants me to live, but that is not who I am."

"It is unfortunate your father does not encourage you or accept you for who you are," Nadesh replied. "My father is quite the opposite. He is an engineer at the military base and he has always expected my siblings and me to attend the university."

"But I don't want to leave," Meena said. "I want to stay close to Mother. If I leave, she will be alone."

"Meena, she will be with Father. She will never be alone. Now, pick up the basket. We must go."

As A'isha listened to them, she thought about her conversation with Basha.

"Nadesh," she said, propping the basket on her hip, "I have two more years until I can leave. Can we keep in touch? You know…in case I need some advice about…about university life. May I write to you?"

"Sure, you may! In fact, I would love that. I'm at Al Akhawayn, the university in Ifrane. Your school librarian can give you the address. Oh, and my surname is Bashir." She furrowed her brow. "Will you remember all of this?"

"Of course, I will. I have researched Al Akhawayn; it has a good sociology program."

"Yes, it does. But if you forget my surname or the name of the university, you can always go to my aunt's house." She pointed at a canopied path. "She lives just over this hill."

"Thank you," A'isha said, placing her hand over her heart.

"You are quite welcome. And remember, if it is Allah's wish for you to leave Ouirgane, you will. Just pray to Allah for guidance and He will lead you. Inshallah."

"Yes, Inshallah!" A'isha beamed and waved goodbye.

"I'm so excited!" A'isha shrieked, pushing open the door to her grandmother's home, causing it to swing back on its loose hinges and slam against the wall.

"A'isha!" her grandmother yelled, clutching the armrest of her chair.

"Oh, Jida, I'm sorry. I didn't mean to frighten you. As-salumu alaikum!" she said, planting a kiss on her grandmother's hollow cheeks.

"My child, you will put your grandmother into an early grave with such shock. What has you so excited?" she asked, closing the Qur'an and pushing it aside. "You act as if you have seen the light of Allah."

"No, Jida," A'isha laughed. "It's even better than that!"

"I want to hear all about it, but first I must relieve myself before I have an accident. You almost made me wet my pants."

A'isha watched her grandmother ease out of her chair, rubbing her thighs. Although Isir was plagued with arthritis, she had retained much of her youthful beauty. Her brown eyes were wide and alert; her crepey, bronze skin emitted a warm glow.

"I will return in a minute," she said, limping toward the door. "I have a surprise for you." She slipped her feet into her sandals, hurried out the door, and shuffled toward the outhouse hidden behind a fig tree at the far end of her yard.

A'isha plopped onto the dusty blue mat at the center of her grandmother's one-room abode. She leaned back on her elbows, stretched out her legs, and smiled at her thoughts of Nadesh. Looking around the room, she inhaled its warmth and soothing scent of cinnamon, and relived snapshots of time—seeing herself run toward this room, seeking safety. Since the age of eleven, it was this room A'isha would run to after an argument with her parents. Her grandmother would wipe away her tears, give her steamed goat milk flavored with a tab of butter, and offer her the solace of wisdom in the form of parables: "Allah could have made the world in one day, but he took seven. You must be patient, my child. Behind every cloud there is a silver lining, and after every storm a calm will follow. A'isha, you must have faith." Her grandmother's home was a source of comfort. It was the only place where she ever felt safe and accepted.

She sighed and looked at her grandmother's mattress, unevenly stuffed with fleece. Then, she swept her eyes toward the firepit, counting the logs her grandmother uses to prepare her meals and temper the cool air that swoops down from the mountains into her home. *Soon, she will need more.*

In this room, her grandmother raised her four daughters. But as a child, she had lived a nomadic life, moving with her parents and five siblings from one plateau to another, along the edge of remote Imazighen villages. Although communal families welcomed them, Isir moved with her parents to wherever the weather chased them, to places where fertile soil could be found. Friendships were difficult to sustain, so Isir often felt lonely, despite her siblings' constant chatter. As a youngster, she vowed to live a different life, one that would provide her own children with the stability she hungered for.

Upon marrying at the age of nineteen, she helped her husband build this room and in it, she raised A'isha's mother and her three aunts, one of whom died from Typhoid Fever at the age of two. Three days before the death of her youngest daughter, Isir's husband headed to the forest to gather timber, so he said, in anticipation of winter. But he never returned home. Isir soothed her aching heart by telling herself it was the drink that stole him away from her—not his mistress nor a leopard. And so, she vowed to remain in her home, hoping Allah would return her husband to her someday.

"So, tell me," her grandmother panted as she entered the room, "what has you so excited?"

"I met two girls from Asni and one of them attends the university in Ifrane. Her name is Nadesh."

"If they live in Asni," her grandmother asked, drying her hands on a frayed towel, "what are they doing here in Ouirgane?" She removed the pastilla and a jar of freshly picked berries from A'isha's basket.

"They're visiting their aunt. Their brother usually brings her to them, but he is at the military school, and so they came with their parents."

"What is the name of this aunt?"

"I don't remember, but they said she lives here, in Ouirgane."

"I see. Come, sit by the fire. I made your favorite—papaya juice and walnut biscuits."

"Oh, Jida, shukran!"

A'isha removed her sandals and sat in one of the wrought-iron chairs at the small wooden table next to the firepit. Her skin tingled from the embers' heat.

Isir smiled as she eased onto the chair, listening to A'isha say, "Yummy!" with each bite of the biscuit. Isir's moist eyes scanned A'isha's face and the strands of hair that escaped her hijab. She placed her hand upon her granddaughter's wrist.

"Your mother sent a note to me. One of Tayseer's sons delivered it…I can never remember that child's name. Anyway, the note said that you and your father got into another argument a few days ago. You have him sick with worry."

"It is not me who causes him trouble. I want to be honest with my baba and not pretend to be who I am not."

"What do you mean?" Isir asked. She sipped her tea.

"I…I don't know," A'isha said, lowering her eyes. "If I…"

"If you what, my child?"

She looked at her grandmother, winced at her tangled thoughts, and lifted the mug to her lips.

"In the Qur'an," Isir said, softly, "Allah tells us that a woman can become educated if that is her wish." Her husband's face flashed across her mind. "The Qur'an also tells us that the husband must support his wife and children, even if his wife is wealthy."

"But that is not my concern, Jida."

"Then what worries you?"

"What if I don't want a husband? What if I don't want children?"

"If that is so, you will break the lineage of this family and the tradition of Islam."

"And that is what I fear." She moved to the edge of her chair, gripping her mug. "I'm afraid I will become an outcast, and everyone will turn their back on me."

"Why don't you want a husband or children?"

"Because I…I…think I…" She slumped back into her chair and looked at the floor.

Isir stood up, groaning at the pain in her hips. "We all must figure out who we truly are," she said, stoking the fire. "Allah has made each of us different. We are not meant to be the same."

"I don't know," A'isha sighed, staring at a swirl of ashes the flames released. "I don't know what I believe anymore."

Her grandmother returned to the table. "A'isha, you must search your heart, and you will find the answer you seek. You must have the courage to be honest—first with yourself and then with Allah. But He already knows your struggle. He is just waiting for you to turn to Him."

A'isha looked at the fire, groping for the courage to tell her grandmother what she already knew. But shame prevailed and lowered her eyes.

"It is time for you to return home. Thank you for bringing the meal to me. I am sure it is delicious. Tell Basha I said so."

"Of course, it's delicious. Basha prepared it, how could it be anything else?" A'isha said, slipping her feet into her sandals.

Isir chuckled, pulling a cloth out of her pocket. She dabbed her eyes and held onto A'isha's arm until they arrived at the door.

"Goodbye, Jida," A'isha said, hugging her grandmother.

"Maa'a Allah. May God be with you," her grandmother whispered. She watched A'isha walk down the path until she approached the bend and could no longer be seen behind the wisp of the Tamarisk tree.

A'isha walked home with a reluctant gait, kicking pinecones along the way. Strolling along the river, she listened to its flow upon a bed of stones while gazing at the jagged edges of mountaintops etched against the blue sky. She picked up a twig of cedar and inhaled its earthy scent, pondering her grandmother's words, 'We must be true to who we are.'

"What does that mean?" she wondered, "to be true to who I am."

Tsewang

Tsewang and Tadashi hurried toward the monastery. In the eyes of the Rinpoche, lateness was among the greatest insults a monk could commit toward the monastic order. Tadashi stirred a trail of dusty soil with each step as he tried to keep up with Tsewang, but as usual, he was always a few steps behind his spry and long-legged friend.

"Will you eat your lunch today, Tsewang?" he asked, panting.

"No, you may have it again."

"The pounds you are losing, my friend, are the pounds I am gaining from eating two lunches each day," Tadashi replied, patting his paunch.

"Well, I am delighted that one of us has an appetite."

"I am hoping that your desire to eat will return to you someday soon, Tsewang."

"Yes, Tadashi. I, as well."

When they arrived at the monastery, Tadashi placed Tsewang's sandals next to his own and hurried up the stairs, following Tsewang through the massive red doors. They hurried down the drafty corridor, sprinting upon its warped and water-stained floor. They passed wooden doors of faded red hung loosely on rusty hinges; doors easily rattled by wind. When they arrived at the prayer room they bowed and sat upon cushions near the threshold. The room was filled. The novices and monks settled into silence as the chime of the tingsha bells vibrated. They closed their eyes and began to chant in slow and equal measure, the Sanskrit mantra for compassion, Om Mani Padme Hum.

The Rinpoche's chant thundered across the room as he meandered between rows of ordained monks. Tsewang kept a slight bow of his head, and through partially closed eyes he watched the Rinpoche walk toward the front of the room, close to the altar, where the youngest among the novices sat. He stopped and stood in front of a child named Bakti. Tsewang shook his head. *He is just seven years old.* The Rinpoche pushed his toe onto the boy's shin. The child kept his eyes closed and responded with a rigid nod. Bile eased its way up Tsewang's throat, filling his mouth with a burning bitterness of rage. Wiping away tears, he lowered his head and recited the mantra of compassion, Om Mani Padme Hum.

He forced himself to pray and he tried to meditate, but before Rinpoche placed the lotus flower upon the altar, and before the final clang of cymbals and chiming of the tingsha to signify the end of midday puja, Tsewang dashed out of the room. He ran down the dim and damp hall, unaware of the splinters piercing his feet or of the whispered calls for his return by his friend, Nanda. He bolted through the massive red doors and ran down the bluff toward the raging waters of the Paro Chhu River. Mud splattered onto his kasaya as he ran along the river's edge, and pebbles rolled, clinking beneath his feet. Tears streaked down his windswept face as he whimpered and wailed. He ran as fast and as far away from the monastery as he could, running to wherever his heart would lead.

Gasping for air, Tsewang arrived at a meadow of rolling hills laced with lilies and stalks of lavender. He continued to run across the meadow, to its center, where he stopped, stretched his arms and fists into the air, and squinted at the powder-blue sky. He screamed, "Buddha, why! Why do you cause us to suffer like this? Tell me, why do you teach us to believe karma exists when those who abuse us do not suffer as we do? Why do you allow this, Buddha? Why? Mahakala! You are the Deity of Protection! Our guardian. Why do you allow the children to suffer? To be robbed of our dignity by those who are supposed to care for us! Why? What have we done to deserve this, Buddha? We are just children! We try to obey your teachings. We honor you. But you do not protect us. You allow us to be mistreated by the very people who are supposed to love us. Why is this so?"

Tsewang fell to his knees, bowing to the deities in rageful submission. Ravaged by anger and sadness, he sank and lay on the ground. His body jerked and writhed as he grabbed and yanked at his kasaya, squirming and pounding his fists into the earth, sobbing uncontrollably, gasping for air. Images of his mother flashed before him, and he curled up, pulling his knees into his chest, overwhelmed by his longing for her embrace. He yearned to hear his mother's voice. Rocking back and forth, clutching his robe, he screamed, "Mother! Mother, where are you? Please, Mother, I need you!" Visions of his siblings flooded his mind, and he thought of his dog, Nugai. He pounded his fist into the ground. "Buddha! Lead me to my family!" he demanded. "Lead me to my family or I will find them on my own." Tsewang's tears flowed freely, like the waters of the Paro Chhu, and he lay in the meadow, hidden beneath stalks of lavender, upon a bed of lilies.

"Where have you been, Tsewang?" Tadashi asked, his voice bubbling with frustration as he followed his friend, passing the bedroom they shared with two newly arrived novices. Tsewang put his finger over his lips, motioning to Tadashi to stop talking. In silence, they tiptoed up the steep and narrow staircase that led to the attic, listening to the scurry and screech of rats within the hollow walls. Once inside, Tadashi eased the door into the jamb, whispering, "Please don't squeak," while Tsewang reached for the candle and matches they kept hidden high up on a rafter near a rusted vent. He lit the candle, stuck it onto a tin plate, and placed it on the floor. Then, he tiptoed across the wooden planks, splintered and unevenly spaced. He grabbed the mat they concealed between two beams, unfurled it with a firm shake, and plopped onto it with a grumble.

"Nanda and I have been looking all over for you," Tadashi said in a breathless whisper. "We were worried sick that you were lost in the darkness. You are in big trouble, my friend. Rinpoche wants to speak to you at once. You are lucky to have returned so late into the night. Surely, he is asleep at this hour."

"Asleep?" Tsewang said dryly, rubbing his feet, "Lucky man that he is, he should be dead."

"He knows you left puja before he rang the final chime. The sound of you running like a loon down the hall distracted Rinpoche so much that he dropped the lotus into the candle bowl instead of the water, and the lotus burned to a crisp. He is blaming you for destroying his offering to Buddha!"

"The poor lotus. It is Rinpoche that should burn to a crisp," Tsewang replied, pulling a splinter out of his foot.

"You missed dinner. You must be hungry. I hid a slice of bread for you in my pocket. I even smeared a bit of fig jam on it. Here, you must eat." He removed the wax paper and handed the bread to Tsewang.

"I do not want food. I want to leave this place. I am going to find my family."

"Find your *family*?" Tadashi said, placing the bread on the mat next to Tsewang. "And how do you suppose you will do that? You have not seen or talked to them in eight years. You don't know if they are in the same home or if they have even remained near Thimphu. And if they are still there, how will you know which path will lead you to them?"

"I will figure that out when the time comes." He stood up and faced Tadashi.

"So, you are telling me you will venture out into the forest without knowing which way to go? A snow leopard will eat you alive before nightfall."

Tsewang thought of the countless nights he had spent as a child, wondering if such was the fate his father had suffered. The thought produced an ache in his belly, still.

"I will find them," he replied.

"And when do you intend to leave this place, Tsewang?" Anger raised his voice. "This place that has been the only home you have known?"

Tsewang tightened his sash. "I am going to leave before morning puja, before the sun has a chance to rise."

Tadashi grabbed Tsewang's arm. He pulled him close and hugged him tightly.

"Please don't leave me," he begged. He lay his head on Tsewang's chest and cried. "Please, my friend, please do not leave me alone. You are all I have."

Tsewang stroked Tadashi's head and kissed his cheek.

"Please, Tsewang, do not leave me here, alone. What will I do without you?"

"Tadashi, I will always love you," he said, holding him closely, "and I will see you again."

They looked deeply into each other's eyes. Tears dripped onto their robes as they cried in silence. Tadashi kissed his lips, softly. Tsewang held his hand as he walked to the candle and blew on the flame. In the light of the moon, they lay on the mat and embraced for one last time.

As the sun transformed a charcoal sky into brushstrokes of turquoise and tangerine, roosters crowed, and cranes glided along glistening snowcapped peaks. Banners of colorful prayer flags danced in the wind. Bells chimed, cymbals clanged, and dungchen horns bellowed across the valley, beckoning novices and monks to rise for morning puja.

As he had every morning for the past six years, Tadashi called out to his friend before he opened his eyes, "Tsewang, Tsewang, are you awake my friend?"

But this morning, his friend did not reply.

A'isha

Sitting on a bolder across the road from her home, Saira watched A'isha saunter up the hill with her hands shoved into the front pockets of her yellow jumper.

"Why are you not wearing the hijab I made for you, A'isha?" Saira asked.

"I wear it all the time. Today I just chose this one, that's all." She plopped next to Saira and planted a kiss on her cheek while Saira tugged on her eyelashes and wiped dust from her eye. A'isha watched her, charmed by her beauty—her flawless champagne complexion, her high cheekbones, and her lips, bow-shaped and full. Like A'isha, Saira was tall and slender but moved gracefully with the stealth and poise A'isha lacked.

They watched an elderly man lead a mule up the hill, balancing sacks of olives on its back. With a swath of cloth that once was white, he dabbed beads of sweat off his creased and weathered brow. He nodded at the girls and whispered "Assalamu alaikum" as he passed them, hunched over, trudging up the slope and around the bend, dressed in a mahogany tunic coated with kicked-up dust of arid soil.

"Basha said you were looking for me," A'isha said. "Did you gather mint?"

"Yes, I waited for you. Where were you?"

"I had to take food to my jida." She hopped off the boulder and extended her hand to Saira. "Let's go for a walk."

Saira blushed as she placed her hand in A'isha's, concerned that her actions might reveal the truth of their friendship to the neighbors. But excitement trumped concern, and she was too enticed to let her go. They walked downhill, past A'isha's home, and arrived at an undulating path along the riverbank, where women veiled in black were washing clothes and bathing babies. Their suspicious eyes followed A'isha and Saira, coercing them to muster a smile and bow their heads in deference to women who made them feel exposed, dirty, and naked.

At a distance, they could see a group of boys playing dinifri near the forest edge, beneath needled arms of pine that lured the girls into a lush and mingling scent of nectar, honeysuckle, and wild. Their solitude reignited arousal between them, a familiar sensation they indulged in secrecy that made them feel alive and giddy. To A'isha and Saira, their love for one another was unquestionably natural, but they knew if the nature of their friendship were ever revealed, they would fall prey to the village's scorn, shun, and shame.

Together, they meandered down a canopied path of amber soil, deep into a thicket of juniper bushes and evergreen trees. Saira teased A'isha with a tug on her hijab and ran ahead with her friend in the chase. They flitted through the forest, ducking branches, and circling trees; the crackle of leaves and snap of twigs beneath their sandals filled the gaps between their laughter. They arrived at the small pond they often bathed in and placed their feet into the coolness of its emerald water. A'isha removed her hijab and laid it on the ground, then she removed Saira's. She scooped water into her palms to quench Saira's thirst, and then her own. Saira lifted her abaya and swayed her feet in the water as she watched A'isha scale a tree and gather in her hijab figs she would feed Saira, filling her with the sweetness of its flesh.

They cuddled on the damp soil, listening to a blend of birdsong and silence. A'isha moved her fingers through Saira's hair and stroked her face with a loving touch. Embracing her with a gaze that relinquished a need for words, she caressed Saira's lips lightly with her own. They marveled at the ease with which nature unfolds—a colony of ants carrying fragments of bark, the intermittent hop of a lone frog, the flutter of a butterfly's wings. A shift in sunlight covered them with an evening shade and told them it was time to leave. They laced their sandals, brushed dust off their clothes, covered their heads with their hijabs, and walked out of the forest slower than they had entered. They arrived at their village as the adhan echoed from the minaret, "Allahu Akbar." Allah is the Greatest. Looking at each other, they inhaled deeply, then released it all with a subtle sigh.

"Where have you been, A'isha? Your sister is doing her homework. Have you completed yours?" her mother asked, stirring a steaming pot of lentil soup.

"Yes, Mother. I have a test in a few days; I will study tonight."

"Very well, because if you want to attend the university, you will need good grades."

"Yes, I know," she grinned, unable to mask the thrill in her voice. "I have just two more years before I can apply."

Her mother placed a lid on the pot and motioned for A'isha to sit with her at the table. She put her hand on her daughter's and said, "My child, I know your father does not encourage your dreams, but it is not because he doesn't love you. He loves you very much. He just wants you to follow the traditions of our ancestors and honor our culture. He is old-fashioned and set in his beliefs, so you must not argue with him."

A'isha shook her head. "But it isn't only Baba who refuses to support my dreams."

Aaminah released her daughter's hand. "Are you telling me that I don't either?"

"Mother, when have you ever?"

"A'isha, when have I not? Have I ever told you that you cannot go to the university?"

"No, but nor have you ever told me that I should. Mother, whenever Baba threatens to hit me or throw me out of the house when I say I don't want a husband, or that I want to leave Morocco, you never support me. You never speak up for me."

"But that does not mean I don't encourage your dreams. You must understand that I am from another generation, from the generation of wives who do not contradict their husbands— ever." Aaminah sighed. "No, I don't understand why you do not wish to marry, and I do not understand your friendship with Saira. Neither do I understand why you wish to leave Morocco, but I will never get in your way."

"Ommi, if you want to understand, why don't you ask me? Why don't you show that you care?"

Aaminah stared at A'isha and eased to her feet. "Maybe I already know the answers, but I'm just not ready to hear you tell me." She returned to the stove and stirred the steaming pot of soup.

Her words were as soothing to A'isha as they were unfamiliar, as it was a rare occasion that Aaminah showed any emotion, especially love. She provided her family with hot meals, clean clothes, and a tidy home, but conversations were as scarce as a warm embrace. Her father's disappearance when she was four, and her sister's death that same year, carved into Aaminah a sense of unworthiness borne of abandonment, and left her crippled with a fear that deadened her ability to sense the needs of others, including her own. For years, she witnessed her mother sit on a stool and gaze at the snowcapped mountains as she prayed to Allah for her husband's return. Trapped in despair, Isir remained unavailable to Aaminah and her sisters, even in the wake of their sibling's death. Often, Aaminah would tug on the hem of her mother's apron and tell her, "Mother, I am afraid," hoping her own grief would be lifted, and that her longing would be quelled by hope. But her wish was left unfulfilled, and then one day she no longer hoped for anything at all.

When A'isha entered her bedroom, Basha was not doing her homework, but reading the Qur'an. The sight filled A'isha with a mixture of sadness and rage, and the intensity of both was as alarming to her as it was freeing. She saw in her sister a dismissal of her potential, of her life's promise. At that moment, she wanted to grab the Qur'an out of Basha's hands, run to the side of the road, rip the pages from the bind, toss them into the valley below, and watch them float into the abyss. She wanted to return to the kitchen, grab that stupid ladle out of her mother's hand, clutch her shoulders, and shake her until her teeth rattled…until her heart opened and enabled her to simply feel. She wanted to return to her grandmother's home, push her goat aside, kick open her door, and yell loud enough for the ancestors to hear, "Get up, woman! Your husband will *never* return." And she wanted to run to the river, to the women whose eyes are all she sees, and lift their veil to release them from the imprisonment of hidden beauty. "You are free! You are free!" she would say, and she would dip their babies into the river and lift them above her head, offering them up to the ancestors who would bless them with the gift of acceptance and tell them, "You are loved." And she would return home to her mother, who would cradle her and tell her the same, at last.

"What is the matter with *you*?" Basha asked, watching A'isha stand at the doorway. "Why are you standing there, staring at me?"

"I…I was trying to remember where I left my textbook. Have you seen it?"

"Isn't it right there, on the dresser?"

A'isha removed her hijab, kicked off her sandals, lay on her bed, and opened her textbook. She heard her father enter the house, arriving from the shop later than usual. Without greeting his wife, he walked toward his daughters' bedroom. The stomp of his footsteps echoed throughout the house. He kicked open their door with such force that it slammed against the wall and swung shut before he could enter. He kicked it open again.

"A'isha, I just saw Josiah." His chest expanded and contracted rapidly as he tried to catch his breath between words that were ablaze with rage. He continued, "He told me that he and his friends saw you and that girl enter the forest. Could that be true?"

A'isha closed her textbook and moved to the edge of her bed. Basha sat up and eased toward the edge of her own.

"Tell me, A'isha, is it true?"

"Yes, Baba, it is true. Saira and I went for a walk after I returned from bringing food to Jida."

Slowly, he walked into their room, balling his fingers into fists. His knees touched hers as he looked down at her, extending his fingers and balling them into fists.

She tried to stand.

"Sit down!" he screamed. "And do you know what else Josiah told me? He said that he and another boy followed you into the forest, but you could not hear them because you and that girl were running and laughing like two wild hens until you arrived at the pond."

A'isha's eyes moved from her father's fists to the bedroom door, begging her mother to enter.

"Tell me, A'isha, what were you doing with that girl at the pond?" His voice was low, menacing. "Tell me!"

A'isha stood up and rushed toward the dresser, moving as far away from her father as she could.

"I'll tell you, Baba, if you want to know. I will tell you." Her eyes brimmed with tears. "Saira and I were lying together on the ground. I fed her figs and brushed her hair. What is so wrong with that, Baba, tell me. If you must know, I love Saira, and she loves me."

Aaminah appeared at the door. Basha stared at her sister, wide-eyed.

"What do you mean you '*love her*?'" her father asked, his face twisted with scorn.

"Exactly as I said, Baba. I love Saira. She is the reason why I do not wish to marry Samir. She is the reason why I don't want a husband."

"Are you telling me…" he squinted, tightening his fists, "that you are a…a…?"

Aaminah moved into the room and stood behind her husband, staring at A'isha.

"You are a disgrace to this family! The ancestors will curse you for your unclean ways—you *and* that girl. May Allah have mercy upon your soul."

Glaring at his daughter, he pointed to the door. "Get out," he said in a controlled rage. Saliva foamed in the corners of his mouth. "Get your things and get out of my house, now."

A'isha looked at her mother, silently begging her to say something. But Aaminah bowed her head and walked away.

Basha whispered, "Baba, please don't."

"Shut up, Basha!" he yelled, glaring at A'isha.

Tears streamed down A'isha's face as she picked up her hijab and gathered her uniform, schoolbag, and books. She slipped on her sandals and looked at her sister, trying to console her with a nod and faint smile. She walked to the front door, opened it, and stood at the threshold.

"Get out of here!" her father screamed. He pushed her onto the road and slammed the door shut. A'isha looked over her shoulder and gazed at the door, then lowered her head and entered a darkness, hollow and opaque, peering at the road ahead, defused by a moonlit sky.

Tsewang

Tadashi ran out of the attic and down the stairs toward the bedroom he shared with Tsewang. He pushed open the door and stared bug-eyed at the cubicle that once held his friend's toothbrush and soap. He spun around to check the hook that once held his kasaya. *Did Tsewang really leave me?* Panic surged through him. His heart banged against his chest. He swiped his forehead with the back of his hand, removing beads of sweat. His feet slapped against the wooden floor and his kasaya flapped in the wind as he sped down the vast corridor. He ran into the meditation room, spinning from side to side wildly with unblinking eyes. He rushed to the dining hall, gripping the door jamb with both hands to steady himself, frantically scanning the room, searching for his friend. The stack of wet breakfast bowls and burning sticks of frankincense on the altar informed him that he had missed morning puja. *What time is it?* Running toward the massive red doors, he saw at the end of the corridor, Rinpoche exiting his bedroom. Tadashi's panic morphed into an unbridled fear. He lowered his head and slowed his pace to a tentative, calculated walk.

"Tadashi," Rinpoche said, picking specks of lint off his burgundy kasaya, its sash tied loosely across his paunch, "you were not present for morning puja. Where were you?"

"I…I overslept, Rinpoche. I apologize. It will never h-h-happen again."

"Where are you running to?" he asked with a mocking smile.

"I…I am trying to join my brothers for pindapata."

"Pindapata? Without your alms bowl?"

He raised his brow. "That is right! I was looking for my bowl and that is why I am late."

"Are you sure it is your bowl that you seek? Or perhaps you are looking for your friend, Tsewang."

"Oh, no, Rinpoche. It is my alms bowl I am looking for."

"Ha! Well, if you're looking for Tsewang, do not waste your time. He is gone."

"Gone, sir? What do you mean?"

"Puran saw him leave this morning, before the sun touched the sky." He folded his arms and leaned on the door jamb. "I am told he had a bundle on his back and that he might have stolen bread and grains from the pantry. Do you know where he intends to go?"

"No, sir. I…I have no idea."

"Very well, do not fret," he yawned. "We are better off without him. He was not a good novice and besides, we now have one less belly to feed."

Tears welled in Tadashi's eyes. He lowered his head. "Rinpoche, I must leave if I wish to join the procession. Goodbye, sir."

"I will see you at midday puja. Do not be late."

Tadashi bowed and pushed open the massive red door. He walked slowly until he arrived at the bend in the road, then ran as fast as he could. He ran to the meadow, the only place he and Tsewang had ever felt safe, where they spent countless hours debating the principles of Buddhism—the virtues of acceptance and surrender, detachment and impermanence, the path of least resistance, and Samsara, the cycle of life.

Tadashi ran into the heart of the meadow and fell to his knees, hidden by stalks of lavender near the very spot where Tsewang had last lain. His soul was wretched over the loss of his dear friend. Vomit hurled out of his mouth. His body shook violently, wracked by the agony of Tsewang's departure, and by the despair he had harbored since his father's disappearance. Clutching his kasaya, he wailed, "Tsewang, why did you leave me? Why did you leave? Father, why did you leave? Where did you go? Why did…?" Birdsong picked up where his words trailed off, carried away by the soft breeze that caressed his soul and eased his breath back into his body.

He lay until the midday sun stung his face and awakened him to the clang of cymbals and the roar of dungchen horns, signaling the start of afternoon prayer. He peeled himself off the ground and walked along the gushing waters of the Paro Chhu River with his head hung low, pulling himself toward Pali Sholing. He stood at the base of its stairway and looked up at the massive red doors. He placed his foot on the step, paused, and turned toward the forest. He walked the path, scanning the soil in search of Tsewang's footprints. When he arrived at the forest edge, he paused and peered between the trees. Wiping his tears, he inhaled deeply and turned toward the monastery. As he ascended the steep, splintering stairs, he moaned and whispered, "Oh, my dear Tsewang…what have you done? What am I going to do without you?"

***

By midday, Tsewang was well into his journey. It was a warm day in April, and the sun sparkled upon snowcapped peaks as Alpine Swifts flapped their elegant wings of onyx and pearl across the powder-blue sky. Golden sunrays tossed silver shadows between soaring evergreen trees, touching the chestnut soil while pine needles scattered in the occasional swirl of a soft forest breeze. The screech of an eagle mingled with the rustle of leaves as Tsewang walked along a path, stopping to pluck figs and berries to quench his hunger. The rushing waters of the Paro Chhu faded into a distant din as he moved more deeply into the forest of the Himalayas.

Pushing aside branches of purple rhododendrons and dislodging his kasaya from the intermittent snag of juniper bushes, Tsewang created a path for himself where once there was none. Wandering in silence, he listened to the coo of a snow partridge and to the rhythm of his heart. The earthy scent of moist soil comforted him, and he inhaled deeply. Tsewang ascended and descended the steep slopes of the mountain, climbing and crawling along its terrain. As daylight transformed into dusk and an obsidian sky cloaked him in darkness, he curled under low-lying branches of evergreen trees and rested his head upon his burlap sack. The hiss and slither of a snake beneath deadened leaves, the grunt of wild boars, and the binturongs' clawing on tree trunks into a canopy of leaves punctured the silence and rattled the stillness as Tsewang lay there, listening, fear seizing his breath.

At dawn, he arose from a sleepless night, nibbled on bread he had gathered from the monastery, and continued his journey. He walked for hours without direction but with purpose. Thirsty and exhausted, he tossed his head back with a yawn and noticed a cluster of nuts in shades of yellow and brown that hung just under the fronds of palm. Tsewang dropped his sack, removed his kasaya and sandals, and scampered fifty feet up the tree. He plucked several and tossed them to the ground, then sat cross-legged and curiously examined each one. He chose the smallest and placed the bitter-tasting bean into his mouth.

Within minutes, a burning sensation surged through his body. An overwhelming sense of warmth and exhilaration caused him to urinate in his underpants. He gazed at the sky that seemed to shift from blue to purple to pink, and the trees appeared to sway without wind. Overcome by a burst of energy, he jumped up and ran wildly through the forest, leaving his kasaya, sandals, and sack behind. He laughed uncontrollably at images of a burping Buddha and the unclothed body of Rinpoche blown beyond the stars by a sudden gale. The euphoric effects of the betel nut lifted his sadness in a way that prayer and meditation never had, and he skipped among the trees, offering up his gratitude. "Thank you, Buddha," he said aloud. "Thank you for leading me to this magical medicine. I have never felt happier in my whole life! Thank you!" He danced and twirled and sang in a broken melody, the mantra of compassion, Om Mani Padme Hum.

But as the sunset pitched a blaze of honey upon the forest, fatigue set in, and his ecstasy wore off. Tsewang sat naked upon a boulder with his head hung low. *Is this the joy that Father sought? Is this the seed that caused him to become lost in the forest and abandon his children?* Tsewang returned to the betel nut tree, climbed its trunk, plucked several more, and placed them in his sack. He slipped his feet into his sandals, wrapped himself in his kasaya, tightened the sash, and lay under the tree.

The sun rose and the sun set…the seasons changed. Spring stretched into summer and Tsewang spent each day chewing betel nuts, spinning in ecstasy. At night, his fear would succumb to weariness, and he slept deeply, no longer fearful of the movement of wildlife that surrounded him. He remained close to the betel nut tree, plucking from it daily—not only for the bliss that distracted him from life but to quell the growing ache in his bones that beckoned his need for more.

The tree and betel nuts also conceived within Tsewang a closeness to his father that he had not felt since he was five, when his father bid farewell to his family and disappeared into the forest, "searching for betel nuts" as his sister, Takuma, often said. For Tsewang, that which stole his father from him became the link that reconnected them, and so he remained close to the betel nut tree. He slept beneath its branches and leaned against it for support when his twirls of ecstasy caused him to fall. And when his hunger pangs became too strong to ignore, Tsewang would leave the tree to gather figs and berries nearby, and promptly return to the tree to eat in its shade. He would lie on his back and rest his feet upon the trunk as he savored his fruit, gazing at the fronds of palm that protected him from the sun, and sometimes from the rain, wondering if his father could have cared for him the way he felt cared for by the betel nut tree. At times, he thought about Tadashi and the novices, wincing at pangs of guilt and sorrow. There were moments when he would think about his mother and whisper the names of his siblings.

But with each passing day, as his consumption of betel nuts intensified and became his sole focus, Tsewang's thoughts lingered less on his father, Tadashi, and all the boys he left behind. In time, he thought even less about his family, for whom he abandoned his monastic life to seek.

A'isha

"Grandmother, it's me, A'isha. Please open the door." Her plea was but a whisper obscured by the grunt of wild boars roaming the hills of Ouirgane.

"A'isha? Is that you?" Isir asked as she opened the door, wrapping her frayed terrycloth robe tightly around her thin frame, clutching it at her neck. "What are you doing out here at this hour?" An icy chill followed A'isha into the room, causing her grandmother to shiver.

"Oh, Jida!" A'isha shrieked. "Baba told me to leave."

"What do you mean he *told you to leave?*"

"He told me to get out of his house," she wailed, slumping into a chair.

"Look at me, child! What happened over there?"

A'isha peeled her schoolbag off her shoulder and dropped it onto the floor. The firepit's simmering embers flickered tangerine shadows across the room. Isir searched A'isha's face for an answer, then shook her head and huffed, "I don't understand why you and your father cannot live peacefully." She limped toward a tin box, poured milk into a pot, and hung it on a hook over the firepit. Stirring the milk, she listened to A'isha whimper.

"My child," she said, dropping a pat of butter into each cup, then easing into her chair, "tell me what happened."

"Baba was in a rage when he came home. He said Josiah saw Saira and me in the forest."

"When was this? When were you and Saira in the forest?"

"Earlier today, after I returned home from my visit with you."

"Hasanan taba…very well, go on."

"Baba screamed at me, asking what we were doing in the forest. And so, I told him."

"What did you say?"

"I…I…told him the truth." She lowered her head and wept, gasping between sobs.

Her anguish tugged at her grandmother's heart. She reached for A'isha's hand and held it. "What did you tell your father, my child?"

A'isha looked into her grandmother's eyes. "I told him the truth, Jida…that I love Saira. I told him why I do not want a husband or children. I told him I do not want to marry Samir because I love Saira."

"A'isha, are you telling me that you are—"

"Yes, Jida. I am not the same as other girls. I'm not the same as Basha. I do not like boys, Jida. I like girls."

Her grandmother stood up and yelped at the surge of pain in her hips. She tightened her sash and stoked the fire, gazing at the flames. She leaned the poker against the wall and returned to the table.

"A'isha, you are not telling me something I have not suspected. So, I will not pretend I am surprised—just as I believe your parents were not surprised." She chuckled. "I mean, they may have been surprised that you told them, but not by what you told them."

A'isha removed her hijab and eased back into her chair.

"So, what are you going to do, now?"

"What do you mean, Jida?" she asked, wiping her tears.

"You have declared who you are to your parents and Allah. I am sure everyone in Ouirgane will find out if they don't already know. You will be treated differently. They will disown you, A'isha. Not because of who you are, but because the Qur'an tells them it is what they must do. And so, I am asking you, what will you do, now?" She wrapped her hands around her mug and sipped her milk.

"I don't know. What should I do, Jida?"

"The answer to that question can only come from you. Now that you have decided to speak your truth, you must decide if you will walk in your truth."

"Will you turn your back on me? Now that you know I am…"

Isir placed her hand on A'isha's. "My child, the Qur'an teaches us that *we* don't reveal the truth, the truth reveals us. But we are not taught that what is true for me, may not be true for you. And so, there is not—nor could there ever be—just one truth."

"Grandmother…"

"Who are we…who am *I* to judge you? Who, besides Allah, has the *right* to judge or condemn anyone? No, A'isha, I will not turn my back on you. You are my grandchild, and you are a child of God. My blood runs through your veins. Why should I ever do such a thing?"

A'isha bowed her head and wept.

"Lift your head, A'isha. Lift your head and dry your tears. You must be strong and trust that all is well. You must have faith and know that after every storm there is a calm, and that the sun will shine tomorrow…it always does. Now, it is late, and you must get some rest. In the top drawer is a nightgown, put it on and come lie down."

Isir limped to her bed and covered herself with the quilt. A'isha gulped her milk and removed her sandals. She washed her face and put on a floral gown she found in the dresser drawer, then lay beside her grandmother and slipped into a deep and dreamless sleep.

***

Weeks turned into months and A'isha's parents did not arrive at her grandmother's house seeking her whereabouts, asking her to return home as she had hoped. She missed listening to Basha gush about Youssef as they lay on their beds in a moonlit silhouette. She longed to hear her mother's voice and her whistling blow with each sip of hot mint tea. Despite the ache that gripped her heart each time she thought about that awful night her father demanded she leave, whenever memories of his musty scent and gap-tooth smile escaped her heart, she missed him too. And she missed their goat, to which she would often raise her fist and shout, "I'm going to throw him over the cliff one day!" in response to its incessant "*maaaa*" that distracted her from reading or awakened her at sunrise.

Each day, as she walked to school and just before the Headmaster chimed the final bell for dismissal, A'isha would send a silent prayer to Allah, asking Him to allow her to see Basha and her mother, hoping they would be in her grandmother's home upon her return from school and say, "come home to your family, we miss you." She asked Allah to grace the people in her village with compassion, hoping that He would touch the hearts of her teachers and the souls of the women who bathe their babies in the river, so they would speak to her and acknowledge her presence once again. But her prayers remained unanswered. Her mother never appeared at her grandmother's home, and Basha and Saira remained absent from school. Taunted by lingering guilt, A'isha often wondered, *were they sent away because of me?*

She attended her classes in isolation. Her peers were instructed to reject her, to keep a physical distance lest they become tainted by her immoral ways, and her teachers led by example. The village's collective shuns cast A'isha into a shadow of invisibility which chased her away from school each day, and into the refuge of her grandmother's home. She would slam the door, sighing in sadness and exhaling with relief, then greet her grandmother with a kiss. Hastily, she would peel off her uniform, stomp on it, and kick it into a corner with all her might before hanging it on a hook behind the door. She would slip into the comfort of her grandmother's purple abaya and work in the yard, planting seeds and pulling weeds with her jida at her side.

Together, A'isha and Isir farmed their patch of land. They tended to her brood of chickens and her goat, Ali. On weekends, they would harvest mint and lentil by day, and at dusk, they would remove their shoes and ease their toes into the cool, damp soil as they gathered olives and limes along the forest edge.

***

"Jida, allow me to gather the mint. You must not bend. I can see it causes pain in your hips."

"I am fine," her grandmother panted, plucking stalks of mint. "I have been harvesting the earth for fifty years," she said, straightening her back, grimacing at a jolt of pain, "and I am not going to allow an ache in my hips to stop me from living my life."

She handed A'isha a bundle of mint and limped along the dirt path toward her home, peering into the forest, wondering if her husband might return home on this day.

The pungent scents of turmeric and thyme wafted through their home as they prepared a meal in the warmth of the fire's glow. Each absorbed in private thoughts as burning wood crackled, intermittently tugging at their attention. Isir thought about her husband and A'isha thought about Saira as they removed the hot, doughy khobz from a pan suspended above the firepit, and slathered each piece with goat butter. Dipping it into their hearty bowls of lentil soup and sipping on sweet papaya juice Isir prepared as a surprise for A'isha, they enjoyed their meal, smiling at each other until Isir shifted her eyes toward the firepit and began to speak with a distant look in her eyes, as if she was looking at something only she could see.

"A'isha, things happen for a reason."

"What do you mean, Jida?" she asked, raising her cup to her lips.

"Sometimes, we don't know why people leave us or why they even come into our lives. But if we trust in Allah we will know, in time. He will reveal the reason." She shifted her eyes toward A'isha and continued, "Things happen to teach us lessons that are meant to strengthen us and make us grow. And until we learn what we must, the lessons will come to us over and over, through different situations and different people. And until we learn what we must, we need to be patient with life, with Allah, and with ourselves."

A'isha listened to her grandmother as they finished their meal. They washed their dishes and prepared for bed, each nestled in the solitude of their inner lives and private thoughts. As her grandmother's words echoed in her mind, *things happen to teach us a lesson,* she was suddenly overcome with a sorrow she had harbored in her heart since the day her father opened the door, pointed to the road, and demanded that she leave. Her sadness twisted her stomach, weakened her knees, and moved her to sit by the fire, wondering, *what lesson is Allah trying to teach me?*

As darkness relinquished its grace to the glimmer of dawn, Isir awoke as she had each morning, to the rooster's crow. She brushed her teeth and re-braided her long, silvery hair before awakening A'isha.

While A'isha dressed for school, Isir embraced the majesty of the mountains from her porch, swaying gently in her rocking chair, and inhaling the chill of morning wrapped in dew. Gazing at the mountains that cradle her home, she sang nasheeds, songs that celebrate Amazigh culture and proclaim Islamic history, religion, and beliefs. A'isha sat on a low stool close to Isir, sipping tea and eating a biscuit, listening to her grandmother sing, feeling inspired by her morning melody. Isir kissed her granddaughter on both cheeks and gave her a small burlap sack that contained walnuts, an apricot, and a palmful of figs. She hugged her and said, "Kuni amnah ya hafidati. Be safe, my granddaughter." When A'isha approached the bend in the road, just before the Tamarisk tree hid her from view, she looked back at her grandmother. They exchanged a wave and a smile, and her grandmother whispered, "Kuni amnah ya hafidati."

Later that day, as A'isha walked home from school along a dirt road at the forest edge, she thought of the math question that had stumped her in class, and her heart pounded as she recalled her peers' hisses and giggles each time the teacher ignored her raised hand. Attempting to shift her attention to a more pleasant thought, she whispered, "I love Geography," and named the countries she planned to see.

Muffled chatter and a sinister laugh interrupted her thoughts, causing her to turn her head sharply toward the forest. "Who's there?" she yelled. Darting her eyes between the forest and the path ahead, she walked slowly, listening intently.

The crunch of leaves beneath footsteps in the forest sent a shiver down her spine. Beads of sweat formed on her brow, and her palms grew clammy and cold.

"Ha hiya," hissed a deep and hardened voice.

"Yes, there she is," another repeated.

A'isha spun around, dropping her books. She squinted into the forest. "Who's there!" she yelled.

Two boys appeared from behind the trees. A tall, skinny boy whose pock-marked face resembled the moon, and a short, rotund boy with deep-set eyes that pierced his world, but did not see it.

A'isha stared at them. *They were in the schoolyard today.*

"What are you doing with that hijab on your head?" the stocky boy snarled, curling his fingers into fists.

"What kind of stupid question is that?" A'isha asked. "What do you want with me?"

"Why would we want anything with you?" the pock-faced boy snarled. "You don't like boys. You're the mithlia who likes girls."

"Mithlia?" she spat. "Who do you think you're talking to? Have you ever thought your mother might be one?"

They walked toward her slowly, tossing their knapsacks to the ground.

"Mithlia, we are talking to you," the stocky boy said. "Maybe we can *make* you like boys."

"Yeah, maybe all she needs is a long hard one to change her mind," his friend jeered.

Keeping her eyes fixed on the boys, she bent down, grabbed one of her textbooks, and said, "If you touch me, you will regret it."

"Are you threatening us?" the pock-faced boy hissed.

The other laughed. "Yeah, what are you going to do with that book? Force us to read it?"

"I am telling you," A'isha glared, "if you touch me, you will be sorry."

The pock-faced boy leaped at her and grabbed her arm. The stocky boy snatched the book from her hand and threw it to the ground. He yanked at her hijab. "Take this off your head! You are not Muslim. You're a sinner."

They grabbed her wrists and pulled her toward the forest.

"Mother!" she screamed, dropping to her knees. "Mother! Help me!"

They grabbed her hair and pulled her to her feet. "Stand up! We're going to teach you how to like boys."

The pock-faced boy squeezed her wrist with one hand and unfastened his belt buckle with the other.

"Get off me!" she yelled. "Mother! Please come!"

"Shut up!" he hollered, tightening his grip, and digging his nails into her flesh.

She dropped to her knees. They dragged her across twigs and pebbles, then yanked her to her feet and pulled her deeper into the forest.

"Get off me!" she screamed. Twisting her head over her shoulder, she cried out, "Sir, please help me! Help me!"

The stocky boy spun around, tripped on a tree root, and fell. A'isha pulled her arm away from him, tightened her fist, and swung. "UGH!" she growled with a swooping force, punching the pock-faced boy in his face and knocking him to the ground. Blood shot from his nose, splattering across his shirt and on her socks. She lifted her leg and stomped on his groin with all her might. "Ow!" he hollered, grabbing his genitals and curling into a fetal position. As the stocky boy scrambled to his feet, she leaped toward him and kicked him in his ribs, knocking him back onto the ground. She pounced on him and grabbed his hair with both hands. Banging his head into the earth, she yelled, "Why!? Why!? Why!?" and pounded her fists into his face. "I hate you! I hate you! I hate you!" she screamed, her eyes bulging, her hair flailing wildly across her face. The pock-faced boy clambered onto his feet and backed away, fumbling to fasten his belt. His eyes widened with each punch A'isha landed on his friend's face.

A'isha eased to her feet and pointed her finger at his bloody face. "If you *ever* touch me again"—she panted— "I will kill you." She drew mucus from the back of her throat, rolled it on her tongue, and spit it into his face, splattering his eyes with a mix of saliva and blood, then turned and walked away.

"C-C'mon. L-l-let's go," the pock-faced boy mumbled, lifting his friend off the ground.

They walked to the forest edge and stared at A'isha as she gathered her scattered books and torn hijab, then stomped toward their knapsacks and grabbed one off the ground. "Uggh! Take your garbage!" she yelled, throwing it at them. The stocky boy watched her, holding his bloody hand over a bulging, battered eye. His bottom lip hung like a slab of beef on a hook.

The pocked-face boy walked toward her, wiping his nose with the back of his hand. "We will see you tomorrow," he muttered, picking up his knapsack.

A'isha cocked her head, walked toward him, and pressed her finger into his chest. "You come near me again," she calmly said, "and I will kill you."

He backed away with his eyes fixed on her. "Let's go," he said, handing his friend a knapsack.

A'isha glared at them until they turned around and disappeared into the forest.

She looked at her books and torn soiled hijab, then fell to her knees. She lifted her head toward the sky and screamed, "Allah! Why must I suffer like this? Why do you allow bad people to roam the Earth? I have done *nothing* except be who I am. Why are you punishing me?" She sobbed and lay on the ground until the sun lifted its warmth and left her in its shadow, alone at the forest edge.

"Jida? Jida, I am home," she called out. Her voice was heavy with exhaustion, edgy with lingering fear. She placed her books and hijab on the table and swept her eyes across the room. Her grandmother's cup of mint tea was untouched, and her blanket was neatly folded. *She did not take her afternoon nap.* A'isha's brow creased with concern as she exited the house. She walked toward the back of their home, stopping to pat Ali. She inhaled deeply, lifted her head, and walked further into their yard.

And there, beneath the fig tree, A'isha saw her jida sprawled on the ground, clutching a bundle of mint. Her mouth was open, and her chin was in an upward tilt. Her eyes held a dignified stare as if she were finally beholding the one she had yearned for. A'isha gasped and ran to her grandmother. "Jida! Oh, my jida!" she wailed, scooping her into her arms. "Why did you leave me?" she asked, over and over, crying inconsolably, cradling her grandmother with a gentle sway upon the patch of land they lovingly toiled together.

Tsewang

"I tell you, Kasim, pain is inevitable, but suffering is optional," Dabir said, skipping over puddles of mud, twigs, and branches tossed about during the violent rainstorm of the previous night. The scent of honeysuckle and pine lingered in its wake.

Kasim tightened the sash of his saffron kasaya around his lanky frame and passed his hand over his shaven head. "What is the difference?" he replied. "It seems to me sir, that pain and suffering are the same. So how can one be inevitable and the other optional?"

"Just think about it for a moment, Kasim. Surely, in this life, we will feel pain. Whether it is pain in the feet from walking many miles on rugged terrain, or pain in the heart that is felt from the death of a loved one. Pain is—"

"Yes, yes, I know. Pain is pain. But how is pain not the same as suffering? When we are in pain, we are also suffering. Is that not true, sir?"

Dabir lifted his chin, clasped his hands on his paunch, and knitted his brow. "Are we really—"

"Are we really what? Not suffering when we are in pain? Is that what you mean?" Kasim asked, wringing his hands as his eyes scanned the forest, privately quelling his fear of it.

"Kasim, if you would allow me to complete my thought, perhaps you will understand the meaning of my words."

"Yes, my regrets. Please continue, sir." He bit down on his fingernail.

"As I was saying, with everything in this life, the pain we feel is determined by our perception and interpretation of the external event that produced it. If we choose to view a painful event as one that calls for suffering—which, in all actuality, is an extension of pain, but not pain itself—well then, that is what we will have. We will have suffering. However, if we choose to experience a painful event without extending it into suffering, then we will not suffer, we will only feel pain. Suffering, what Buddha referred to as dukkha, is an extension of the original pain and it is quite unnecessary. We cannot choose to feel pain, but we can choose to extend it into suffering, or not. Therefore, pain is inevitable, and suffering is optional."

"Alright," Kasim said, scanning the forest, and walking closely behind Dabir. "I think I understand. It makes sense."

Dabir stopped, turned around, and looked at Kasim. "Of course it makes sense. How could it not?"

They continued to wander through the forest, debating the lesson of the day and contemplating Buddhist principles, a daily ritual they began five years ago when Kasim arrived at Dechen Podrang, a monastery in Thimphu, at the age of eleven. Dabir, twenty-six years older than Kasim, assumed the role of his preceptor, his mentor, only because it is customary for ordained monks to take under their wings orphaned boys who appear at a monastery hungry and alone.

Dabir's calm and pensive presence would often become rattled by Kasim's nervous and doubtful demeanor, and his attempts to quell the boy's disposition were futile. Yet, Dabir perceived this challenge as good fortune bestowed upon him by Buddha himself. For he believed that Kasim was not sent to him as a punishment for his immoral ways, but as an opportunity to strengthen two important virtues with which he was weakest: Kshanti Paramita, the perfection of patience, and Dana Paramita, the perfection of generosity. So, despite the constant wrangling he endured with Kasim, he did not petition Rinpoche to reassign the child to a fellow monk, although he often prayed that he would, then beg Buddha for forgiveness for his selfish ways.

"Well, sir," Kasim said after a few moments of quiet reflection which challenged his need for incessant chatter, "I believe today's lesson is a good one and yes, I am beginning to understand the difference between pain and suffering."

Dabir removed his eyeglasses and dabbed his nose with a handkerchief as he watched the morning fog waft across the forest. Then, he looped his eyeglasses behind his ears and looked at the white clouds floating across a pristine, powder-blue sky.

"You know, Kasim, in the five years we have worked together, I have seen you grow in ways that, well, surprise even me. Especially when I think of the unruly and distrustful manner with which you approached me on the day we met." He patted Kasim's shoulder, stepped over a puddle, and continued down the path.

"Really, sir? It pleases me that you notice my effort. I am really trying to be a good monk."

Dabir raised his finger. "Correction, you are a novice." He turned around and looked at Kasim. "You have yet to achieve the status of a monk, and from the looks of it that will take quite some time."

"Yes, sir, I know that is true. I misspoke. I am a novice, not a monk. And I suppose, regarding suffering, I have caused much of my own. As a child, I often sat by the lake behind my parents' home and…and…*did you hear that?*" He cupped his ear.

Dabir turned around and frowned. "Did I hear what?"

"That sound…what is that?" His eyes grew wide.

"I don't—"

"Shhh!"

Dabir glared at him. "How dare you shush me?"

"Sir, I do not mean to be disrespectful, but I heard a sound that could be the growl of a wild boar or even a mountain lion. I do not wish for us to be eaten alive."

"I don't hear a sound other than your voice. Perhaps if you stop talking, I will hear the sound you speak of."

"Oh, no! I heard…see! Did you hear that?" Kasim shrieked, grabbing Dabir's arm.

"Shh," Dabir replied, jerking away from Kasim. He placed his finger on his lips and crouched. Kasim crouched, too.

A voice called out. "I am over here. Please…"

"Oh, yes, I hear it now," Dabir whispered.

"Who is there!" Kasim yelled.

Dabir bolted upright. Kasim slapped his hand over his mouth, muffling his laughter.

"What do you find funny?" Dabir hissed.

"I'm sorry I frightened you, sir."

"You are most immature! When will you—" He cupped his ear. "Did you hear that?"

"Yes, I hear it," Kasim gasped.

"Help me. Please, help me."

"Who is there?" Dabir hollered.

"It is I, Tsewang."

Kasim and Dabir looked at each other wide-eyed. *"Did he say Tsewang?"* Kasim whispered. "Do you know who that could be?"

"I have no idea."

"Who would be here, *alone?*" Kasim asked, scanning the forest.

Dabir walked off the muddy trail, toward the voice. Kasim followed.

"Over here…I am here."

They squeezed between clusters of rhododendrons, walked across a shady clearing carpeted with pine needles, and then peeked over a band of juniper bushes.

"Oh, my dear God! In the name of Mahakala!" Dabir cried.

"My dear brother!" Kasim gasped, wide-eyed. "What has happened to you?"

Tsewang, lying on his back in his underpants, partially immersed in a pool of mud, squinted at them. His hair, draped across his face and shoulders, was caked with soil and fragments of bark. His leathery, sunbaked skin hung onto his jaw and settled into the hollow of his cheeks. The outline of his ribs moved with each shallow breath, the empty scoop of his belly did not. One arm stretched above his head as if he were reaching for something he could not see, the other was tucked by his side. His hand clung tightly to decaying leaves and onto the wetness of earth as if he were afraid to let go. His empty gaze rested upon drifting white clouds, and the heavens gazed back, upon a young man stripped bare of cloth, spirit, and mind.

"What shall we do?" Kasim begged, kneeling at Tsewang's feet.

Dabir wiped dry mud from the corners of his mouth and held his hand. "Are you feeling pain? Can you walk?"

"I am not in pain, but I don't know if I can walk," Tsewang whispered. "I cannot remember…I cannot remember the last time I walked. I am thirsty."

"We have no water, and I do not know where the nearest source might be," Dabir said. "We are about one mile from town."

"Where do you come from, my friend?" Kasim asked, horrified by the sight of the emaciated soul.

Tsewang closed his eyes and dug his fingers into the mud, clenching the earth.

"Do you hear me?" Kasim asked, panic rattling his words.

Dabir placed his hand on Tsewang's forehead and rubbed the crown of his head. Tsewang inhaled and opened his eyes.

"My name is Tsewang, and I am from Pali Sholing, a monastery in Paro."

"*In Paro?*" Dabir shrieked.

Tsewang closed his eyes and nodded.

"Mahakala surely has been watching over you, my child," Dabir quivered. "You have traveled many miles and over extremely dangerous terrain. *From Paro,* you say? You are now in Thimphu. That is a great distance."

"Thimphu?" Tsewang whispered.

"Yes, the capital of Bhutan," Dabir replied.

"Are you able to walk?" Kasim asked. "We can bring you to our home, to Dechen Podrang, where we can feed and clothe you."

Tsewang rolled onto his side. Dabir helped him sit up and moved hair out of his eyes as mud and water dripped from his mane. Kasim placed his hand under one arm, Dabir held the other, and together they raised Tsewang to his feet. Weakened by thirst and hunger, his knees buckled, and he began to cry.

"Do not weep, my friend," Dabir said, softly. "We are here to help you. Mahakala, the Deity of Protection, has sent us to save you. So, you must not feel sorrow. Instead, you should rejoice."

His kasaya and sandals lay under a tree nearby. Kasim twisted rainwater out of the kasaya while Dabir eased Tsewang's feet into his soaked sandals. He wrapped his arm around his waist and was saddened by the press of Tsewang's protruding ribs against his wrist. Tsewang leaned on Dabir, rested his head on his shoulder, and began his journey out of the forest. Kasim walked behind them, carrying Tsewang's kasaya; and his burlap sack, brimming with betel nuts, remained in the wilderness.

Between evergreen trees and twisted vines, streams of morning sun stretched toward them and lay warmth upon their backs. They followed the path that would lead them out of the forest as Dabir chanted the mantra of compassion, Om Mani Padme Hum. In the distance, they could hear the blow of dungchen horns and the beat of the choenga drums, beckoning novices and monks for meditation and prayer. Tsewang listened to the familiar sounds of long ago as he staggered out of the forest, toward the city of Thimphu.

A'isha

A'isha removed her sweater, placed it upon her grandmother's bosom, and lay beside her in the moist soil beneath their fig tree. She caressed her head and held her closely, rocking her gently, weeping, and whispering into her ear, "My jida, my dear jida, why have you left me all alone? What am I going to do without you?"

Ali lifted his head toward the sky and released a long, mournful "Maaa." He lowered his head, lifted it again, stretched his neck, and repeated his cry, informing the Kingdom of his loss. As if he understood the sorrow that had befallen A'isha's heart, he walked over to her and rested his head upon her shoulder. Grunting, he dropped his head to her knees and licked away the blend of blood and soil, then lifted his eyes to hers as if to ask, "Who did this to you?" The warmth of his breath and the brush of his whiskers soothed her. "Maaa," he cried, lowering his head and nudging her elbow with his damp nose, saying to her in the only way he could, "Get up, A'isha. Go get help."

"Okay, Ali, I'm going," she moaned, wiping her tears. She eased her grandmother onto the ground and Ali remained at her side, gazing at A'isha as she walked toward their home, stumbling, looking over her shoulder at her grandmother. She yanked a blanket off the bed and returned to the yard. A'isha sobbed as she knelt next to her grandmother and unfolded the blanket upon her body. She hugged her and whispered, "I'm going for help, Jida," then kissed her forehead and lifted the blanket onto her grandmother's face.

She retrieved a clean hijab from the dresser drawer, covered her head, splashed water on her face and wiped it dry, then returned to the yard. She tucked the blanket under her grandmother's feet and shoulders and patted Ali's head. "I will be back, Ali. You stay with Jida."

She ran out of the yard and down the dirt road from which she waved goodbye to her grandmother just hours before. Downhill, she ran past the Tamarisk tree and around the bend, traversing a small wooden bridge. Uphill, she ran on the undulating path of amber soil, along the river. Beneath her moan and whimper, A'isha could hear the water rumble. The river seemed to beckon her, and she was tempted to respond. Shifting her eyes from the river to the road, then from the road to the river, she continued to run along its edge, toward the only place her heart would lead—her parents' home.

Whimpering and weeping, her windblown tears streaked her face, and her hijab fell onto her shoulders as she ran across the red hills of Ouirgane. At a distance, she could see the village's cluster of cantaloupe abodes. "Mother, Mother…" she moaned, slowing her pace as she approached the village. At the entrance, she hid behind a tree, panting. She covered her hair with her hijab and peered at the main road, lined with weathered tarps of makeshift shops and donkey-drawn carts stacked with baskets of lemons, cinnamon sticks, saffron, and thyme. She listened to the cluck of chickens and the hollow, rhythmic whoop of a whipped carpet draped across slackened twine.

"Allah, make me invisible," A'isha whispered, as she had each morning during her walk to school. She eased away from the tree, wiped her tears, lowered her head, and stepped into the village. She walked past contemptuous eyes, eyes that pierced her through the slits of black niqabs. The eyes of women who carried sheaths of mutton in one arm and clutched the hands of their children in the other, hissing through veiled lips, "Look! The kafir has returned. Has she no shame?"

A'isha clenched her teeth and her fists, fighting the urge to lift her head and scream, "Who gives you the right to judge me?" But instead, she ran. She ran past the butcher shop and the barber, and past the shop owned by her father and Amir, ignoring men sitting in doorways shooing flies and idling hours with nicotine and tea. Waving the hem of their pastel tunics in search of a cool breeze, they peered at the girl who bestowed upon her family an unrelenting shame that spilled into the village and tainted its name.

"Mother! Mother!" she yelled as she approached the home she once knew, banging on an unresponsive door until her strength escaped her, and she could yell no more. She hoisted herself onto a wooden crate and stretched her neck to peek through the window of chicken wire mesh. The furniture had been removed and the clay walls that once confined her were bare. Like a cocoon abandoned by the butterfly, so too was their home—a hollow shell of the lives it once held. She eased off the crate and sat on it. She stared at the ground, bewildered, brushing her hands against her uniform, wiping sweat off her palm, and rubbing blood off her knuckles with the hem of her navy-blue skirt. *Where are they?*

She bolted to her feet. "Saira would know!" Her calves burned as she ran up the steep hill toward her home, curving a bend and passing the boulder she and Saira often sat upon, sharing dreams and making plans until the sun set at the rooster's crow. She approached Saira's home and froze. *I have not seen her. I am sure she has gone away too.* She peered at her home and gasped when the door opened. Saira's grandmother limped out, tossing grains at her brood of chicken. "Sayadati," A'isha called out. But when the old woman looked her way, A'isha ducked behind a juniper bush, then spun around and ran, slapping her feet against the ground as she ran downhill to her family's home. She plopped onto the crate and sighed, gazing at the suspended swirls of arid soil her footsteps left behind in a funnel of tangerine glow. Her knees ached as droplets of blood caked and crusted around her open wound. Her throat was parched, and the lingering taste of blood made her cough and gag.

Amir…Amir would know what happened to my family. She jumped to her feet and trudged up the steep hill, passing a woman bent beneath the weight of mustard greens bound upon her back. She turned onto a wooded path, toward the home of her father's business partner and lifelong friend. *I have not seen Amir in a year. I wonder if he has moved away too.*

"Amir!" she called out. "Amir, it's me, A'isha."

A phlegmy cough approached the door. "A'isha," he said, raising his brow and clearing his throat. "What are you doing here?"

His large brown eyes smiled, deep-set in mocha skin that contrasted his silver hair. Everything about Amir was large—his hands, feet, and broad shoulders. His strapping presence contradicted his gentle, almost effeminate ways, and it was this blend of qualities that lent to his popularity among the adults and children of Ouirgane.

He stepped aside, gesturing for her to enter. "Please, come in." He put a cigarette to his lips, sucked smoke into his lungs, and extinguished the ashy remnant in a clay bowl outside his door.

"Oh, Amir!" A'isha cried, wrapping her arms around his waist, and hugging him tightly.

"What's going on?" he asked, his voice quivering with concern. He put his arm around her shoulders and led her to the kitchen table. "Sit here. I will get some water for you."

He returned with two glasses and lit another cigarette, lowering onto a chair across from her. A'isha gulped the cool water, then stared at the empty glass. She could not look at him.

Amir raised the cigarette to his lips, surveying her bruised knees and shredded, blood-stained socks. "A'isha, what is going on? What happened to your knees? What has happened to you?"

"My jida has died. And I…I…" She dropped her face into her palms and wept.

"Enna lillah wa enna elaihe Rajioun," he replied, his voice heavy with compassion. He repeated his condolence in English, "We belong to Allah, and to Him we shall return," then said, "I am so sorry, A'isha. When did this happen?"

"Today," she sniffled.

He leaned forward. "Where did she die? Where is she?"

"I found her…" She raised her head and looked at him. "She's lying on the ground behind our home."

Amir rubbed his cigarette into an ashtray, blowing a stream of gray smoke above his head. "Who is with her?"

"She's alone. Where is my family? I went to their home, but it's empty."

Amir blinked away tears, recalling the last time he had seen Isir, at the celebration of Eid al-Fitr. *She was a robust, youthful woman. Always kind.*

"Amir, are you listening to me? Please tell me, where is my family?"

"Your family left the village many months ago, A'isha." He patted her hand. "I don't know where they are, but we cannot worry about that now. We must focus on burying your grandmother." He stood and adjusted his kufi. "As you know, she must be buried within one day."

"But how will I bury my grandmother without my family? They need to know she—"

"As I said, A'isha, the Qur'an tells us our deceased must be buried within twenty-four hours. You know this."

"Yes, but—"

"Do you know when she died?" He placed their glasses into the sink.

"It had to be while I was in school. She looked healthy this morning. She waved goodbye to me."

"Well, we must hurry. We don't have much time before sundown."

He rushed toward the door and as he slipped his feet into his sandals the adhan bellowed from the minaret, "Allahuuu Akbar…Allahuuu Akbar." He checked his watch. "Ya Allah!" he exclaimed. "Don't tell me it's already five o'…this stupid watch!" he yelled, tapping on it. He huffed, "La hawla wa la qu wat illab illah" and glanced at A'isha, recalling her parents rarely spoke to their daughters in Arabic. He repeated his appeal to Allah in English, "There is no transformation or power, except through Allah."

He repeated it in Arabic, hoping to quell his mounting anxiety over the sudden confluence of events: A'isha's return, the death of Isir, his ambivalence with involving himself in Nabeel's family matters, his resurging anger and grief over Nabeel's abandonment, his desire to forgive Nabeel, his concern for his wife and daughter in Fez, his unpreparedness—once again—for the Asr and, of course, his stupid, unreliable watch.

The call for prayer continued, "Allahuuu Akbar… Allahuuu Akbar."

Amir kicked off his sandals. "Wait right here, A'isha. I will return shortly."

He hurried into his bedroom, unfurled his sajadah, positioned it toward Mecca, knelt on it in salah, and hastily whispered, "Allahu Akbar, Allah is the Greatest."

A'isha listened to Amir praying and imagined her father doing the same, *somewhere in these mountains.* As she sat at the table, her mind raced from one vision to another: from her grandmother lying on the ground beneath the fig tree, to the boys in the forest, to her family's empty home, to her mother, Basha, and Saira, then back to Amir. She recalled her grandmother's words the night before, as they shared lentil soup and khobz, "Things always happen for a reason, A'isha. You must look for the lesson."

"Come, A'isha. Let's go," Amir said, lighting a cigarette and slipping his feet into his sandals. The sun leaped at them as he opened the door; they squinted at the stretch of butterscotch rays spilling upon the red hills of Ouirgane. They walked in silence, sorting private thoughts. A'isha did not know where they were going, and she did not ask.

"As-salamu alaikum," Amir said solemnly, greeting his neighbors.

"Wa-alaikum salaam," they replied, staring at A'isha, glancing at her knees, and raising their brow at Amir.

They arrived at the shop. Amir opened the door with a firm push, and the musty scent of motor oil and stale tobacco greeted A'isha before her eyes could adjust to the dark room of damp wood and moist cement. She remained at the threshold. A sliver of sun stretched over her shoulder and welcomed itself in, nestling its warmth upon her back. Amir reached toward the dangling, unshaded lightbulb and pulled the chain. A'isha swept her eyes across the room as if seeing it for the first time.

"Wow," she whispered. Memories flashed like snippets of film, one frame at a time. She saw herself, the little girl with unruly jet-black hair, too young to wear a hijab, sitting on a stool beside her father, plucking a scab on her knee. And she saw herself slap her hands over her ears to muffle the sudden clang of her father's hammer against a stirrup. She saw herself look up at him and say, "Be careful, Baba," patting his thigh with dimpled fingers, worried that he might swallow one of the nails he held between his teeth.

She saw her father working on the saddles and sandals villagers brought to him for repair. She could hear him say, with a wink and a wide, gap-tooth smile, "A'isha is my little helper," then turn to her and ask, "Do you see the blue babouche over there? Please bring them to me." And she saw herself hand him the shoes and ask, "Baba, may I shine the saddle?"

She was proud of her father and, as a little girl, knew he was proud of her too. She did whatever she could to see his eyes sparkle. She always wanted to make him smile. He did, at times, but that was so long ago.

Why do people change? Had Jida ever talked to me about that?

She rubbed her eyes and returned her attention to Amir as he pushed aside rolls of fabric. She moved further into the shop and glided her hand along her father's workbench, wanting to organize his tools and cans of mink oil scattered about. She recalled her excitement and pride whenever she arranged her father's tools at the end of the day.

"No, A'isha," she could hear her father say as he patiently held his hand on the chain, waiting to turn out the light, "Leave them as they are. They will be in a mess by this time tomorrow."

"But Baba, I want you to have a neat shop," she would reply, looking up at him, crinkling her nose with a whine. "Your customers will be happy."

"Alright, A'isha," he would say with a chuckle, "if it is that important to you, line them up if you want." Then, he would lean on the doorjamb and smoke a cigarette as he watched the people of Ouirgane move about.

She recalled how she would say, "Look, Baba! I'm finished!" and he would toss his cigarette to the ground, extinguish it with a quick twist of his foot, and settle his eyes upon her as she looked up at him, searching his face, seeking his smile, hoping to see a sparkle in his eyes.

BOOM! The thud of dead weight slamming onto the cement floor startled A'isha and jerked her away from the memory of her father and back to Amir. He was sifting through rolls of fabric—saffron, mahogany, and turquoise—which he would eventually fashion into djellabas and sell to the wealthy women of Marrakesh for a hefty profit. Moving bundles here and there, he paused occasionally to ease his breathing and to dab sweat trickling on his brow.

"Aha! Here it is," he said, panting and smiling as he yanked at a fold of white cotton cloth wrapped in plastic. He tucked it under his arm, stepped over the rolls of plastic-covered fabric scattered across the floor, turned toward A'isha and said, "Let's go."

A'isha glanced around the shop and gazed at her father's workbench, subduing her desire to arrange his tools. Amir yanked the chain at the dangling bulb, waited for her to exit, then shut the door.

They walked the backroad of Ouirgane, past her school, along a ridge high above the amber, sloping valley dotted with almond trees, rosebushes, and cantaloupe abodes.

"I did not know your grandmother well," Amir said, softly, "but whenever I have been in her company, she always had a kind word for me." He lifted his eyes toward the sky. "Now, she is with Allah and her soul will rest in peace, Inshallah."

"Amir, what are we going to do about my family?" A'isha asked, quickening her pace, wishing he would slow down. The torn skin on her knees burned. "Shouldn't we try to find them?"

"No, A'isha. As I said, I do not know where your family is. We must focus on burying your grandmother. Tell me, do you know of a woman who can help us?"

She stopped walking. "What do you mean?"

Amir turned around, waving his arm. "Please, keep moving, we don't have much time before sundown."

"Amir, what do you mean?" she asked, running toward him. "What woman? Why do we need help? You and I can manage, can't we?"

He turned to her with an encouraging smile. "I can bury your grandmother," he said, "but I cannot cleanse and shroud her. A woman must do that. Now, do you know who can help us?"

A'isha frowned. *There is no one.*

"She must have a neighbor, yes?"

"No, we don't." *What are we going to do? Where is my mother?* She wanted to scream.

They walked along the riverbank until they arrived at a bend, then traversed a small wooden bridge and walked uphill.

"We are not far from my jida's home," A'isha said.

They passed a forested path partially hidden beneath a canopy of willow trees.

"Wait!" A'isha shrieked, startling Amir. "There's a woman who lives just over that hill."

"Which hill?" he asked, patting the breast pocket of his dusty, brown tunic.

"The one we just passed."

"What woman? Who is she?"

"The woman…she is the aunt of two girls I met on this road." She placed her hand on her forehead and searched the sky. *It was so long ago…what are their names?*

"Which girls? Who are they?" Amir asked, lighting a cigarette.

She walked toward Amir and lowered her voice. "The day Baba asked me to leave his home I brought food to my jida, and I met…Nadesh! Yes, that's her name. Their names are Nadesh and…and…Meena!"

"And they live over that hill?" he asked, squinting his eyes, protecting them from the smoke that escaped his mouth with each word.

"No, *they* don't live there, but their aunt…their aunt does."

"What is her name?"

"I…I…can't recall. I never met her."

A screech echoed across the valley and pulled their attention toward the sky.

"Look, that's a Bald Ibis," Amir said, squeezing out his words between phlegmy coughs. "I have not seen one since I was a child."

A'isha blocked a sunray with her hands as she watched the enormous bird flap its glossy, black-feathered wings, and swoop across the sky.

"It is quite unusual to see one of those here in Ouirgane," Amir said. "I wonder if it is trying to tell us something." He glanced at his watch, dropped the cigarette onto the ground, and extinguished it with quick twists of his foot. "It's getting late. We must go to the woman's home and see if she can help us."

A'isha gazed at the circling Ibis.

"Did you hear me?" he asked. "We must go to her home and see if she can help us."

They walked in silence, listening to the Ibis screech.

Dead leaves and splintered bark crackled beneath their feet as they walked up the canopied bluff. They could see at a distance a clay cottage covered in a patchwork of naked vines.

"Is that the woman's home?" Amir asked, panting.

"I don't know."

A'isha followed Amir as they trudged up the bluff; she listened to his breathless pants as they approached the house.

"You should stop smoking."

"Perhaps one day I will. Salaam?" Amir called out. "Salaam?"

The door opened to a slit, revealing a woman with two long braids of black hair streaked with gray. "As-salamu alaikum," she said, then patted her head. "Astaghfirullah. I will return, please wait." She closed the door.

"Does she look familiar to you?" Amir whispered.

"No. I have never seen her," A'isha said, scanning the forest, listening to the chirp of a lone bird, and wondering what lay beneath the intermittent rustle of fallen leaves.

The door creaked open.

"As-salamu alaikum," the woman said, partially hidden behind the door. Her braids were concealed by a black hijab, and she had changed out of her pink bathrobe and into a beige abaya. She greeted them, this time, with a smile. Her large eyes were framed by long lashes; her crepe skin was sun-kissed and coral. Amir was struck by her beauty.

"As-salamu alaikum," he bowed, wiping his brow. "Pl--please, may we enter?"

The woman stepped aside and welcomed them in. The firepit and warmth from smoldering embers reminded A'isha of her jida's home. The woman's resemblance to her grandmother—her petite frame, the slight bend of her posture—tightened A'isha's chest. She wanted to touch her.

"My name is Amir, and this is A'isha. We are from a village not too far from here."

"Salaam. My name is Hira."

Amir turned to A'isha. "Tell me your grandmother's name."

She jerked her head back and pursed her lips. *How could he forget her name?*

"It's Isir," she replied, rolling her eyes and turning to Hira, "Her name is Isir."

"Yes, of course," Amir said, frowning at A'isha. He turned to Hira. "Do you know her?"

Hira shifted her eyes from Amir to A'isha, then back to Amir. "*Isir?* No…no, I don't recall." She lowered her eyes and said, "I rarely leave my home."

A'isha cleared her throat. "Maybe your nieces have mentioned her to you."

"My *nieces*? How do you know my nieces?"

"I believe I met them one day last fall. One attends the university in…in…*Ifrane*?"

"Yes," Hira smiled. "My niece, Nadesh."

"Yes, and her sister is—"

"Meena," Hira added.

Amir looked at his watch and bit his lip. *We have two hours before nightfall.* "Sayadati," he interrupted, "we have an urgent matter."

"Well, please have a seat."

"We really don't have—"

"Are you thirsty?" she asked over her shoulder, pushing past the red damask that hung in the doorway to her kitchen.

Amir sat on the small, brown sofa and glanced at his watch. Hira returned with two glasses of water.

"Shukran, Sayadati, barak allah fik," Amir said, reaching for the glass. "May Allah bless you."

Hira sat next to Amir. A'isha stood beside him, listening to him gulp the water. She held her glass but did not drink.

"This child," Amir said, tilting his head toward A'isha, "her grandmother passed away today."

"Aw, my child, I am sorry for your loss," Hira said. "But do not worry, she is with her Creator and is at peace."

Amir nodded. "She lives just down the road. Is that correct, A'isha?"

"Yes, not too far from here."

"And we need a woman to shroud her, to prepare her for burial. There is no one to help us. We are wondering if—"

Hira shook her head. "Oh, no, I cannot. Her husband was…I mean my husband was…" She shifted her eyes away from Amir and onto the door.

"Sayadati, did you know Isir? Did you know her husband?"

"Oh, no. I…I don't believe I did. I misspoke. I meant *my* husband. I have not buried anyone since he passed."

Amir pushed back his kufi and scratched his head. "I see. Sayadati, as you know, the Qur'an instructs us to bury our deceased within one day. We need your help."

She gazed at the floor, rubbing her hands.

"Ma'am, do you hear me? Sayadati, please. Nightfall is approaching. Will you help us?"

Amir's voice faded into a distant din as A'isha stared at the Yaz hanging above Hira's door. She recalled the pride in her grandmother's voice whenever she spoke about the Yaz. "It is our flag, A'isha," she would declare, "the flag of our ancestors. It means 'free man' and it symbolizes the Imazighen people. Blue represents the Mediterranean Sea, whose shores have been inhabited by the Imazighen for thousands of years. Green represents the land that has been cultivated by the Imazighen since Prehistoric times. Red represents eternal life, and yellow represents the Sahara, but also joy and gold."

As A'isha stared at the Yaz, she felt a warm caress on her cheek. She placed her hand on it. "My jida," she whispered, "do I have the courage to shroud you alone?"

"What did you say, A'isha?" Amir asked. "Are you okay?"

"Yes," she nodded, staring at the Yaz. "I'm okay."

Hira stood up. "Very well, where is her home?"

Amir jumped to his feet. "It's just down the hill. Is that right, A'isha? A'isha! Do you hear me? Your grandmother's home…it is nearby, yes?"

"Yes," she replied, pulling her eyes away from the Yaz. The glass of water slipped out of her hand and shattered. "Oh, my! I'm sorry. Please forgive me," she said, bending to pick up the shards of glass, wincing at the pain in her knees.

"Do not worry," Hira said, rushing into the kitchen. She returned with a cloth and handed it to A'isha. "Please do not cut…what happened to your *knees*? Allow me to clean and bandage your wounds."

"No, I am fine…really."

Amir glanced at his watch. "So, will you help us?"

"Yes…yes, I will."

"Shukran! Thank you, ma'am."

A'isha went into the kitchen, dropped the pieces of glass into a garbage pail, then returned and sopped up the water, moving about as if alone in the room.

"A'isha, did you hear? She will help us."

She looked up at Amir and frowned. "Yes, I heard her."

"We will need the Qur'an and the Duas," Hira said. "I will bring mine. Please excuse me for a moment."

"Amir," A'isha whispered, easing to her feet, "I think I can shroud my grandmother. Maybe we don't need Hira."

"I understand why you want to, A'isha, but shrouding requires specific steps. It is a ritual that Hira is familiar with."

"And you're not?"

"Yes, I am, but as I told you, I cannot shroud your grandmother. Allow Hira to help us."

"But there's something about her that I don't—"

"Don't what?"

"That I don't like. I don't feel comfortable with her. I don't know what it is."

"Do you think she…"

Hira returned to the living room wearing a white kaftan and a white hijab, clutching the Qur'an, the Duas, and a white pouch. She took the cloth from A'isha, placed it in the sink, and walked to the door. "Shall we leave?"

"Yes," Amir nodded. "Come, A'isha, let us go."

A'isha led them over the bluff and down the wooded path to her jida's home. The sun had settled behind the mountains and a dusky breeze rustled stiffened leaves.

"She's back here, on the ground," A'isha said, as they walked along the side of the house.

Ali ran toward A'isha and nudged her thigh with his nose, then stretched his neck and released a mournful, "Maaa." She patted him, kissed his head, and led Amir and Hira to where her jida lay.

"We must bring her inside," Amir said as they approached Isir. He bowed his head and spoke Arabic words A'isha did not understand, then lifted Isir off the ground. Her body was stiff. Her bones pressed into his arms. "A'isha, please open the door," he panted.

Hira removed the blanket from her body, folded it into a rectangular mat, and placed it on the floor. Amir lowered Isir onto it, positioning her head toward Mecca. Hira retrieved the cast iron pot from the firepit and handed it to Amir. "We will need plenty of water," she said, then turned to A'isha. "Do you know where we might find more pots?"

"My jida keeps them in the yard," A'isha said, staring at her grandmother. "We use them for harvest."

"Show me where they are," Amir said. "And the water well…where is it?" He followed her out the door.

Ali ran toward them, nudging A'isha's thigh as she collected the bowls and jars her grandmother stored in the shed and placed them on the ground. Amir eyed the shovel leaning against the wall.

"The well is over there," A'isha pointed and returned to the house. She stared at her grandmother through the screen door, envisioning her on the front porch, rocking in her chair, sipping tea, and gazing up at the mountains that frame her home while humming nasheeds to honor Allah and the ancestors, "Who died so we could live," A'isha whispered, repeating her grandmother's words. She entered the room, lit the lantern, sat in her grandmother's chair next to the firepit, and wept.

"You must be strong, A'isha. We must prepare your grandmother. The angels are waiting," Hira smiled. "Go fill the pots. Bring as much water as you can."

Amir entered the room carrying jugs of water and placed them on the floor next to Hira. "Come with me, A'isha. Help me bring in the others."

When they brought in the last two jugs of water, Amir pushed back his kufi and scanned the cluster of jugs and bowls filled to the brim.

"A'isha," he said, clearing phlegm from his throat, "the cemetery is much too far from here. We have no way to bring your grandmother to it. I am sure Allah will understand if we bury her here, beneath the fig tree."

"She would prefer that," A'isha nodded, "and so would I."

"Very well then, I will prepare the ground," he said, shifting his eyes between Isir, Hira, and A'isha. A vision of his wife flashed across his mind. He closed his eyes and whispered, "Thank you, Allah," then bowed and closed the door behind him. He returned to the fig tree, pushed the shovel into the ground, looked toward the sky, and said, "And thank you for sending Hira to us."

A'isha clutched the package of white fabric against her chest, rocking back and forth in her chair. Tears streamed down her face as she gazed at her grandmother. "My jida," she cried, "what am I going to do without you?"

Softly, Hira sang a nasheed for the dead as she removed Isir's shoes, "The hour has come for your soul's return. Life's journey is done. Now the long-promised question has come: How did you worship the Lord of the worlds? Did you submit with your heart and your soul? How did you answer the One who was sent as a mercy to you? Enna lillah wa enna elaihe Raji'oon. Surely, from Allah do we come, and to Allah we shall return." She looked at

A'isha. "Get up, my child. You must change your clothes. Do you have a white kaftan and hijab to wear?"

"I think my jida has one," A'isha sniffled, wiping her face with the hem of her skirt.

"I am sure she does," Hira said. "She is a woman of Islam."

She removed Isir's stockings, repeating the nasheed, "The hour has come for you to return…"

Then, she unbraided her hair.

They moved about in silence. Amir opened the ground, and Hira prepared Isir for burial. She gazed at her with a faint smile. *You're the lucky one. The angels are waiting for you.* She removed her clothing and swaddled her in the flap of the blanket. She looked at A'isha. "I have told you; you must change your clothes."

A'isha peeled herself off the chair. She sifted through the dresser drawer and found a long, white cotton djellaba and hijab. She went into the kitchen and removed her uniform, eased into the gown, wrapped the white hijab around her head, then knelt next to Hira at her grandmother's head. Hira removed the blanket. Isir's skin was taut and blueish-gray.

"Oh, my jida," A'isha winced, touching her grandmother's shoulder.

Hira placed her hand behind Isir's head and lifted her back to a semi-sitting position. She pressed on her belly in downward strokes. Fluid from her bowels and bladder oozed out onto the blanket, then expelled with a final, violent swoosh. A'isha gagged. Bile crept up her throat and vomit filled her mouth as the pungent odor of feces, urine, and decay permeated the room. Clenching her teeth, she stretched her neck and gulped. Hira lay Isir flat on the blanket, then lifted her again and pressed firmly on her belly with downward strokes. A mix of brown, yellow, and black gelatinous fluid squished and gurgled, propelling out of Isir onto the pile forming between her legs.

As she stroked and emptied Isir's intestines, Hira said, "A'isha, in the white pouch are cubes of camphor. Take one and hold it to your nose." She continued to press on Isir's stomach until bubbling, moist air sputtered from her body, and nothing more.

Hira eased to her feet and unfolded one of the sheets she had brought with her. She lay it on the floor, closer to the bed. "We can cleanse her now. Take your grandmother's ankles and help me lift her onto this sheet."

A'isha choked back vomit as they moved Isir onto the sheet. Hira balled up the blanket and placed it outside the door as A'isha held the camphor to her nose. She glanced at her grandmother. Wracked with guilt, she put the cube of camphor on the floor. Hira knelt beside A'isha and covered Isir's genitals with a white cloth, then dropped camphor into the bowls and jugs of water that surrounded them.

"The Qur'an tells us to start at the upper right side and then the upper left side, then the bottom right, then the bottom left," she said. "But first, we must wash her head."

She removed a bottle from her pouch and lathered Isir's hair. She rinsed it with the camphor water and repeated this process three times. A'isha refilled the bowls and jugs with clean water, patting Ali and nodding at Amir with each return to the yard.

"The Prophet Muhammad tells us that a woman's hair should be parted into three braids. Come, A'isha, help me braid your grandmother's hair."

A'isha sopped puddles of water with a towel, then knelt next to Hira.

"At the time of burial," Hira whispered as they braided Isir's hair, "the angels are present. The camphor gives a good aroma and is very pleasing to them. It also keeps the insects away from the body."

With Isir's hair in three braids, they proceeded to cleanse her, following the Qur'an.

"A'isha," Hira said, dabbing Isir's body with a white towel, "check to see if your grandmother has another white djellaba. If not, this sheet will do."

A'isha sifted through her grandmother's drawer. "She does!" she exclaimed, relieved she was not wearing the gown her grandmother needed. She unfolded it and placed it on the bed.

Hira smiled. "The angels will always provide in times of need. Inshallah."

She dabbed Isir's body dry, humming a prayerful nasheed, asking for Allah's guidance and forgiveness.

"There," she said, glancing at A'isha, "now that her hair and body are cleansed, we can shroud her. Let us lift her onto the bed."

"I can do it," A'isha said. She lifted her grandmother and cradled her as if carrying an infant, holding her close to her bosom while Hira spread onto the bed the white fabric Amir brought from the shop.

"My jida," A'isha whispered, "thank you for caring for me." She kissed her forehead and lay her in the center of the cloth.

Together, Hira and A'isha eased the gown over Isir's head and worked her arms into the sleeves. Hira wrapped her braids around her head and placed her right hand upon her belly, then her left hand over her right, following the Qur'an.

"She is ready, A'isha, and the angels are pleased. Allow me to shroud her."

A'isha moved to the foot of the bed, and Hira lifted the first of three white cotton sheets.

"The hour has come for your soul's return," she recited, softly, "and life's journey is done." She pulled the shroud over Isir's feet. "Now the long-promised question has come." She shrouded the right side of her body. "How did you worship the Lord of the worlds?" Then, she shrouded her left. "Did you submit with your heart and soul?" she recited, shrouding Isir's head. "How did you answer the One who was sent as a mercy to you?"

A'isha bowed her head and wept.

Hira lifted the second sheet, repeated the process, and again with the third. She removed three long pieces of twine from her white pouch and tied one around Isir's neck.

"Enna lillah wa enna elaihe Raji'oon," she whispered, then tied another around her waist. "Surely, from Allah, do we come," she said, tying the final piece around her ankles, "And to Allah, we shall return."

Through the screen door, Amir watched in silence, blinking away tears.

"Amir," Hira called out, "The deceased is prepared. Please help us."

He entered the room and lifted Isir into his arms. A'isha held the screen door open and followed Amir and Hira to the yard. Ali swung his head toward the sky and released a long, mournful "Maaa," then dropped his head and trotted at A'isha's side. They stood beneath the fig tree, at the edge of the shallow grave.

As Amir lowered Isir into the ground, A'isha wailed, "Jida, please don't leave me!" Hira placed her arm around A'isha's waist and drew her close, as Amir positioned Isir onto the right side of her body, facing Mecca, in honor of Qibla.

A'isha dropped to her knees and screamed, "My jida! Please don't leave me! I'm all alone!"

Hira knelt over Isir and placed twigs of myrtle in the folds of her shroud to please the angels. She stood, lifted A'isha to her feet, and held her hand.

With bowed heads, Amir recited the burial prayer. His voice weighed with sorrow. "Bismillah wa ala millati ra sul illah." He repeated it in English, "In the name of Allah and the faith of the Messenger of Allah. From Allah we come and to Him we shall return. Inshallah."

He placed upon Isir branches of pine and the bark of cedar he had gathered from the forest, creating a lattice shield between Isir and the earth he had removed. He pushed the shovel into the mound of soil and showered it upon Isir until the mound was gone.

"A'isha, when you find a marker place it here, at your grandmother's head," he said.

She nodded, gazing at her grandmother's grave.

Amir raised his head and smiled at the twinkling stars dotting the moonlit sky. "The angels have welcomed her home," he said, then turned to A'isha. "What are you going to do?"

She wiped her tears. "What do you mean?"

He leaned the shovel against the fig tree. "You may come home with me if that is your wish."

"Or you can come home with me," Hira said.

A'isha looked at her grandmother's grave, and she looked at Ali. "I thank you both, but I will stay here."

Hira placed her hand on A'isha's shoulder. "Are you sure? You are welcome to—"

"Yes, I'm sure. Thank you," A'isha replied, forcing a smile, "but this is my home, and it is here where I will remain. And anyway, Ali needs me, and so do the chickens." She looked down at her grandmother's grave. "And this is where my jida would want me to be."

"Well, my child, if you change your mind, my home is yours," Hira said with a warm smile.

Amir nodded, "And mine, too."

"Come, let us help you clean up," said Hira.

"No, please. It is late and you have done enough for me. I can handle it."

A'isha went into the house and retrieved Hira's Qur'an and duas, then led them along the side of the house and out to the road.

"Thank you both for helping me…me and my jida."

Amir hugged her. "No need to thank us, A'isha. If you ever need me, you know where I am." He turned to Hira. "I will walk with you to your home."

"Shukran, Amir," she replied. "A'isha, we shall leave."

"Shukran, Maa'a Allah," A'isha said, hugging Hira, then Amir.

Amir smiled. He knew she spoke Tamazight, but it was the first time he heard her speak Arabic.

A'isha watched them walk down the moonlit path until they turned the bend at the Tamarisk tree, then she peered into the forest across the road. She lifted her face and searched the sky. "My jida, why did you leave me alone?" she whispered, then wiped her tears and walked toward the yard. Ali was standing near Isir's grave.

"Come, Ali, you may sleep in the house tonight."

Ali stretched his neck, released a long bleat, and trotted toward A'isha. He stopped at the threshold and looked up at her.

"Yes, Ali, you may come in," she said, patting his hind. He looked back at Isir's grave and entered her home.

The smell of death moved about the room. Ali lay at the door, watching A'isha gather the soiled sheets and towels and place them in a pile near the shed. His eyes followed her as she mopped the floor with fresh camphor water. She lit the logs in the firepit and heated water while she examined her wounded knees.

In the kitchen, she emptied the kettle into the zinc tub and eased into the warm water. She bathed her body and patted it dry, then slipped on a turquoise kaftan and lay on her side of the bed.

"Good night, Ali," she said; and blew at the lantern.

Stretching her arm to where her grandmother would lay, she moved her hand back and forth against the cool sheet until her eyes fluttered and closed.

"Good night, my jida," she whispered. "I will miss you."

She slipped into a dreamless sleep where she remained, until the rooster's crow awakened her to the dawn of a new day.

Tsewang

Rinpoche! Please come quickly!" Kasim shouted as he and Dabir stood at the bottom of the steep stairway looking up at the monastery's massive red door. Monks and novices clutched their mala beads and lifted their saffron kasayas to their knees as they ran toward them, some from the garden with tools in hand, others from the meadow with sutras. They gathered around, gasping at the frail and broken boy whose face was obscured with matted hair caked in mud. His head hung low with weakness and shame. A tall and slender monk adorned with a beauty mark on his cheek that resembled a splash of dark chocolate remained on the periphery, observing with a glint in his bespectacled eyes the plight of the newcomer and the excitement he produced.

"What do we have *here*?" Rinpoche asked breathlessly, drying his hands on a frayed cloth, and looking down at the crowd.

"We found him lying in the forest. He says he is from Pali Sholing…from Paro," Dabir said. "Please, sir, let us bring him to my room. He can rest there. May we?"

"Yes, of course," Rinpoche smirked, folding his flabby arms over his paunch.

The monks and novices followed Kasim and Dabir as they held Tsewang and ascended the steep and splintered stairs of faded yellow. "Someone, please, get water!" Dabir cried as they walked along an echoing corridor lined with red doors hanging on loose hinges. They arrived at a room across from the shrine, where candle flames flickered, and sticks of myrrh released ringlets of smoke toward a beamed ceiling blackened with soot.

Two novices, as young as six and seven, stacked pillows and swept the floor silently, unmoved by the stir across the hall.

Kasim opened the door to the small, austere room. It consisted of two mats, each with a quilt fashioned out of yak wool, neatly rolled where heads lay. The mats were separated by a low stool splattered with the candlewax of a white stub attached to a small tin plate. To the right of the door were four wooden cubicles that held a toothbrush, toothpaste, a dwindling bar of soap, and a jagged shard of mirror. Dabir lowered Tsewang onto one of the mats while monks and novices gathered at the doorway, their faces etched with awe and sadness.

Kasim dropped Tsewang's wet kasaya onto the floor and took the glass of water from a novice. "Kadrin chhe la," he said to the boy, and closed the door with a bow.

"You will stay in this room with me so I can look after you," Dabir said as he removed Tsewang's sandals. "You must shower and cleanse your body…your hair. The bathroom is just two doors away." He sat next to him. "But first, you must eat. You will have soup and begin to regain your strength." He looked up at Kasim. "Please go to the kitchen. Warm some of the soup served for lunch yesterday and bring it here. I am sure you will find some crackers in there, too."

"Consider it done!" Kasim said, poking out his chest and raising his chin, eager to please Dabir. He hurried out of the room and raced down the corridor, but as he approached the kitchen he slowed his pace to a crawl and his skin grew clammy. "Lord Buddha," he whispered, "please do not let Rinpoche see me."

Dabir stood up and removed his bathrobe from a hook. "Here, you may put this on. You will soon feel better. Buddha will see to that."

"Ugh," Tsewang moaned, attempting to stand, but the ache in his bones was unbearable. He slumped back onto the mat.

"You are in pain, my friend," Dabir said, opening the robe and guiding Tsewang's arms into it. He tied the sash, eased to his feet, and handed Tsewang the glass of water.

"Thank you," he whispered, and gulped the water until the glass was empty.

The door swung open and slammed into the cubicles. Dabir gasped and spun around with his hand splayed across his chest. "Kasim! Is an animal chasing you? Why do you insist on entering a room like a maniac?"

"Please forgive me, sir. But I have his soup, and I found some crackers," he said, flashing a broad smile. He sat next to Tsewang, scooped a spoonful of soup, and blew on it.

"I think he can feed himself, Kasim," Dabir said.

"Why, of course he can," he blushed.

Tsewang sat up and leaned against the wall. Kasim handed him the bowl and spoon.

Dabir closed the door and eased onto the mat across from Tsewang, then groaned at a knock on the door. "Kuzuzangpo? Who is it?"

The door opened slowly, releasing a long, slow creak. The slender, bespectacled monk with the birthmark on his cheek entered the room. He was holding a clean and neatly folded saffron kasaya. He locked his eyes with Tsewang's as he placed it near his thigh. "Tashi Delek," he said with a bow, then quietly exited the room.

Tsewang stared at the door. *I've seen that face before...that birthmark.* He raised the spoon to his lips and returned his attention to Dabir.

"Well, all I am saying, Kasim," Dabir said dryly, "is who would have ever thought *he* could be so considerate. And who does that kasaya belong to, anyway?"

"Sir, as you have taught me," Kasim replied, "wise men do not judge; they seek to understand."

Lukewarm water dribbled onto Tsewang's mud-streaked body. He scrubbed his skin raw and tried to remember the last time he had bathed. Washing and rinsing his mane with a sliver of soap, he lifted it off his shoulders and looked at it, baffled by its length. He exited the shower and dabbed himself dry, clenching his teeth as he worked his arms into the robe. When he returned to the room, he was thankful that Dabir and Kasim were nowhere in sight. The silence soothed him, and the warm soup and long shower had made him drowsy.

A cool breeze feathered through the open shutters, mingling with the bronze of an afternoon sun. His teeth chattered and goosebumps prickled his skin as he eased his arms out of the robe and lowered onto the mat closest to the door. Scanning his body as if he were seeing it for the first time, squinting with parted lips, he inspected scabs on his knees and elbows, picking at the gooey edges until pain shot his hand away from one wound and onto the next. He wrapped his hand around his big toe to numb the dull throb. Pus oozed into his palm with each squeeze as he tried to recall how his nail was torn off. He passed his hands along the length of his inner thighs, each suffused with oblong bruises that looked like a blending of blackberries and blood. *How did this happen?*

He slipped into the kasaya, grimacing from the ache in his shoulders, and lay on his back with his fingers knitted upon his protruding belly, filled with warm soup of lentil and rye. He inhaled deeply and remembered the forest. A tear escaped from the corner of his eye and trickled into his damp, tangled mane. The scent of Nag Champa, a blend of burnt wood and dampened earth, wafted from the shrine into his room and calmed his mind. The chime of tingsha bells soothed his heart. From the distant hills, Tsewang could hear the monks' solemn mantra to Ganesh, the Hindu God who destroys all obstacles, "Om Gum Ganapatayei Namah," and it lulled him into a deep sleep as he moved into midnight, dreaming of his mother and his beloved dog, Nugai.

***

The dungchen horns thundered across the hills of Thimphu as they had each morning at 4:00 a.m. The moon shimmered like a translucent pearl suspended in an obsidian sky, lending light

103

through slats into empty spaces. Tsewang opened his eyes, vaguely recalling how he had arrived at where he lay. He listened to Dabir yawn and mutter words he did not understand, but his voice reminded him of Tadashi's morning greeting, "Are you awake, my friend?" Tsewang rubbed his eyes. *He would ask me that question every morning. Of course, he knew I was awake. I wonder what Tadashi meant by that question, 'Are you awake, my friend?' I wonder if he is well.*

Dabir stood up, stretched and yawned, and grabbed his kasaya off the hook.

"Good Morning, Tsewang," he said, tying his sash, turning toward him, smiling. "I do not have to ask if you slept well, for surely you did. Your snore sounded like a lion's roar." He chuckled. "I brought a glass of water for you, but I could not shake you hard enough to awaken you. So, I left it here on the stool."

A spark of flame flashed across the room as Dabir lit the candle and extinguished the matchstick with a slow and steady blow. "How are you feeling?" he asked, handing Tsewang the glass of water.

What is his name? Tsewang wondered. He turned his head toward Dabir.

"I am well," he replied, propping onto his elbow to reach for the glass. Pain shot through his arm. "Ouch!" he yelled, spilling water onto the mat. He drank until the glass was empty and handed it to Dabir.

"I see you are still feeling pain."

"Yes, I have bruises on my body, and I cannot recall how I got them. I must have…" He eased onto his back. "Anyway, thank you for allowing me to rest in your room."

"It is my obligation to do so," Dabir said. He collected his toothpaste and soap. "I…I am…" He turned toward Tsewang. His smile faded, and he held Tsewang's eyes with his own. The candlelight flashed shadows across their faces. "You appeared awfully close to death. I have never been so frightened in my life. But our loving protector, Mahakala, kept you safe and here you are. I am grateful to him and to Buddha that we found you. This morning, I will offer a special prayer of gratitude to both for guiding Kasim and me to you. You may want to do the same." He placed his hand on the doorknob and lowered his eyes to the floor. "It is nearly time for morning puja, and we must not be late."

Monks and novices entered the prayer room in silence. They approached the altar and bowed deeply before sitting in lotus position upon mended red velvet cushions. Tsewang eased onto one closest to the door. A novice chimed a prayer bell to announce Rinpoche's entrance into the room; his face was solemn as he bowed at the altar and placed a white silk khata upon the portraits of Guru Rinpoche and the White Tara Thangka. He released a lotus flower into the offering bowl and placed his hand upon a tureen of apples and oranges in a prayerful way. He lit the butter lamps, bowed deeply, touched his forehead with his praying hands, and sat on a cushion at the dais. Sitting at the left of Rinpoche, a monk circled the rim of a ghanta with a mallet, while another struck a dorje with his hand; and to his right, a monk drummed a damaru, while another blew into a kangling horn. Each instrument tossed a vibration onto the faces of monks and novices as they advanced mala beads between their thumb and forefinger after each whispered prayer. In unison, they bowed their heads and sat silently; then shifted to the chant for compassion, Om Mani Padme Hum. Morning puja had begun.

Tsewang bowed his head. *I cannot recall the last time I prayed.* His hair fell forward, hiding his face. *This is not who I am anymore. I do not belong here.* The forest flashed across his mind, competing with the lull of the monks' mantra, "Om mani padme hum…Om mani padme hum." He squeezed his eyes until they hurt, trying to blink away visions of sloths and bears clawing up pine trees and musk deer foraging through brush. He opened his eyes, looked around the room, and closed them. He could see the stealth leopards he hid from beneath juniper bushes and upon branches of Oak. His heart pounded. He flinched at the gray wolf that flashed across his mind, the one that chased him up a tree. "Mother!" he moaned, releasing his panic into the monks' chant for compassion, "Om mani padme hum."

His palms moistened and his throat tightened as he relived his empty search for water. And in the backdrop, he could hear the chant of compassion, "Om mani padme hum." He squirmed. His thighs ached upon the thin cushion. His legs cramped, locked in lotus position as his mind returned to the forest and his hunger, thirst, and fear. He saw the betel nuts. In the backdrop, he could hear the chant of compassion compete for his attention. His eyes welled with tears.

He shook his head, panting and whispering, "I do not belong here," and choked back a scream emerging from his heart as the roar of kangling horns and the beat of damaru drums tangled with howling gyalings, ringing dorjes, and the clang of cymbals. Each pitching a penetrating, vibrating cacophony that raped his ears, mimicked his confusion, and taunted his soul, fueling his urge to get up and run.

Then it stopped. Silence seeped into the room. The monks and novices stood up, bowed, placed their mala beads around their necks, stacked their pillows, and exited the room. They retrieved their alms bowls from the kitchen and awaited Rinpoche's release. He pulled open the massive red door and an impatient chill forced its way in, eclipsing the warmth of the sun. The monks descended the steep stairway.

"Now it is time for pindapata, Tsewang. I'm sure you practiced pindapata at Pali Sholing, yes?" Kasim asked. "Here, you will need this," he said, extending an alms bowl.

"Thank you. Tell me, what is the name of the brother who has welcomed me into his room?"

"Ah, his name is Dabir. He is my preceptor. If you stick around long enough, perhaps he will become yours."

If I stick around long enough…ha! "And I'm sorry, what is your name?"

"My brother, my name is Kasim. Do you even know where you are?"

"Not exactly."

"You are in Dechen Podrang, just outside the city of Thimphu."

"I see. Thimphu, you say?"

"Yes, Thimphu. You came a long way. You told us you are from Paro."

"Yes, I am. Well, yes and no."

"What do you mean?"

Tsewang glanced at the monks lining up on the pebbled pathway, adjusting their kasayas and glancing at him from the corner of their eyes.

He lowered his voice. "I lived in a monastery in Paro, but that is not where my mother lives. She lives in…in…"

"Tsewang!" Rinpoche yelled from the door.

The monks gasped and fell silent.

"Surely, you cannot take part in pindapata with an unshaven head. Come here! The rest of you, it is getting late, you should have begun minutes ago. Be on your way, now!"

"Y-yes, of c-course," Kasim stammered, grabbing the alms bowl out of Tsewang's hand. "Go with Rinpoche, you may join us tomorrow. Go!"

Tsewang ascended the stairs, gripping the banister and grimacing with each step. He stood next to Rinpoche and watched him glare at the monks. His paunch and stubby toes reminded him of Tadashi. The bulge of fat on the nape of his neck reminded him of Buddha. They watched the monks secure their alms bowls in their left arm and walk in silence and single formation along the path that would lead them into the heart of Thimphu. When they turned the bend and were no longer in sight, Rinpoche snapped, "Come with me! I want to talk to you."

Tsewang followed him down the drafty corridor.

"Sit there," he said, pointing to a low stool and yanking open a drawer. "I must shave your head if you are going to remain with us."

Tsewang looked around the kitchen and recalled the hours he had spent scrubbing the floor at Pali Sholing, years before he was tall enough to reach the countertop and cupboards.

"I hear you are from Paro, from Pali Sholing. Is that so?" Rinpoche asked, rummaging through a cubicle, sifting through utensils.

"Yes, that is where I grew up," Tsewang replied, groping his hair.

"Tell me, how did you end up in this condition? How did you end up in the forest, *supposedly* near death?" he asked, approaching Tsewang with shearing scissors and a white tablecloth used to cover the altar on special occasions. He held the scissors between his teeth, wrapped the cloth around Tsewang's shoulders, and then gripped the shears as a hunter would a spear. Tsewang pulled away, looking up at him, wide-eyed.

"What do you think I'm going to do, stab you? Sit up!" Rinpoche yelled. "I asked you a question. What were you doing in the forest?"

"Well, sir, I ran away."

"Why would you do that? And run into the forest of all places," he snorted, scanning Tsewang's hair as if he were searching for something he was afraid to find.

Tsewang lowered his head. "I want to find my mother, my family."

"Find your mother! Is that why you ran into the forest…to find your *mother*?" Rinpoche tossed his head back and laughed. "What is she, a wild boar?"

Tsewang raised his head and looked at Rinpoche. "I want to find my mother and I…I had to leave because…"

"Because of what?" he snapped, grabbing a clump of hair, releasing it with a huff, then grabbing another. Tsewang winced.

"I arrived at Pali Sholing when I was seven years old. I am now sixteen…I think."

"You *think*? Are you telling me you don't know how old you are?" He grabbed a clump of hair and cut it off.

Tsewang hunched his shoulders, feeling the blade graze against his scalp. He watched his hair tumble onto the sheet. "I seem to have lost count of the years, I guess."

"And so, do you know how long you were in the forest? Or did you lose count of that, too?"

"Given that I am here on this stool, I suppose I wasn't in the forest long enough," Tsewang replied, slipping his hand from under the sheet and catching a tangle of hair just before it fell to the floor.

"You're a sly one, I see. You are the kind of boy Buddha warns us about," Rinpoche said, grabbing and chopping off another clump of hair.

Tsewang watched it tumble to the floor.

"You still have not answered my question. Why did you run away from Pali Sholing? You said you wanted to find your mother, but what was the other reason? You started to say something, what was it?" He grabbed another clump of hair and chopped it off. Tsewang hunched his shoulders to his ears. "Be still!" Rinpoche yelled.

"Sir…I…I don't…I ran away because…" His thoughts drifted to his last argument with Tadashi, the one about Satya, the virtue of truthfulness. *How truthful should I be?* he wondered, catching another clump of hair before it tumbled to the floor, then easing his clenched hand beneath the sheet.

Rinpoche released a handful of hair, moved in front of Tsewang, and folded his arms. "You don't *what?* What *don't* you know, Tsewang? Or better yet, what *do* you know?"

Tsewang stared at him, clutching his tangled mane beneath the sheet. He bit onto his bottom lip. He could hear Tadashi's voice, "We must take the path of least resistance, Tsewang. You must remember that the root of all suffering is our resistance to what is."

And then he heard his own voice. "Sir, I left Pali Sholing because the headmaster, the Rinpoche, is abusing the novices," he looked into Rinpoche's eyes, "…and he abused me."

"What do you mean, *he abused you?*" Rinpoche sneered, glaring at Tsewang, gripping the scissors so tightly that his fingers tingled.

"It is as I said. He abused me. He has tormented me since I was seven years old."

"In the name of Jampelyang!" Rinpoche hollered, raising his face toward the ceiling, "Please punish this child's tongue!" He dropped the scissors, grabbed Tsewang's shoulders, and shook him. "How dare you say such a thing! Chana Dorje will strike you with the swiftest of thunder and make you disappear if you say such a thing ever again! Do you hear me!?"

Tsewang's sullen eyes grew icy. Images of the child he once was flashed across his mind, the child who silently begged Buddha to pry him from Rinpoche's grip. And as he stared at the man who stood before him, his sadness morphed into a silent, seething rage. "Why do you react so strongly to what I am saying, Rinpoche?" he asked. "Why do you respond this way?" He tilted his head with a wry smile. "Do you not believe me?"

"Are you mocking me, boy?"

"No, I am simply asking you a question." He straightened his back, lifted his chin, and spread his feet firmly on the floor, the flaps of his kasaya parted. "Answer me, Rinpoche. Why do my words trouble you so? Is it because what I am saying raises concern in you…or perhaps fear?"

"Fear? How dare you! How dare you come into my monastery and taunt me? You are nothing but an orphaned child—a throwaway!"

His words sliced through Tsewang. He tightened his grip on his clumps of hair. "Why does my truth trouble you, Rinpoche? Why are you asking me to dishonor Satya?"

"Dishonor Satya? I would never do such a thing! But your so-called truth is nothing but a lie!"

"How do you know? What do you know about that which I speak? Why are you so quick to deny what I am saying about the abuse the novices are forced to endure? What do *you* know about that, Rinpoche?" Tsewang pulled his feet together and stood up. Clumps of hair tumbled to the floor.

Rinpoche stepped back; he had not noticed Tsewang's height until now. He looked up at him. "How dare you come here and start trouble? You—a throwaway! Have you forgotten that I am the Rinpoche of this monastery?"

"No, I have not forgotten," Tsewang replied, picking up the scissors. But I am telling you this: I and every other novice at Pali Sholing have been abused! Do you hear me? Violated!" he screamed.

Rinpoche's face twisted with disgust. "How? How have you been violated—*abused*—as you say?"

"Sexually! That is how! We have been forced to do things that…that," Tsewang looked away and lowered his voice to a pleading whisper. "They made me do things that have caused me to question if Mahakala and Buddha even exist." The room spun; his knees weakened. He eased onto the stool and gazed up at Rinpoche. "If Mahakala is our protector, how could he allow such a thing to happen? How could he allow the children to be treated so badly?"

"I do not—I *cannot*—believe my ears! I know nothing of what you speak!" Rinpoche screamed.

Tsewang sprang up, glaring at him, tightening his grip on the scissors.

"Well, you may not believe your ears, but you better believe me! I am telling you the truth. I know what I have experienced for the past eight years. And I know that it is still happening, even as we speak. I am certain of that! Who knows, maybe the novices at Pali Sholing aren't the *only* boys who are being abused."

"What do you mean by that?" Rinpoche scowled, balling his hands into fists.

"Exactly as I said. Maybe other boys are suffering in the same way." He lowered his voice and moved closer to Rinpoche. "What I *do* know is that it must end—it *will* end." He untied the sheet around his neck and shoved it into Rinpoche's hands. "I swear to you, even with the last breath I take, I will make known what is happening to the boys."

Tsewang held the scissors and his tangled hair in one hand as he touched his head with the other, feeling the random, scattered connections between scalp and hair. He locked his eyes into Rinpoche's as they stood inches apart, their hearts pounded against their chests. With flared nostrils and clenched teeth, they glared at one another until Rinpoche inhaled and lowered his eyes. Tsewang nodded and smiled, then turned and walked out of the room without a bow. Pounding his feet onto the hollow, wooden floor, he stormed toward the room he shared with Dabir, passing two novices, leaving an echo of footsteps in his wake.

A'isha

Allah, please make me invisible.

Gone were the days when A'isha would whisper these words as she approached the village upon her arrival for school. No longer did she bow her head to avoid the eyes of women who peered at her through the slits of their black niqabs, attempting to inject into her veins a daily dose of guilt and the burden of their own shame. Anger did not curl her fingers into fists as she walked across the hills of Ouirgane, taunted by the boys who followed her from school, tossing pebbles and kicking dirt at her, yelling, "Qadhir! Mithlia! Ahira! Dirty! Lesbian! Whore!" For they finally left her alone. The probing eyes of men, trailed by their seductive smirk, no longer made her feel naked, vulnerable, and empty. Their perception of her did not determine her worth…no, not anymore, nor was her identity shaped by their manly needs. After her jida's death, A'isha returned to school uncloaked by shame. She walked through the village with her head lifted, no longer whispering, "Allah, please make me invisible."

She did not seek her family, nor did her eyes wander in search of Saira; their abandonment occupied less space in her heart. She granted herself the freedom to forgive. Without her jida, she eased into a new version of life, accepting that she was her own protector, her sole provider. Each day, upon her return from school, she would peel off her uniform and slip into her grandmother's turquoise kaftan. She would brush Ali's nose and giggle at his "maa" of delight. She would feed the chickens, extract their eggs, and hoist water from the well. She would toil the earth behind their home, immersing her hands deep into the cool, moist soil, pulling weeds and planting seeds to sustain its fertility and reap its harvest. Balancing a basket upon her hip, she would walk barefoot toward the forest edge (she loved the feel of the damp earth between her toes), and she would gather limes, almonds, and bundles of mint, receiving the Earth's offerings while Ali followed her, nudging her thigh intermittently, wanting her to stroke his nose.

In the chill that arrives with dusk, she would sit on the porch wrapped in her grandmother's chador and watch the sun set behind the mountains' silhouette, rocking in her chair and sharing figs with Ali, humming nasheeds her grandmother had taught her. Sometimes, when the river was tranquil and welcoming, she would enter it and gather stones of onyx and slate, then return to her home and lay them upon her grandmother's grave. "This is for you, my jida. I miss you so." She kept a tin can of freshly picked wildflowers at the head of her jida's grave, near the pinecones she had collected and laid in the shape of a J.

On Saturdays, she would sweep out the firepit, mop the floor, shake out the tattered rug her jida had kept at the foot of her bed, and gather water from the well to wash her uniform and hijabs in the large zinc tub. And on Sundays, she would prepare soup and khobz with the vegetables and herbs she harvested from her garden, and with the flour given to her by Abdullah, the village grocer. She brewed jugs of mint tea with lime and topped them with cinnamon, how her jida had taught her. By sunset, she would bathe in lukewarm water and settle into her pajamas. With a steaming cup of mint tea, she would sit on her bed and study for exams in the warmth of crackling embers, soothed by their tangerine glow.

It was on a Saturday morning, a month after her jida's death, that Amir decided to visit A'isha. *After all*, he thought, *she is no longer a child. What could Nabeel say?* As he walked along the high ridge of Ouirgane, he gazed at the valley below, at the amber soil that sloped in waves between rosebushes and juniper trees. When he arrived at the river, he inhaled deeply and smiled at the slivers of sun that dipped into the water and moved to the rhythm of its flow. He gazed at the river as he eased onto a boulder upon its bank and wiped beads of sweat off his brow.

"Allah," he said, as he swept his eyes across the blue sky, "the beauty You create is without bounds. To You, I give praise. I ask You to strengthen and forgive me for where I am weak. With humility, I ask for Your mercy. Inshallah."

He raised his eyes toward the crescent mountains that cradle Ouirgane and thought of Nabeel.

"It was the worst mistake of my life," he whispered, shifting his weight upon the boulder and rubbing the ache in his knees. Squinting at the sun, he flinched at the image of Nabeel's face that flashed across his mind, and he recalled the last time he had seen his friend, the day he learned Nabeel tossed A'isha out of his home.

He had been sitting at the kitchen table when his wife rushed in with a basket of damp clothes and dropped it into the sink.

"Amir! I was at the river and Samar told me awful news—just awful!"

"What did she say, *this* time?" Amir sighed. He was not fond of gossip.

"She said a big commotion happened at Nabeel's house last night. Something about him throwing A'isha onto the road. I don't know for sure," she said, wringing her hands, "but you should go check on them." She scanned his face for a response as she lowered into the chair beside him and raised his cup of tea to her lips.

Amir moaned as he recalled that day. "Why did I go to his house? I should have kept my nose out of his business."

He raised his eyes toward the sky, patted his breast pocket, retrieved his cigarettes, lit one, held it between his lips, and recalled the moment he arrived at Nabeel's house.

"How *dare* you come here and chastise me as if I am some child?" Nabeel had screamed. "How dare you tell me how I should manage my family?"

"I am just telling you that there are other ways to deal with A'isha besides throwing her out of your house."

"This is none of your business, Amir. Do you even know why A'isha is no longer allowed in my home? Do you even know what she did—who she is? No! you don't. You just—"

"Well, maybe I do know!" Amir shouted. "What makes you think I don't know?"

Nabeel's eyes widened. "What does it matter, anyway? What does it matter what you know…what *anyone* knows!" Nabeel hollered.

Amir peered at him and nodded, "I have been telling you that for years, Nabeel."

They stared at each other; Aaminah stared at them.

"What do you mean by that, Amir?" she had asked, walking toward them. "What do you mean you have been telling Nabeel that for years?"

"Stay out of this!" Nabeel shouted.

"Tell her, Nabeel! Tell her what I mean!" Amir hollered.

Nabeel glared at Amir, shook his head, and threw his hands into the air. "I am finished with this. Get out of my house!" he shouted, pointing to the door.

"Is this how you handle your problems," Amir yelled as Nabeel swung the door open, "by throwing people away? By denying the truth?"

"What truth?!"

Amir lowered his voice to a whisper, "You know *exactly* what I am talking about."

"I do not! Go away! You are no longer welcome here!"

Amir backed out of the house and onto the road. Nabeel followed him, tightening his fists. Basha and Aaminah remained near the door. Their eyes brimmed with tears, filled with the same despair that twisted Amir's face as Nabeel screamed, "Go! You must leave. Do not come back here!"

Amir spun around. He gasped and his legs weakened when he saw his neighbors gathered, at a distance. Their heads shook in disbelief and their mouths gaped in horror as they watched two elders, who were a source of spiritual guidance for so many, speak to each other with such dishonor.

"What, in the eyes of Allah, would cause Amir and Nabeel to behave like this?" a woman whispered, cradling her crying child.

"I cannot imagine," replied another, "but whatever the reason, Allah's heart aches for them."

They lowered their heads and walked away as Amir turned toward Nabeel and pleaded, "Please, Nabeel, do not do this to us. I love you."

Nabeel clenched his teeth, glaring at Amir. Aaminah approached him and placed her hand on his elbow. "Nabeel, let us go inside," she said, quietly.

"Do not touch me!" he shouted, yanking his arm away from her, and ripping the seam in his tunic. He tightened his fists and scowled at his neighbors, then pounded his feet into the earth as he returned home. He waited for Aaminah to enter, and slammed the door shut.

Amir stared at the dirt that swirled in Nabeel's wake. He wanted to fall onto his knees and scream, but his neighbors' prying eyes weighed on him. He spun around. "Excuse me, excuse me," he begged, pushing through the crowd, "Please, let me through, let me be."

The memory of that night made Amir shudder. He eased off the boulder, tossed his cigarette onto the ground, extinguished it with a few quick twists of his foot, and proceeded toward A'isha's home. He walked along the river, listening to the water's rumble. "It is turbulent today," he said, then returned his thoughts to his fallout with Nabeel.

A quiet sadness had settled upon the village after that day, a stubborn stillness unmoved by the Mu'addin's calls for prayer, unshaken by the rise and fall of the sun. The demise of Amir and Nabeel's friendship was whispered about. Speculations of truth lingered on the lips of women along the river, and among the men who tend to their shops in the heart of the village. Their customers dispatched the news to neighboring villages, and to the grazing nomads of the plateau who received the gossip as warily as they accepted the eggs and olives brought to them as a nod toward kindness. The merchants of Marrakesh returned to the medina without Amir's beaded abayas and were baffled by the reason why. The news of the ending of Nabeel and Amir's friendship whipped around Ouirgane like the sands of the Sahara and was viewed as a greater disruption to the spiritual cohesion of the village than the news of A'isha and Saira's illicit friendship.

Amir had become ashamed of his conduct and was convinced the village had lost every ounce of respect it once had for him. *Rightfully so*, he insisted and refused to leave his home. With his wife visiting their daughter, Hakima, at the madrasa in Fez, she was unaware of the monumental disturbance he had caused, nor was she there to encourage him to get out of bed.

A week had passed before he mustered up the courage to return to the shop. *The merchants must have arrived by now, seeking the abayas I have yet to bead. I must return to the shop. After all, life goes on.* The walk seemed longer than usual. He greeted his neighbors with a reticent smile and meekly avoided the friendly banter he had once enjoyed.

He approached the shop and fumbled the key into the lock. "Please do not get stuck today," he whispered, and pushed the door open. He hurried in and eased the creaking door back into its warped jamb. His eyes moved across the abandoned room of sifted sun. His chest tightened as he gazed at Nabeel's tools scattered upon his workbench. He folded his arms and leaned against the door. Tears stung his eyes as he recalled the last evening they spent together in the shop—the night Nabeel arrived home and found Tayseer's son, Josiah, lurking near his home, eager to tell him, "I saw A'isha and Saira in the forest today."

That same night, Nabeel had hung the CLOSED sign in their window earlier than usual so they could enjoy a bottle of wine the merchant from Marrakesh brought for them, as he had on each visit, in exchange for a favor or two. He recalled with a smile how Nabeel pulled on the chain attached to the unshaded lightbulb that dangled from the ceiling and darkened the room. Nabeel took him by the hand, and they retreated to the rear, exhaling with relief as Nabeel uncorked the bottle. Chuckling at the pop of released tension, he filled their glasses to the brim.

Lounging upon bundles of black organza and burgundy silk, they had raised their glasses and recited with satisfaction, a Moroccan proverb, "The first glass is as bitter as life, the second glass is as strong as love, the third glass is as gentle as death." With a wink, they clinked their glasses and sipped. Tossing their heads back with hushed laughter, they reminisced about their opening day and relived the pride they shared fifteen years ago, as the village gathered with fruit and pastilla to celebrate their success.

And as they drank the wine, they moved onto their secret fears and silent dreams, as they often had, and shared their innermost selves until the bottle was dry.

"What time is it, Amir?"

"I have no idea. Have you heard the Mu'addin?"

"You know it is difficult to hear anything back here," Nabeel said with a wry smile.

"Well, I suppose we should leave, yes?" Amir asked, hesitantly.

"Yes, my friend, it is time."

Their eyes spoke the words their mouths could not, and they arose in a gradual unfolding that revealed a confluence of age, reluctance, and regret. They stood in shadows tossed by moonlight and glanced at each other one last time before they exited their shop and locked the door.

If I had known that would be our last night together, Amir thought as he stared into the river, *I would have...I should have...* He shook his head and tugged his mind back to his memory of that night.

Hoping nightfall would conceal their longing and boozy merriment from the men who linger in their shops well into the night, Amir and Nabeel stepped onto the road and were relieved to be greeted only by the sound of silence penetrated by a rooster's crow. They walked together along the barren road of shuttered windows and dormant dust, inhaling the cool of evening dew, and released into it the musky scent of red wine cloaked in piety, as they privately asked Allah for His forgiveness, and wondered when the merchant from Marrakesh was due to return.

The memory of that evening saddened Amir as much as it aroused him. He yearned for Nabeel, for his touch. He looked at his groin as his erection grew. Walking became difficult, so he stopped, lit a cigarette, waited a moment, and then continued toward A'isha's home. His physical response to Nabeel produced a guilt that crept from his bowel, seized his throat, and filled his mouth with the bitterness of bile. "I am such a hypocrite," he whispered, grabbing his kufi off his head. And his guilt morphed into rage as his thoughts of Nabeel shifted to a less erotic memory.

After their argument, Nabeel did not return to the shop. Amir would arrive each morning hoping to see him at his workbench, but his hope was futile, and his prayers remained unanswered. He threw himself into tedious tasks around the shop to distract himself from Nabeel's absence, but everything reminded him of Nabeel—his messy workbench, the buttery scent of his saddle soap, his stool that squeaked with every turn. "Why don't you wipe some oil on that thing?" Amir would often ask, feigning frustration. "Then how would you know when to look up at me and smile?" Nabeel would reply with a wink.

Amir's heart ached each time he entered the shop. *I should just sell it*, he often thought, *but what if he returns?* And so, he trudged to the shop each day. By the third week, he awoke with renewed energy and had even begun to greet his customers with a smile. That is until Shahid had arrived for a visit.

"As-salāmu alaikum, Amir," he said, flashing a jagged row of tobacco-stained teeth. He was a thirty-year-old man with a bend in his posture brought on by his love for cheap wine. A black kufi covered his thinning hair, and a dusty tunic hung on his bony body which hungered for a good meal and affection.

"Wa 'alaikum al-salaam," Amir replied glumly, plopping beads into jars.

"I have not seen you in quite some time, Amir. How have you been?" Shahid asked, furrowing his brow with mocked concern.

"I have seen better days. What brings you here?" *This gossipy opportunist. I wish he would go away.*

"Nabeel…have you seen him?" he asked, removing his kufi, and placing it on the glass countertop.

"No, I have not seen him. Have you?" Tension tightened his words.

"In fact, I *have* seen Nabeel—him and his wife. They were…" Shahid paused and scanned Amir's face.

"Well, go on, they were what?" Amir asked. He adjusted his kufi, picked up two jars of beads, and walked toward the back of the shop.

"He cut a deal with me," Shahid said. "He wanted to trade his furnishings for one of my mules."

Amir spun around. *"His furnishings?"*

"Yes, you know…pots, bedding, a rug…stuff. Most of it was quite old, but—"

"But why would he want to give you his…why would he need your mule? Did you trade with him?"

"Well, of course I did. Why wouldn't I? He needed my mule, and I could always use…well, it doesn't matter. Anyway, I was told he left the village one day last week. I hear he left so early that even the roosters were still asleep."

"Is that so?" Amir walked toward Shahid and pushed a large jar of sequins to the end of the counter. It slammed against the wall.

Shahid raised his brow. "That was close! You would've had quite the mess if that jar had cracked."

Amir grabbed spools of thread out of a bowl, dropped them onto the counter, and assorted them, tossing them into tin cans, doing what he could to conceal the tremble in his hands and to hide his eyes from Shahid, 'the troublemaker,' as he and Nabeel had dubbed him years ago.

"Anyway," Shahid said, leaning against the counter, cleaning his nails with a toothpick, "I hear he was with his wife and daughter—and my mule. I was told it was carrying sacks of who-knows-what." He put the toothpick in the ashtray and looked at Amir. "I hope he knows it is an old mare and cannot carry too much weight without collapsing."

Amir lost his patience. He scooped up the remaining spools and dropped them into a can.

"Thank you for stopping by," he scowled, "but I must get back to work."

Shahid tilted his head and smiled.

"Did you hear me? I said it is time for you to leave. I have much work to do."

"Ah, yes," Shahid replied, placing his kufi on his head, "I know you're a busy man and I do not want to get in your way. But I was thinking, now that Nabeel is gone you will need help with the shop, yes?"

"No, I am getting along just fine."

"Well, Amir, you never know…things might change," he grinned, and left as quickly as he had arrived.

Stunned, Amir gasped for air. He walked to the rear of the shop and eased himself onto a bundle of fabric. He pressed his elbows into his knees, wringing his hands, rocking back and forth. He stared at the floor, nauseous, crippled by waves of disbelief and denial followed by anguish and anger. He buried his face into his palms and wept. "How could you leave me, Nabeel? How could you leave us?" he whispered, over and over, vowing he would never involve himself in the business of another man, ever again.

Amir tore himself away from that awful memory, moaning and shaking his head. "So very painful," he said. "It has been many months, and it is still so painful." He wiped his eyes and tossed his face to the sky. "Ya Allah!" he called out, scanning the rugged mountains etched across the cerulean sky. He inhaled deeply and listened to the river's swoosh against its bed of stones. A pain shot across his chest and landed in his back. He clenched his teeth, grimacing. *Could thoughts of Nabeel still cause my heart to ache?* He massaged the dull throb in his chest and proceeded to walk. He could see A'isha's house up the road. *Although I vowed to never involve myself in Nabeel's family, I must honor Allah. He warns us against harboring resentment. Besides, I had no choice. I had to help A'isha bury her grandmother. I could not have turned my back on her the way her father has.* He approached A'isha's home, glanced down at his groin, and released his breath with a slow sigh. *I must forgive Nabeel for what he has done. I must move on with my life.* He knocked on the door. *But I beg of You, Allah, please bring Nabeel back home to me. Inshallah.*

"A'isha? Salaam? Are you here?"

"Amir!" she exclaimed, "I'm back here!"

He smiled at the joy in her voice.

She dropped the shovel and ran past the chicken coop, along the side of her home.

"Maaa!" Ali bleated, trotting behind her.

"Amir! It's so good to see you," she said, hugging him.

He kissed her on each cheek. "It is good to see you, too," he replied, flashing a broad smile.

"Please, come in. I just gathered a bundle of mint; we can have some tea."

She led him through the front door, hoping he noticed the wreath she fashioned out of cork, oak, and fennel. Ali followed them and lay on the rug at the foot of A'isha's bed.

Amir eased onto the wrought-iron chair near the firepit and swept his eyes across the room. "Your home feels lovely, A'isha."

"Thank you," she said, over her shoulder, smiling and washing her hands in the bucket of water she had drawn that morning. She dried them, dropped a handful of mint leaves into a pot, filled it with water from another bucket, and hung it over the firepit's simmering embers. She sat down at the table, then jumped up and retrieved two bamboo placemats and two mugs and spoons, then returned to the table and exhaled with a smile.

"How have you been, A'isha? You look well."

"I'm okay, but sometimes I feel lonely. Ali is good company, but I miss my jida."

"I'm sure you do. But, you must know that her spirit lives on and she is always with you."

"I believe she is. Sometimes, when I'm in bed, reading, the scent of cinnamon fills the room. I think it is her."

Amir nodded, "Bialtabe. Yes, of course, it is her. My mother has been deceased for many years and I still miss her. At times, when I feel her presence, I talk to her."

"Do you, really?"

"Yes, I do. And I encourage you to do the same. Your grandmother will listen and remind you that you are not alone." He leaned back in his seat. "And school? I trust you are still attending, yes?"

"Yes, I attend every day. My classmates don't tease me. Not anymore. But my teachers…the adults…they, well…I'm glad my school is on the back road and not in the village, so I don't have to see those phony people every day."

She removed the pot from the firepit, poured tea into two mugs; then went into the kitchen and returned with a plate of biscuits. "I made these. They're almond biscuits. I made them the way my jida taught me. Please, have some."

"Ah! How could I resist? They are my favorite! Shukran." He bit into one. "Ladhidh! Delicious!"

"Shukran," she replied, settling into her chair. "So, yes, I have just one more year until I can attend a university."

"That is wonderful news," Amir beamed. He lifted the mug to his nose and inhaled the minty aroma. "Ah, this is my first cup for the day. Usually, I would have had ten cups by now!"

"Ana uhibb al-shay," she replied.

"Well, well…this is the second time you've spoken Arabic. I don't recall ever hearing you speak Arabic *or* Tamazight."

"My grandmother has a book that translates phrases like 'thank you' and 'you're welcome.' I read it, sometimes."

"Your father would be delighted to know this. I suppose…" His face flushed.

A'isha looked away and sipped her tea.

"I apologize, A'isha. I didn't mean to upset you."

"You can mention my baba. It's okay, Amir. I'm sure you know why he asked me to leave his house."

"Yes, I do know. I know all about that awful night." He shook his head. "I was not surprised."

"Not surprised by what?"

"By what you told him or by the way he responded."

"Did he tell you? I figured you found out from the nosy neighbors. I thought he would be too ashamed of me to tell anyone."

"He didn't tell me why he threw you out of his house. I found out from…from…"

"You see? I was right. I know I was the talk of the village. I probably still am, even after all this time. That's why no one speaks to me. I'm the pariah. People act like they're angels…like they don't do anything wrong. Well, I haven't done anything wrong. I am who I am. I have a good heart. I just wish having a good heart is enough to be accepted, but it's not. I…I—"

"A'isha, listen to me." He placed his mug on the table. "You must know that the Qur'an admonishes such a thing. But I do not judge you for who you are." He looked at the smoldering embers. "I would be a hypocrite if I tried."

"What do you mean?"

He cleared his throat and looked at her. "I…I…Your father and I…"

"What are you trying to tell me, Amir?"

"Look, I have known you since you were a child, and I have suspected your…your ways…who you are…for quite some time. But that has never changed my admiration for you."

"You *admire* me?"

"Of course, I do. I admire how you speak your truth."

"Thank you, Amir." Tears filled her eyes. "You are one of the few people who ever loved me."

"Your father loves you too, A'isha."

"Have you seen him? Have you seen my family?"

"No, I have not. They moved out of the village months ago. Where to? I do not know. And I hear Saira and her family have also moved…to Imlil."

A'isha eased away from the table, opened the front door, and peered at the forest across the road. "How could my family—my *mother*—leave without telling me? I knew they had moved away…that day I went to their house and saw it was empty…the day my jida died. I have spent so many nights lying awake, wondering where they could be. Sometimes, I wonder if they ever really cared for me. My baba and I…we used to be so close when I was a little girl. And now they went away and left me alone. I miss my sister. I wonder if she is going to school…if she has made new friends. And Saira…" She wiped her eyes.

"A'isha, I know your family loves you. And yes, you and your father used to be close when you were a little girl—like buddies. I know things changed as you got older. I could never understand why he…" He leaned back and shook his head.

A'isha returned to the table.

Amir cleared his throat. "I know he could not accept you for who you are, and it caused so many arguments. I know it was unfair to you. The day I finally stood up to him it cost us our friendship." He looked at the firepit. "I am such a hypocrite."

"You're not a hypocrite, Amir. You're one of the most honest people I know. My father, *he's* the hypocrite—and so is my mother. But I don't blame her, she's just as much a victim as I was. Baba took my home and family away from me, but he stole my mother's voice. Islam stole—"

"No, A'isha. I am also a hypocrite. A perpetrator and victim wrapped in one."

"I don't get it. Why do you keep calling yourself that, Amir?"

"I…I…well, that's another story."

"What do you mean? What's the other story?"

"Perhaps I will explain that to you someday; maybe during our next visit." He dabbed his mouth and stood up, rubbing at the tightness in his chest. "All I can say is things are not always what they appear to be. I'm sure you know that by now. I must be on my way."

"But you just arrived. Please stay a little longer."

"I will return," he said, coughing.

"Are you still smoking, Amir?"

"Yes, I am."

"I wish you would stop. I have always considered you family, and now you're all I have." She looked at Ali. Her mother's face flashed across her mind, stirring her anger.

"One day I will quit smoking. But for now, I must head home. It is quite a walk from the village to here. And just think, you do it every day! Ah, the advantage of youth."

A'isha handed him the two remaining biscuits. "Please, take these."

"Shukran," he smiled, and wrapped them in his handkerchief.

Ali followed them out the door.

"Thank you for coming to check on me, Amir. Next time, I will visit you, if that's okay."

He placed his hands on her shoulders. "A'isha, you are *always* welcome in my home. Do not ever forget that." He kissed her on each cheek and stepped off the porch. "Have you seen Hira?"

"No, but I must visit her. Her niece should be returning home in a couple of weeks."

"Her niece? Where is she?"

"She studies at Al-Akhawayn, the university in Ifrane if I remember correctly."

"Will you pursue your studies there?"

"It's a good school, but I want to leave these mountains." She looked beyond Amir, into the forest. "I used to say that to my baba, but he never…he never encouraged me to do or be anything except a good Muslim woman."

"What do you wish to study?"

She looked at him and smiled. "Sociology. I want to study world cultures."

"Wonderful! Do you want to teach? My wife's sister teaches at the university in Marrakesh. Maybe you can visit her one day. Her name is Ajani al-Kahn."

"Shukran. I will keep that in mind. Who knows? Maybe one day I will teach. But what I *do* know is I want to be a voice for those who have been silenced…for those who have learned to be silent. Do you know what I mean?"

"I'm not sure, tell me more."

She inhaled deeply and lifted her eyes toward the mountains. "I want to speak up for the children and for the women who have been made to feel that they don't matter…that they don't have a right to their lives, or to be who they are." She looked at Amir. "I know what that feels like. My father put me on the street just because I spoke my truth. Some people don't have the courage to speak up and be honest, but I do. And so, I'm going to use my voice and speak for the women and children who have been silenced."

Amir nodded. "You are correct. The world needs people like you…people with courage. And where will you prepare to do this? Where will you study?"

"I might attend the university in Fez; they have a good sociology program. Or, who knows, maybe I *will* leave Morocco and travel to America to study…or India. I wouldn't mind trading in these mountains for the Himalayas. There's a tiny country there, the Kingdom of Bhutan."

"Bhutan? I've never heard of that place." He removed his kufi and wiped his brow.

"Yes, it's high in the Himalayan mountains, near Nepal and Tibet, in Asia. It's a Buddhist country. I learned about it while looking at the world map in school. I had never heard of it, so I researched it in the Atlas book. It's fascinating…the country, the people, their religion. It's called the 'happiest place on Earth.' I'd love to learn more about it. I'd love to travel there one day."

"Hmm, Buddhists. The world is a big place and knowing you, you will see it. Inshallah!"

"Yes, Inshallah," she smiled.

He placed his kufi upon his head and took her hands into his. "Whatever you choose to do with your life, A'isha, I know you will be successful. You will achieve your goals. I am proud of you, and you should be proud of yourself, too." He hugged her. "Give my regards to Hira. I hope to see you soon."

"Yes, you will. Ahbak ya Amir," she called out, waving goodbye.

He turned around and smiled. "Thank you, A'isha. I love you, too."

The afternoon sun settled on his shoulders, cloaking him with warmth. He followed his shadow, stretched before him. A Bald Ibis circled and swooped between drifting white clouds; the beg in its screech echoed across the valley. A'isha called out to Amir, "Idhab maa'a Allah." Go with God. And as her grandmother had each morning, she waved goodbye until he approached the bend and could no longer be seen behind the wisp of the Tamarisk tree.

Tsewang

The steady beat of damaru drums echoed across Thimphu Valley, beckoning believers for midday meditation and prayer. The blended scents of patchouli, barley soup, and steamed yak milk wafted through the monastery's windows and along its hollow halls, settling into empty rooms. Monks and novices kicked off their sandals, lifted their kasayas to their knees, and ran up the yellow, splintering stairway. Some were returning from school, others from toiling in the fields. As they entered the massive red doors, they hushed their laughter and faded their smiles as they walked in single file to the communal washroom to prepare for puja and a midday meal. Kasim headed straight for Dabir's room. He was eager to see Tsewang.

"In the name of Buddha!" Kasim gasped. "What happened to your hair, Tsewang?"

He poked his head out the door and looked down one end of the corridor, then the other. Lifting the door by its knob, he eased it into the jamb, trying to silence its grating squeak. He spun around. "Tsewang, who did that to your *hair?*"

Tsewang rolled onto his back, then sat up, grimacing, biting on his lower lip. He folded his legs in lotus position, ran his hand across his scalp, and shrugged his shoulders. "What's wrong with my hair?" he asked dryly.

"What's wrong with your *hair*?" Kasim shrieked. "Are you *serious*?" He grabbed the shard of mirror from the cubicle and stretched his arm toward Tsewang, not wanting to move too far from the door. "Take a look at yourself!"

Tsewang held the mirror to his face and smiled. "As I said, what's wrong with my hair?"

"Your head's a mess! You have one bald patch next to a patch of hair ten inches long! Your whole head is like that! It looks like…like a jigsaw puzzle!"

Kasim scanned Tsewang's blank face, then splayed his hand on his chest, tossed his head back, and shot howling laughter into the air. Tsewang stared at him, his eyes stoic and aloof.

"I will get a pair of scissors," Kasim said, lowering onto the mat across from Tsewang. "*I'll* shave your head and help you look…look sane."

"Help *me* look *sane*? Ha!"

"Well, I mean I'll help you look like the rest of us. You know…with a completely shaven head. There is no way Rinpoche will allow you to walk around here with your head looking like that."

"To hell with Rinpoche," Tsewang said, placing the shard of mirror on the floor. He stretched out on the mat, folded his arms behind his head, and squinted at the ceiling. "To hell with him *and* Buddha."

Kasim bound to his feet, pounced toward the door, and grabbed the knob. "How could you say such a thing? Rinpoche is our spiritual leader. He is our guide. You mustn't speak about him as such. The deities will punish you."

"The deities?" Tsewang replied, closing his eyes, "They cannot punish me any more than I have already been punished." He turned his head and looked at Kasim. "I have learned to fear nothing and no one."

"The *deities*? Punished *you*? How could that be? They are the reason why you were found in the forest. They led Dabir and me to you. They have protected…" He stretched his neck toward the door. The boom of damaru drums and the chime of tingsha bells echoed from the prayer room. "Tsewang, puja has begun. We will bring trouble to ourselves for being late. We must go. I…I must go. Please allow me to shave your head after puja. I will even skip midday meal to help you."

He opened the door, bowed, and left the room. But just before he closed the door, he stuck his head in. "And remember," he said, "if we aim to please Buddha, we must aim to please Rinpoche." He pulled the door shut, hurried across the hall, and entered the prayer room.

Tsewang stared at the door, then rolled his eyes and shook his head as he listened to the monks' chant for compassion. Their voices, deep and solemn, throbbed the walls and pulsated the mat on which he lay. "Om mani padme hum. Om mani padme hum." He sat up, looked around the barren room, and then peered at the sky through the bare window. He picked up the shard of mirror and scanned his reflection, moving his hand across his head, feeling the juxtaposed patches of scalp and hair. He leaned his face closer to the mirror and peered at the image that stared back at him—the lightly bearded, bruised young man with eyes of onyx, jutting cheekbones, and a chiseled chin. A version of someone vaguely familiar to him. Opaque yet translucent, exposed yet masked. He frowned at the image, but it seemed to smile back at him. "Who are you?" Tsewang whispered, moving his face closer to the shard of glass, peering at the alternating patches of scalp and hair. "Who did this to you? Why?"

He eased off the mat, grimacing at the ache in his thighs. He placed the mirror in the cubicle and brushed off his kasaya, clenching his teeth at the pain that shot down his arm with each stroke. He twisted his patches of hair into a tight knot at the nape of his neck, unconcerned about the bald patches that remained exposed. A string of mala beads fell out of his pocket. He picked it up and hung it around his neck, then shook his head and removed it. He held them in his hand, closed his eyes, and sighed; then raised them to his lips, kissed them, and placed them in his pocket. He tightened his sash, opened the door, walked across the corridor, and stood at the threshold to the prayer room.

He looked at the monks and novices draped in saffron kasayas, sitting upon tattered pillows shoulder-to-shoulder with bowed heads, moving their mouths to a monotone chant, advancing mala beads between thumb and pointer after each recitation. In unison, they sustained the vibrational din that weighed the room with each chant, "Om mani padme hum…Om mani padme hum." Their backs were to the door, so they could not see Tsewang. But Rinpoche, who sat at the altar facing the door, did.

"Om mani pad—" he gasped, and watched Tsewang move his eyes across the room as if he were searching for someone, settling his eyes upon each novice, one child at a time, as they sat before Rinpoche in the first two rows.

Within each novice, Tsewang saw himself—the seven-year-old boy who had arrived at Pali Sholing. He also saw within these boys, those he had left behind. He moved his gaze away from the children, away from their frail, hunched shoulders, and he looked at Rinpoche. They stared at each other. Their eyes spoke words their mouths could not, and neither was confused about what each had said. Tsewang nodded at Rinpoche as he moved his hand across his patches of scalp and hair, and then he crossed the threshold. He entered the room, grabbed a cushion from the stack, and stepped among the praying monks. "Excuse me," he snarled, tossing his cushion between two monks, forcing them to scoot apart and carve a space for him. Heads spun with muffled gasps, filling the room with babbled and paused recitations. Rinpoche clapped, "Refocus! Continue at once!"

Tsewang eased onto the cushion and swept his eyes across the altar draped in red damask. He smiled at the candle's flickering flame and the lotus flower afloat in the glass bowl. He shook his head and pursed his lips at the offering tureen of apples and oranges, and he smirked at the Thangka of Mahakala, the Deity of Protection. He closed his eyes and inhaled the musky scent of Nag Champa that wiggled away from the glowing tips of burning sticks and snaked the room in a blue silhouette against a blade of sun that penetrated the room through a lone, circular window and landed at Rinpoche's feet.

He opened his eyes and winked at the monks who sat on either side of Rinpoche, chanting and eagerly awaiting the proper moment to chime the tingsha bell. Tsewang did not bow his head nor remove the mala beads from his pocket. He did not chant. In lotus position, he sat and thought about Pali Sholing. Images of Tadashi flooded his mind—the gurgling sound of his laughter and the way his belly would bounce with each chuckle. He wanted to feel the warmth of his moist skin. He could smell the odor of his early morning breath that seemed to arise from his bowels, and he could see the frown that fell upon Tadashi's face each time he told him to get up and brush his teeth. He relived their walks across the wildflower fields and envisioned their caress upon the mat they kept hidden in the attic. Tsewang longed for Tadashi, the sensation in his groin told him so. And he longed for his mother and his dog, Nugai.

The tingsha bells chimed. He shook his head and squeezed his eyes until they burned, hoping his tears would not escape. The monks and novices stood up, returned their cushions to the stack, and approached the altar with praying hands. "Namaste," they whispered and bowed, and walked past Tsewang as if he were invisible and until he was alone.

Tsewang eased to his feet and tossed his cushion at the stack, causing the neat pile to tumble. He stepped over them and ignored the pain in his ankles as he pounded his feet into the hollow floors of the corridor.

"I'm hungry!" he growled, standing at the kitchen door. A novice dropped his spoon, another choked on his soup, and a monk spilled a cup of scalding tea onto his lap. Muffled pangs of anguish followed by hushes of comfort rippled across the dining hall as Rinpoche rushed toward the door.

"Tsewang, you may not come in here with your head unshaven." He placed his hand on Tsewang's shoulder, nudging him to turn around.

"Do not touch me!" he hollered, pushing away Rinpoche's hand. "Don't *ever* touch me."

Dabir bolted to his feet, knocking over his chair. He glanced at Kasim, and they hurried toward Tsewang.

"Tsewang," Dabir said, "please come with us."

"Yes," Kasim added, forcing a smile, "please, listen to Dabir."

"But I'm hungry," Tsewang scowled.

"Of course, you're hungry. You will eat, but first we must talk," Dabir said, placing his hand on Tsewang's back.

"No! First, I will eat and *then* we can talk. I'm hungry, I tell you."

He shoved past Dabir and Kasim and walked toward the end of the long, wooden table flanked by monks on one side and novices on the other. He yanked out a chair and plopped onto it.

"*Well?* Will I be served, or should I serve myself?" he asked, landing his fists on the table. "I mean, how do things work around here?"

The bespectacled, birthmarked monk stood up with his cup and bowl. He walked toward Tsewang, grinning, locking into his eyes until he passed him and entered the kitchen. *That birthmark,*

Tsewang thought, watching him place his bowl and cup into the sink. *I remember that birthmark.*

"I...I will serve you," Kasim said, glancing at Rinpoche.

Rinpoche nodded and scanned the room. "Continue eating!" he hollered.

The monks and novices lowered their eyes and scooped the soup into their mouths, swallowing without tasting. The clink of utensils competed with anxious silence and obscured the presence of the odd newcomer—the one who dared to resist, and not bow or surrender. Speculation swirled, especially among the novices. *Is he a deity in disguise? For whom else would dare to challenge Rinpoche?*

Kasim placed a bowl of barley soup, crackers, and a steaming cup of chamomile tea between Tsewang's fists.

"Thank you," he said.

Kasim patted his shoulder. "You are quite welcome, my friend."

Tsewang slurped and shoved and chomped on his food like the wild boars he hid from. The novices tapped each other with their feet and hung their heads close to their bowls, hiding their mouths behind spoons and mugs to stifle an eruption of laughter. The monks stared into their own bowls, appalled and frightened by the savage among them. They listened to Tsewang devour his lunch until his bowl was empty, and then he lowered his head.

Rinpoche clapped his hands. "Lunch is finished!"

Chairs scraped against the warped, wooden floor, and tin cups clinked as monks placed their dishes into the sink and headed to the fields. The novices washed the dishes, swept the floor, and wiped the table around Tsewang before returning to their monastic studies.

Dabir and Kasim moved closer to Tsewang. The room was still and silent.

He lifted his head and quietly asked, "May I have another bowl of soup?"

Kasim took the bowl and returned with it filled to the brim, along with a few more crackers.

"Please do not tell the others about this second serving," he said, placing the bowl in front of Tsewang.

"I won't. And don't worry, I will not tell Rinpoche."

They watched Tsewang savor each mouthful until the bowl was empty, then gasped and stared at each other wide-eyed when he stood up, belched, and passed gas as he walked into the kitchen.

"My goodness!" Dabir whispered, shaking his head.

Tsewang returned to the table. "I am ready," he said, patting his belly. "I washed my bowl, cup, and spoon. Thank you for feeding me, Kasim." He turned and headed for Dabir's room.

"So, what's the problem?" he asked, easing onto the mat and releasing a loud, rumbling belch.

Dabir snapped his head back, slack-jawed. Kasim stifled a chuckle and plopped onto the mat across from Tsewang. Dabir clutched his mala beads, raised his head toward the ceiling, and whispered, "Help me, Mahakala." He sat next to Kasim.

"So, you said you wanted to talk to me," Tsewang said, lying down, easing his arm behind his head, wiggling his toes. "What's the problem?"

"Oh, no! There's no problem," Kasim said, leaning forward and patting Tsewang's knee. "We just wanted—"

"Kasim, *please!*" Dabir barked. "Allow me to handle this, would you? Do you remember that I am still your preceptor, and you are my student? Or has that changed?" He removed his eyeglasses and cleaned them with the hem of his kasaya, then looped them behind his ears, cleared his throat, glanced at Kasim with flared nostrils, and turned toward Tsewang.

"Now, Tsewang, yes, there *is* a problem," he said. "In fact, there are a few."

Tsewang sat up and leaned against the wall, folding his legs in lotus position. "Well, what is it?" he asked.

"First, you mustn't belch like that in the presence of others. I think you know that behavior is improper but are pretending you don't know. Or maybe there are two Tsewangs in that bruised body of yours—one who knows right from wrong and the other that does not...or at least *pretends* to not know."

Kasim nodded, "Yes! Yes!"

"Would you STOP nodding your head, Kasim? Must I ask you to leave?"

"Oh, no! Please, sir, I'll be quiet," he said, patting Dabir's knee.

Dabir pushed away his hand, raised his face to the ceiling, and sighed, "Lord Shiva, help me." He inhaled deeply, shifting his eyes between Kasim and Tsewang. "You both must learn that the truth can be heard only when we become still," he said. "Truth emanates from our heart and our heart is a silent teacher. This busyness—this, this rudeness—will prevent you from reaching the stillness within. It will keep the truth out of your reach and serve as a wedge between who you *think* you should be, and who you really are. This…this…" he continued, grimacing, waggling his hand at Tsewang, "this is not who you are. This is not your truth."

"How do you know what is true for me?"

Dabir frowned. "Your hair, my child…how did it become so?"

"Rinpoche did this to me, Dabir. I…I mean, sir."

"Did what to you? What do you mean?"

"You asked me and so I am telling you." He lowered his eyes. "Rinpoche cut my hair like this."

"Well, maybe you should thank him."

"*What?*" Kasim and Tsewang shrieked.

"That's right. This…this hodgepodge…this patchwork of hair and scalp. Perhaps it brings to the fore the conflict that exists within you."

"I…I…don't understand," Tsewang said.

"When did Rinpoche do this to you?" Dabir asked. He threw his hands into the air, "Why would he even *want* to do something like this to you, Tsewang?"

"Sir, while everyone was out on pindapata, he took me into the kitchen and did this to me."

"In the name of Buddha, what would make him do such a thing? I have known Rinpoche for many years, and I have *never*—"he glanced at the door and lowered his voice, "I have never seen him commit such a…a mess! What did you say to him that would make him want to do such a thing?"

"Sir, he asked me why I was in the forest…why I was lost in the forest, and he laughed at me when I told him I was looking for my mother."

"And so, he chopped off patches of your *hair*?"

"No. I also told him I ran away from Pali Sholing, and he asked me why."

"Well, why did you run…" Dabir's eyes shot toward the door. He waved his hand, "Forget it. That's not necessary right now. We are moving away from our focus, which is the condition of your hair." Dabir glanced at Kasim. Kasim gazed at Tsewang, blinking away tears.

Tsewang sighed. "Rinpoche began to shave my head, but when I told him why I ran away from Pali Sholing, he did not finish. I got up and—"

"Truly, Tsewang, if he cut your hair as such, then you must thank him. You must."

"Sir, with respect," Kasim said, pointing at Tsewang, "why should he thank him for doing this to his hair?"

"Yes, why?" Tsewang asked.

"Because he has made visible the struggles of your soul."

Tsewang furrowed his brow, "Huh? What do you mean?"

"What I am saying to you is this: Our external life is an expression of the life we live within." He looked at Kasim, then at Tsewang. "We all live two lives simultaneously—our outer life and our inner life."

Their eyes searched Dabir's.

"The truth you are seeking does not exist in my eyes. You must turn inward. It lives within your heart. Pay attention to what I am telling you. If you continue to seek truth—Satya—by searching your surroundings, you will be forever lost. Satya exists within. One does not know or see Satya, one *feels* it. You know the truth by the way it feels. Do you understand what I am saying to you?"

Kasim and Tsewang glanced at each other, then looked at Dabir and nodded.

"In the meantime, Tsewang, we must shave your head completely. You cannot remain here with your head unshaven." He turned to Kasim. "Please go to the kitchen and get the shears. They're in the top drawer, just beneath the sink."

"No, it's not there," Tsewang said.

"How do you know?" Dabir asked.

Tsewang tossed him a blank stare.

"As I said, Kasim, please go. It is getting late. We must do this before evening prayer."

"Yes, sir," Kasim said, jumping to his feet. He flung open the door. It slammed against the wall and bounced back into the jamb.

"That young man will be the death of me," Dabir huffed.

"Sir, do you want to hear what I told Rinpoche? Do you want to know why I ran away from Pali Sholing?"

"Someday, I will hear your story," Dabir said. He stood up and looked out the window, at the rows of prayer flags fluttering on a bluff. He turned to Tsewang. "You know, my child, we all have a story to tell. And yes, one day I will listen to yours. Perhaps it is no different from my own. But I cannot listen to it today. You must remember, he that knows patience, knows peace."

Kasim's footsteps echoed in the hollow corridor. He pushed open the door. "Tsewang was right," he panted, "it's not there."

"Well, where could it be? Did you check the top drawer?"

"Yes, sir, I checked every drawer, but nope, it's not there."

Tsewang slipped his hand behind his back, between the wall and mat. He felt his ball of hair next to the sharp, cool blade and eased his hand onto his lap.

"That's strange. Very well, I will find another pair." He turned to Tsewang. "And until I do, try to keep the patches of your hair knotted as it is so you can look sane. Just…just try to look sane—like one of us."

Tsewang snickered. "Just try to look sane, you say? Such a strange request."

"What do you mean? Strange? How so?"

"No need for me to explain, sir. I think you already know. But yes, I will keep my hair in a knot. Who knows?" he said, easing off the mat, "Maybe I'll keep it like this forever." He took the mirror from the cubicle and looked at it, turning his head from side to side. "I think it's befitting of me. Bald patches and hair. Don't you agree?" He placed the shard in the cubicle. "I mean…it's me. It's who I am."

"Is it, really?" Dabir asked, opening the door. "Is that your truth?"

Tsewang shrugged, "I suppose it is."

"You don't seem so sure," Dabir replied. He turned to Kasim. "Come, let us leave."

"Where are we going?" he asked.

"Kasim, what do we normally do at this time?"

"Our studies? I thought we could stay here with Tsewang. We could—"

"*Please* come with me."

"Of course. You know wherever you are, I will be!" he said, bounding to his feet.

"Well, I suppose that's a good thing," Dabir nodded. "I suppose."

"Thank you, sir," Tsewang said. "Thank you for your time…for talking with me. And Kasim, thank you for feeding me. You both have saved my life, and you must know that I am grateful."

"Mahakala led us to you, Tsewang," Dabir replied. "Do what you must to show him your gratitude."

"I will try."

"Well, you can start by arriving at evening puja on time. It begins at seven. Until then, you may stroll the fields and introduce yourself to your fellow monks. In fact, there is a monk here who believes he knows you. His name is Doijin. He says he has a nephew at Pali Sholing. You might want to meet him."

"Thank you, sir. I will do that."

Dabir and Kasim exited the room. Tsewang turned toward the window and watched a crane flap its long grey wings across a pristine blue sky, heading toward the tangerine horizon and a yawning sun.

"Doijin…Doijin," he whispered, watching the crane. "Why does that name sound familiar?" He shrugged his shoulders and walked to the door. Just before he crossed the threshold, he retrieved the shard of mirror from the cubicle and peered at it, wondering who he might see. Moving his face close to the image and then pulling away, he smiled and then frowned at who he saw. "Who are you?" he whispered, then placed the shard of mirror in the cubicle, and exited the room with a sigh.

A'isha

"C'mon, Ali, we're almost there," A'isha said, yanking the rope, leading Ali into the heart of the village, passing men in kufis and tunics. Some were smoking cigarettes, leaning languidly on plastic crates in the doorways of their shops; others were stacking olives and oranges atop their donkey-drawn carts, hoping to earn a dirham or two before the sun dipped behind the mountains at the Mu'addin's final call for prayer.

A'isha walked slowly, listening to a merchant exclaim to a woman veiled in black, "Yes, I have curcumin, brought in from Marrakesh just this morning!" The tinkling of a donkey's bell mingled with the grunt of an elderly man yanking at his weathered tarp, revealing a spread of sorghum, prickly pears, and bundles of eucalyptus that released an earthy scent into the summer air.

"Wait, Ali. The sack is slipping," A'isha sighed. "I know it's heavy; we're almost there."

She patted his head and adjusted a burlap sack filled with wreaths she fashioned from oak, cork, and fennel. Squinting against the sun, she peered down the road, toward her father's shop. "Amir?" she called out. "Amir!" she said, waving her hand and pulling on Ali's rope.

"A'isha! What are you doing here?" he asked with a broad smile, watching her approach, tickled by the swagger in her walk. He kissed her on each cheek. "As-salamu alaikum."

"Wa-alaikum-salaam," A'isha said, embracing him, feeling a new thinness of his frame.

"I was on my way to the shop," he said, raising his brow at Ali. "Come with me."

They walked downhill, along the winding, amber road. Amir nodded at the baker and chatted with the woodsman in passing. A'isha smiled at the barefoot children in dust-riddled tunics and tussled hair, laughing in their delight, rolling stones with sticks, keeping score with fingertips in the arid soil beneath a warming sun.

"So, what brings you here on a Saturday? And with…"

"Ali. His name is Ali."

"Yes, of course. And the sack?" he smiled, fishing for the key in his pocket. He shoved it into the lock and said, "Please do not get stuck today." He jiggled the knob and with a firm push, he opened the door. The odor of stale cigarettes and wet cement leaped at them, causing A'isha's eyes to flutter.

"Come in, please. Don't behave as if this place is strange to you. You have spent many hours here as a child," he said, pulling the chain on the bare bulb dangling from the ceiling.

"Yes, I know, but I have Ali." She stood in the doorway, staring at her father's workbench, his scattered tools, and an open tin of mink oil.

Amir leaned against the counter. "So, tell me, what brings you here? Is everything okay at home?"

"Yes, I am fine." She tightened her grip on Ali's rope. "But…but I need money. My shoes are worn, and I'm running low on seeds. Harvest season is just a few months away and I haven't planted anything. And…and I leave for the university in one year. I'm going to need money." She glanced at the sack on Ali's back. "I made some wreaths. I'm hoping to sell them in the market. I…I…" Her heart pounded. She clenched her lip between her teeth and gripped the rope in her sweaty hands.

Amir looked at the sack. "Well, let's see what you have."

"*Really?* Are you sure?" she said, fumbling with the sack's knot. She pulled out a wreath. "See? Do you like it? Do you think I could sell them? Do you think people would want to buy one? I can sell them at a low cost. What do you think?"

Amir took it from her. He surveyed the wreath and held it to his nose. "I love the scent of fennel," he said. He held it up against a wall. "I think it's beautiful, A'isha. Of course, you can sell them. Where do you want to do that? Do you have a place in mind?"

"I suppose on a tarp, near the donkey carts. Or maybe…"

"Or maybe right here!" Amir said, handing her the wreath. "And that way if anyone tries to give you a tough time I can intervene. Your father left many hammers in here, you know." He chuckled and coughed.

"Really? I can sell them here?" she asked, wide-eyed.

"Bialtabe! Of course!" he exclaimed. His smile faded and he pressed his hand on his chest.

A'isha rushed toward him. "Amir! Are you sick?"

He walked to the rear of the shop, gliding his hand along the counter. He eased onto a stool and leaned back onto a bundle of fabric.

"Are you okay, Amir?"

"Yes, yes, I am fine. Perhaps too much excitement." He removed his kufi and fanned himself with it. "A'isha," he coughed, "please go to Nasim in the carpet shop across the road and ask him to give you some water for me."

"Yes, of course. I'll be right back. Ali, you stay here."

She dashed across the road and returned with a glass of water. Nasim followed her into the shop. His sixteen-year-old frame was tall and lean. His lavender tunic was tight against his biceps. He maintained an upright posture (shoulders pressed back at all times), but his eyes held a hint of sadness, and his full lips a pout that contradicted the confidence he tossed through his words and gait.

"Ma al-khabar?" he asked, pushing past A'isha.

"Nothing is wrong with me, Nasim. I just became a bit dizzy with all the good news." He looked at A'isha and raised the glass to his lips.

"And what news is that?" Nasim asked, glancing at A'isha. "I sure hope she—"

"Amir, are you *sure* you are well?" A'isha interrupted. "Your face is without color. Shall I call the doctor?"

He eased off the stool waving his hand. "No, I do not need a doctor." He looked at Nasim. "The good news is you will have a new neighbor."

"*What?* Are you leaving us?" Nasim winced, sliding his kufi off his head.

"No, I'm not leaving, but A'isha is joining our community of vendors and," he put his hand on Nasim's shoulder, "I expect that she will be treated in the same manner we all would want to be treated. Hal tafham?"

"Yes, of course, I understand. But are girls even *allowed* to sell? To be vendors?"

"I don't recall reading anything in the Qur'an that says they cannot. Besides, many of these vendors do things they know are admonished in the Qur'an, and they do them anyway. So, what's the difference?"

Nasim lowered his eyes. "I...I don't know what you are speaking of."

"I'm not so sure about that, Nasim. But if that's the case, hang around here long enough and you will. You are new to this community and are not much older than A'isha. Many of our vendors are old and stubborn and are stuck in their way of thinking. Perhaps you will help them become less rigid, yes?"

"But, but she is also a...a—"

"A what!? Tell me, what is she?"

Nasim gasped. "Nothing, sir."

"Look at me. You spend more time with the vendors than I do. You are here in the village more than I am, lately. I know that they—*and you*—gossip like a bunch of hens." Nasim smirked, thinking about the rumor of Amir's relationship with Nabeel. "So, when they begin to speak nonsense about A'isha, I want you to put an end to it. Do you hear me?"

"Yes, sir, I will do as you ask."

"Shukran. You must teach them to respect her as you would want to be respected. Allah commands that of you—of us all—and so do I. Hal tafham?"

"Yes sir, I understand." He glanced at A'isha, seething. *This kafir…this sinner, how dare she!*

"Very well," Amir said, easing behind the counter, "I must get to work." He removed a jar of sequin from the shelf.

"Shukran, Amir. If you need anything else, let me know," Nasim said, placing his kufi on his head. He turned toward the door, glared at A'isha, and pushed past Ali. He wanted to knock the sack off his back and kick him.

A'isha watched Nasim pound his feet into the earth as he crossed the road. When he entered his shop he spun around, locked his eyes into hers, and slammed the door, causing the knob to slip out and tumble to the ground. He pressed his mouth between the door and the jamb and shouted, "Would you pick it up and put it back in the door?"

She cupped her hand to her ear and mouthed, "*What?*"

"I'm locked in…the knob," he yelled, pointing to the ground. "Put it back in the door and turn it!"

"Huh?" she said, squinching her face. She turned toward Amir, grinning. "How are you feeling, now?" Over her shoulder, she listened to Nasim shout through the door, trying to get a passerby's attention. She bit down on her lip, stifling her laughter.

"…and that's what I must do," Amir sighed. "A'isha, do you hear me? Are you listening?"

"Oh, my apologies, Amir. I was distracted. What did you say?"

"I see. What is Nasim hollering at over there?" Amir chuckled and waved his hand dismissively. "Please do not pay him any attention. All these men—young and old—are quite ignorant. You must not allow them to get in your way. Now, bring the rest of your merchandise in here. You may set up your space anywhere you are most comfortable. As you can see, I have not touched your father's workbench. But if you choose to use it, you may."

Their eyes scanned the emptiness Nabeel left behind, then they looked at each other.

A'isha spun around and stuffed her wreath into the sack. "I can't do this," she said, shaking her head. "C'mon, Ali, let's go."

"What do you mean? Where are you going? You can display your wreaths on this shelf and begin to sell your merchandise today."

"It's all happening so quickly, Amir. I didn't expect…" She looked at her father's workbench. "My baba…he's… Oh, Amir. I can't!"

"I understand your pain, A'isha. I live with it every day. I miss him too, but life goes on. We must mix the bitter with the sweet and trust in Allah."

She lifted her head; tears clung to her lashes. "My jida used to tell me that I must seek the lessons behind the pain." She looked at her father's workbench. "I wonder what… I mean, if I come back, I wonder what the lesson will be for me?"

"Perhaps it is one of perseverance." He took her hands into his. "When we are faced with an opportunity that will help us grow, we must move forward in faith. We must have the courage to do what is best for us, even if it is the more difficult road to take." He looked at Nabeel's workbench, then at her. "Perhaps the lesson you must learn, whatever that is, awaits you here. But the only way you will know is if you take this opportunity."

"Yes, maybe you're right," she sighed. "Thank you, Amir."

"You are welcome, but you do not have to thank me. I love you, and it is by Allah's command that I treat you as I would want to be treated."

She hugged him. "Sa'arak qariba. I will see you soon."

"Yes, I hope so. I am so proud to hear you speak Arabic. Your father would be proud of you, too."

She walked through the village with Ali at her side, along its undulating, winding path. She arrived at the arch that marks the entrance. She turned around and watched the men and women who resembled her mother and father but were not them. Her heart ached. She watched the movement of women beneath black niqabs, with slits and probing eyes, gloved hands, and hidden mouths. She wanted to ask, *Does your veil hide a grin intended for me? Or does it spare me your truth?* She lowered her eyes and looked at her yellow jumper, soiled at the knees, then raised her head toward the men who sought shade in the doorway of their shops. *And you, you men who follow me with curious and accusing eyes of your own, who are you to judge me? You, who sit in salah five times a day, praying 'Ashhadu an la ilaha illa Allah...I bear witness that there is no God but Allah.' Such hypocrisy. You judge as if you are He.*

She looked at the children and listened to their laughter. *How could a loving God create His children to live and experience the tapestry of life, granting us free will to do so, then punish us for choosing to live our truth?*

Does a mother tell her child, 'You can put your hand in the fire if you choose,' then punish him for not making the choice she wanted him to make? Why offer him a choice in the first place? Is that love, or a set-up?

Belonging. To whom does that child belong? Is she who relinquishes the essence of herself out of fear that she will suffer the loss of God's love, more deserving of His love? Is she more deserving of His love because she is afraid to turn inward to seek that which is truth onto her, and her alone? Is she more worthy of His love than the child who, by her unsolicited, God-given nature, has the courage to seek her true self and live fearlessly, with integrity? Who is the better of the two? Who of the two is more deserving of God's love? The fearful or the fearless? Who of the two is less entitled to suffer? Who of the two is less entitled to His love? And who decides that this should be so? Is it God? Is it His word in the Bible? the Qur'an? the Torah?

Who am I in His eyes? I, who have sought truth and have lived by my truth, and have therefore honored His truth? Am I less deserving of God's love because he created me as such, and because I have chosen to not shun it? Am I less loveable? Less deserving of love from the men and the women who profess to be in better favor of God's love simply because they choose to perceive their world, veiled? While I stand unmasked, exposed, and vulnerable? Who is the better of the two? And who gets to decide that is so? Is it the one who chooses to interpret God's word in a manner that justifies their fear and unwillingness to navigate life without the confines of a synthetic safety that, in their minds, entitles them to judge those who do not live life as such, just by virtue of who they are?

I do not take that which is not mine, and I give without expecting anything in return. Am I not worthy of God's love? I love, unconditionally, those who love me and those who have condemned and abandoned me. Am I not worthy of God's love? My purpose in life is to teach the children and be the voice of the silenced. Am I not worthy of God's love? Who are you to condemn me and say, 'No! God loves you less than I, and you will not be welcomed into heaven or paradise on earth,' simply because of who and how I love? What gives you the right to veil and cloak yourself with your interpretation of His word and use that interpretation to condemn me, in service of yourself? In service of your fear? In service of your relinquishment of any variation of life, other than that which you choose and use to condemn me, in service of yourself? What gives you the right to impose your abandonment of self upon me? And to use your interpretation of God's word to justify, excuse, and quell your guilt and frustration for doing so?

I have allowed you to wipe yourself off on me, to inject into my vein the shame and doubt that belongs to you, and only you. I have lived my life feeling less than. I have lived my life owning your business of condemnation and imposition. And now I must find a way to forgive myself for allowing you to use me for your self-indulgence.

Ashhadu an la ilaha illa Allah…I bear witness that there is no God but Allah. If you profess to believe that which you pray, then how, in God's eyes, do you feel entitled to judge me? Why do you choose to reduce me to being less deserving of God's love? I am a living example of the myriad and miracles of His creations. What does your condemnation of me do for you? Why do you use me and my difference from you as your crutch? As the rag with which you wipe off your fear and frustration? Who are you? Who am I? Who is God? What is love? Who are you to make me doubt?

A'isha turned away from the village and walked along the ridge of Ouirgane, gazing at the sloping hills of an arid, amber earth. Cliffs and outcrops freckled with rosebushes and almond trees. She smiled at the swoosh of the river's flow into its crescent and raised her eyes to the sky, listening to the Mu'addin's call for midmorning prayer echo across the valley, "Allahu Akbar, Allahu Akbar." Her eyes followed a Bald Ibis swooping across the gray sky with rhythmic flaps of its long, black-feathered wings. *Should I return to sell my wreaths? Going to school near the village is one thing, but to be in the heart of it, among the people, might be more than I can handle.* "My jida, what should I do?" she asked, watching the Ibis glide onto a jagged ledge and stretch its wings.

She and Ali arrived home. She walked him into the yard, went to her grandmother's grave, and adjusted the tin can of wilting wildflowers. She whispered, "Good morning, my jida." She hoisted a bucket of water from the well and filled the can and Ali's bowl. She removed the sack from Ali's back and brought it into the house, then returned to the yard with a bowl and entered the chicken coop. "Shukran," she said, smiling at the chickens as she collected their eggs. At the doorway of her home, she paused to inhale the scent of cinnamon. *If I didn't know better, Jida, I would think you are here.* She placed the bowl of eggs on the table, removed her hijab, lit the ashen log in the firepit, dropped some mint leaves into the kettle, and hung it above the fire. She thought about Amir. Nasim's face flashed across her mind, and her heart raced. She eased the wreaths out of the sack and placed them on the floor at the foot of her bed. She kicked off her shoes and returned to the rug with a cup of tea, then pulled a bundled sheet from under her bed, unwrapped it, and smiled at her pile of cork, fennel, and oak.

Tsewang

"What are *you* looking at?" Tsewang asked, sneering at a group of monks sitting on the stairs, dusting off the soles of their feet.

"Who me?" one smiled, shaking his sandals.

"No, not you with the big feet. That one. The one with the big nose. You. What are you looking at?"

"Who me?" he asked, touching his nose.

"Yeah, you. You've never seen someone with hair?"

"I don't know what you're talking about," he said, slipping his feet into his sandals.

Tsewang sauntered toward him, jutting out his chin. A group of monks descended the stairs clutching their mala beads. They circled Tsewang. Others shoved their feet into their sandals and walked away.

"Pl- Please. I…I do not want any trouble with you," the monk replied. His hot breath smelled like sour milk and made Tsewang's eyelids flutter.

"Who says I'm looking for trouble?"

"N- No one."

"But if you keep staring at my hair," Tsewang said, pressing his finger into the monk's chest, "there *will* be trouble."

"Okay, okay," he winced. "There won't be any trouble."

A frail, freshly shaven monk with swatches of brown paper speckled with blood on the back and sides of his head tapped the monk's elbow. "Come, let us leave," he said softly. "It is getting late." The group followed him, keeping their eyes on Tsewang, shaking their heads with pinched lips and knitted brows. They crossed the path, climbed onto the bluff, and dispersed amid rows of colorful prayer flags fluttering in the cool breeze.

Tsewang watched them until they were out of sight. He smiled and frowned at once, then lifted his face toward the jagged horizon of snowcapped mountains cloaked in evergreen trees, trees deeply rooted into the face of each in an even exchange of life for beauty. He bowed his head and sighed, then walked toward the remaining pairs of sandals, seeking his own.

He sifted through the sandals, tossing them over his shoulder, high into the air. Some landed on the pebbled walkway, and some hung onto the lilac bush behind him. His mala beads fell onto the earth. He picked them up and shoved them back into his pocket with one hand, tossing sandals over his shoulder with the other. A group of monks descended the stairs, staring at him slack-jawed with awe, fear, and disgust.

Tsewang snapped his head up. "What are you looking at?" Their silent stare fueled his anger and shame. He sneered at them. "I *said*, what are you looking at?"

"What are you doing with our sandals?" asked a slender monk much taller than Tsewang.

"What does it look like I'm doing? I'm looking for mine," Tsewang scoffed, holding sandals in each hand.

"Do you even *have* a pair? Who *are* you, anyway? Better yet, *what* are you?"

Tsewang dropped the sandals. "What do you mean, 'what am I?' What kind of stupid question is that? Obviously, I'm one of you. Don't you see my kasaya? My…my…" He brushed his hand over his head.

"Your what?" the monk grinned, pointing at Tsewang's head and looking back at the group. "Your *mess*?" The monks laughed, tightening their circle around Tsewang. "Do you think wearing a kasaya makes you one of us?"

"No, you fool. I'm not saying that. Of course, this kasaya doesn't make me one of you."

"And your puzzle head doesn't either," another monk jeered.

"Then if you're not one of us, why are you here?"

"That's none of your business," Tsewang scowled. "Who do you think you are, asking me these questions, 'Who am I? Why am I here?' who are *you*?" Anger raised his voice.

"I hear you were found in the forest," the monk replied, looking at the strewn sandals. "Perhaps you should return. You appear to be a better fit for the animals."

"How dare you say such a thing to me! What gives you the right? You don't know why I was in the forest. You don't know why I ran away! How dare you make fun of me?" he hollered, tightening his fists.

The monk moved closer to Tsewang. "Whatever the reason you ran away and ended up in the forest, you still do not have the right to come here and disrupt our lives. Now, if you would—"

"Disrupt your *lives*? Your lives here are already disrupted. As disrupted as the one I left behind. The only difference is I had the courage to leave, and you are still here."

"How do you know what our lives are like? You arrived…when? Just two days ago? What do you know about us?"

"The minute I met Rinpoche I knew this place is no different than the one I ran away from. Yeah, I've been here for just two days, but I can tell you *exactly* what's been happening here for years. For as long as you have been here, I'm sure."

The monks looked at each other.

"Are you finished?" the monk sneered. "If you will excuse us, we have the fields to tend."

They retrieved their sandals from the pathway and off the lilac bush and stood in a circle, whispering and exchanging sandals, then walked away leaving none for Tsewang.

He clenched his fists. "Argh!" he growled, tossing his face to the sky. Tears pooled in the patches of hair behind his ears. He pounded his fists into his thighs, grinding his teeth at the pain in his bones.

"Tsk, tsk."

He spun around. The monk with the birthmark was leaning against the doorjamb, his arms folded across his chest. Tsewang stared at him. The monk stared back with a smirk, then entered the monastery and closed the door. Tsewang plopped onto the stairs and lowered his head into his palms; then twisted around and looked at the door. *Was that Doijin?*

The door swung open.

"There you are!" Kasim beamed, running down the stairs with a pair of sandals in his hand. "I was looking for you. I think you'll need these, yes? They're yours. I fixed the strap, and they are finally dry."

"Thank you, Kasim," Tsewang replied. He slipped his feet into the sandals, noting his big toe had begun to heal. "Where are you heading? And where's Dabir?"

"Dabir is teaching the novices and I'm heading to the labyrinth. Do you wish to come with me?"

"Sure, what else is there for me to do," he said, rolling his eyes.

They crossed the path, hiked up the bluff, and stood before a labyrinth. It was a maze formed by long swaths of fabric—red, blue, yellow, purple, and green—sewn lengthwise onto six-foot-tall pine branches chiseled and sandpapered into pliable poles. When the air was still, the fabrics hung stagnant. But when a breeze swooped down the mountains, the flags would lift and flutter, creating colorful walls of movement that concealed the monks and deepened their solitude as they walked the labyrinth.

"You do know," Kasim said in a hushed tone, "that in here we are to remain silent."

Tsewang chuckled. *That should be quite the challenge for you.*

He continued, "The labyrinth represents a journey to our core--our center—and our return to the world. It is here that we come for contemplation and reflection. I encourage you to use this time to…"—he looked at Tsewang's head— "to search your heart and see what it tells you. I will do the same. Dabir has told us, 'The heart is a silent teacher. The quieter you become, the more you can hear,' do you remember?"

"Yeah, yeah, I remember."

"Wonderful! You may enter first. I will wait to allow the proper space between you and me. I will meet you on the other side."

"And how long is *this* supposed to take?"

"As long as it should," Kasim replied. "Please begin."

Tsewang entered the labyrinth. The flags fluttered in an intermittent breeze. The whoop of a vulture's wings pulled his attention toward the gray sky. He sighed and pounded his feet into the earth until he arrived at the first bend. "This is ridiculous," he whispered. He turned and looked at his footprints, then peeked around the bend at the path ahead. "This is the stupidest thing," he grunted, but continued, making it into a game—touching only the red flags, then turning a bend and touching only the blue, turning another bend, touching only the purple, and then only the green, while moving deeper into the maze.

As he approached another bend, he spun around to see if Kasim was near, and then exhaled and grinned at his solitude. His pace slowed and so did his breathing. He brushed his hand across his head, inching his fingers between the lines of scalp and hair, listening to the voices that arose in his mind: *who are you? why are you here? is this who you really are?* He stopped walking and raised his eyes to the vulture, swooping and circling above the labyrinth. He continued to wander through the twists and turns of the path, lost but unconcerned until he arrived at its end. "Finally," he huffed, and sat on a boulder to wait for Kasim, lifting his eyes toward the vulture circling above, listening to the prayer flags flutter in the breeze.

Are you ready?" Kasim asked, approaching Tsewang with a misty gaze.

This guy looks like he's floating! Tsewang giggled.

"Yeah, I'm ready. Are you okay? You look as if you've seen Buddha, himself."

"Are you making fun of me, Tsewang?"

"No, I'm not making fun of you." He softened his voice, "You saved my life. I would never do such a thing."

They walked away from the labyrinth, toward a high ridge of mocha brown earth. An echo of laughter drew their attention to the monastery in the valley far below. Tsewang smiled at the novices as they exited the massive red doors and scrambled down the steep stairway, having completed their studies.

"It reminds me of Pali Sholing," he whispered.

"What did you say?" Kasim asked.

"Nothing…nothing at all."

They walked in silence, passing a group of monks returning to the monastery, the group Tsewang encountered at the stairs. All but one ignored him. The monk he had called 'big nose' nodded and smiled. Tsewang nodded back at him and continued walking with Kasim until they arrived at the end of the path, stopping at the edge of the forest.

"We should head back," Kasim said, muffling a yawn. "I am sure Dabir has found a pair of shears and is waiting for you."

Tsewang touched his head. "I don't know if I want to do that."

"Do what? Shave your head? You cannot stay with us if you keep your hair as such." He took Tsewang's hand in his. "Please, let him shave your head."

Tsewang eased his hand away. Kasim continued, "If you do not shave your head, what will you do? Where will you go?"

"I had no intention of coming here, let alone staying. I left Pali Sholing to find my mother, not to come here and be bullied by Rinpoche."

Kasim stepped back. "Rinpoche isn't bullying anybody. He has been only kind to us. Why do you hate him? What has he done to you?"

"The question is not what has he done to *me*?" Tsewang replied, tightening his sash, "but what he is doing to the novices."

"What do you mean, '*doing to the novices*'?"

"Exactly as I said. I'm sure he is no different than the Rinpoche at Pali Sholing and—"

"What has he done? The Rinpoche at Pali Sh—"

"Nothing! I do not want to talk about it!"

"About *what*?"

"Forget it! You said we have to return. Well then, let's go."

"But…but…I want to hear what you have to say, Tsewang. What happened to you?"

"Nothing! Don't ask me any more questions." He spun around and walked to the edge of the ridge. He gazed down at the valley, walking along the edge. Pebbles rolled off with each step he took.

"Tsewang, you're walking too close to the edge. If you slip and fall you will kill yourself. Please move away from there."

"Maybe death isn't such a bad idea," he whispered, staring at the valley below.

His mother's face flashed across his mind. *Tsewang, my child,* he heard her say. "Mother where are you?" he called out, moving his eyes across the valley and lifting them to the gray sky. "Mother…" He looked over his shoulder at Kasim, then at the valley below, and again at Kasim. He eased closer to the edge, clenched his teeth, and inhaled. Behind him, he heard his mother's voice, *Tsewang, my child, don't!* He looked over his shoulder and peered into the forest; then backed away from the edge and returned to the path.

Kasim exhaled, squeezing his eyes shut. "You harbor so much pain in your heart," he said, stretching his hand toward Tsewang, pulling him close and hugging him. "I can feel it," he whispered, "I see it in your eyes." He released him, blinking away tears. "I will pray to Mahakala to help you heal."

"I told you, Kasim, the deities cannot do anything for me. I have lost all faith in them."

"I will pray for you, anyway."

They walked silently, glancing at each other intermittently until they approached the labyrinth. Tsewang pointed at it. "We're not going through this thing again, are we?"

"That would be silly, wouldn't it?" Kasim replied. "But" he continued, pointing his finger upward as if he had stumbled upon a magnificent idea, "if you need more time to contemplate, and I truly think you do, then yes, we can walk the labyrinth again."

"No, that's quite alright. If I need to contemplate I can do that anywhere, I suppose."

Kasim laughed. "Ah, so you *do* have a brain beneath that mishmash of hair and scalp."

They walked along the perimeter of the labyrinth, bending beneath branches of pine and poplar, raising their kasayas, and easing between pink and ruby rhododendrons. They arrived at the pathway leading them off the bluff and into the valley. Tsewang descended quickly, grunting at the ache in his thighs. Kasim panted, trying to keep up with him. They arrived at the monastery, kicked off their sandals, and hastened up the stairs. Tsewang pulled open the massive red door.

"Tsewang," Kasim whispered, "please remember what I told you."

Tsewang stopped at the door to Dabir's room. "And what's that?" he asked.

"To allow Dabir to shave your head so you may stay. If you do not, where will you go?"

"I…I am going to my…to my…" He lowered his head, entered the room, and closed the door.

Kasim walked across the corridor and entered the prayer room. He lit a candle and bowed with praying hands at a brass statue of Buddha. "Namaste," he whispered, then eased onto a frayed pillow and sighed.

Tsewang awoke, stretching and yawning. He looked at the window above his head; the sky was gray and hollow. He lay, recalling the labyrinth and thinking of his walk along the bluff with Kasim. He glanced at Dabir's mat and bolted upright. He patted his head, feeling the patches of hair and scalp. *I must get out of here!* He eased the door open and peeked down the corridor, relieved no one was in sight. He tiptoed out of the monastery, shuffled down the stairs, and retrieved his sandals. He held them in his hand, lifted his kasaya, ran across the path, and up the bluff with elongated strides.

He stood before the prayer flags, billowing in the soft breeze. He looked over his shoulder at the monastery and entered the labyrinth. He walked through the maze until he arrived at its core. He lowered onto his shins and watched the soft movement of each flag, unsure of what he should think or do, unaware of how he felt, confused about what he wanted to say. He ran his hand across his head, moving his fingers between the lines of scalp and hair. *What should I do? What would Tadashi do?*

He eased off his shins, sat on the ground, and folded his legs in lotus position. Bowing his head, he closed his eyes. *This…this is what Tadashi would do.* He pressed the palms of his hands together and whispered, "Namaste." He inhaled deeply and continued, "Namaste, Lord Buddha. I need your help. First, please forgive me for conducting myself in a manner that is against everything you stand for. But I am asking for your help. I am lost and I don't know what to do. I know you are watching me—you and Mahakala—and I know you both sent Dabir and Kasim to lead me out of the forest…thank you. And now I am here in Thimphu, and I am still lost. Should I allow Dabir to shave my head? I don't want him to. It was not my intention to arrive at this place. Should

173

I stay here, or leave at this moment? If I stay, how will I know when to leave? More than anything in this world, I want to see my mother. Would you please help me find her? I will do whatever you want if you lead me to my mother. To you, Lord Buddha, I pray. Namaste."

Tsewang thought of Dabir's words, "The quieter you become, the more you can hear." And so, he sat there and waited. He waited to hear something, anything. The silence became louder, and his heartbeat slowed. In the distance, the chime of tingsha bells echoed and blended with the beat of the damaru drums. The brash blowing of the duncheon horns resounded across the valley, weaving a vibrational cacophony throughout the labyrinth. A prayer flag brushed across the sole of his foot, tickling him. He opened his eyes, slipped his feet into his sandals, and wandered amid the prayer flags, listening to the sounds beckoning believers to evening puja.

He exited the labyrinth and walked the path leading him into the forest. He arrived at the evergreen border and shifted his head from side to side, peering between and beyond the trees. "The quieter you become, the more you can hear," he whispered. He stopped moving and waited for his heart to speak, wondering if he could trust what it might say. Moments grew into minutes before he sighed and walked toward the sound of cymbals, horns, and damaru drums.

When he arrived, the monks and novices were in the prayer room, advancing mala beads and chanting Tayata Om, the mantra for healing all suffering. He pulled a pillow from the stack and sat near the threshold. He removed the beads from his pocket and joined his brothers in the chant. He looked up at Rinpoche and grinned. Rinpoche tossed a stern nod at him and continued to lead the monks and novices in the Tayata Om mantra. "II Tayata Om Bekandze Bekandze Maha Bekandze Radza Samudgate Soha II. May the many sentient beings who are sick, quickly be freed from sickness. And may the sickness of all beings never arise again." Rinpoche ended puja with a final prayer. Everyone stood up and bowed with their palms pressed together. "Namaste," they said in unison and exited the room, prepared for the evening meal.

Tsewang remained seated as the monks and novices brushed past him. Once the room was empty, Dabir retrieved a pillow and sat by his side.

"I am delighted that you have returned. We were hoping you would."

"Really? Even with my hair as such?"

"Yes, even as you are." Dabir cleared his throat and continued, "Rinpoche has asked me to tell you that you are welcome to stay and that you may keep your hair as such until you decide which direction you will take—until you know what you want to do, or who you want to be."

Tsewang raised his brow, not knowing if he should smile or frown. "Why is he being so kind to me? I don't know if I should trust it."

"My child, perhaps it is not Rinpoche that you should fear or doubt, but the part of you that has learned to be fearful and mistrusting."

"I don't understand," he replied, rolling his mala beads between his fingers.

"What I am saying to you is this: when a person or an experience has given us reason to be on guard, our fear and mistrust, *in that instance,* can help us survive. But if we do not let go of fear and mistrust the moment those feelings are no longer justified, if we do not release them the moment that experience has ended, then we begin to deal with everyone through that filter. And when we do that, the tools that were once a means of survival become a hindrance and block us from seeing goodness in those who we believe we should fear but have given us no reason to be fearful."

"But how do we know when to let go of the fear? How do we know who to trust?"

"Your heart will tell you so. It's not a knowing, but a feeling. However, a more important question is this: can you trust your heart?"

Tsewang shifted his eyes to the shrine and gazed at the flickering flame. "Yes," he said, smiling faintly, "I think I understand."

"Good, if you choose to remain with us, we may continue this discussion. But for now," he chuckled, "let us go to evening meal before there is no food left."

They walked the damp, echoing corridor toward the dining hall. Tsewang's mouth watered at the wafting aromas of barley soup and chamomile tea. A burst of thunder and crackle of lightning shook the walls, and a deluge of rain pounded against the roof and shutters. He thought of the labyrinth and the forest. They arrived at the dining hall, pausing at the threshold. Two seats awaited them next to Kasim, and across from 'big nose.' The monk with the birthmark was seated at the far end of the table, to the right of Rinpoche. Dabir and Tsewang glanced at each other and entered the room. They eased onto their chairs, listening to a crack of lightning and roll of thunder, ignoring muffled laughter and veiled stares, ready to receive the evening meal.

A'isha

With school closed for summer vacation, A'isha had time to focus on two things: making wreaths to sell in the village and completing her college applications. In September, she would begin her last year of secondary school and needed to save as many dirhams as possible to leave Ouirgane. The sale of her wreaths was slow but steady. Some customers bought them simply because they could not resist the scent and beauty it added to their wooden doors. Others bought them at Amir's plea. "But she is just a *child*. Please give her a chance," he would say to those who confided in him their condemnation of her, despite their whispered rumors about his questionable relationship with Nabeel.

It was on a Tuesday morning when A'isha decided to stop by Hira's home to gift her with a wreath three months after her jida's death. Her excitement and pride put a bounce in her step as she sang her grandmother's favorite nasheeds until she arrived and knocked on her door.

"Sayidati? Sayidati, are you home?"

"A'isha, is that you?" Hira called out. She opened the door and flashed a broad smile.

"As-salamu alaikum," A'isha beamed. "It's so good to see you."

"Ah, my child, please come in. Wa-alaikum salaam," Hira gushed, tucking her hair into a navy-blue hijab. She kissed A'isha's cheeks. "It is so good to see you, too. I think of you often." She sniffed the air and hurried toward the kitchen. "Please sit," she said, over her shoulder, "I was just brewing some tea."

A'isha sat on the brown velvet sofa, placed her satchel near her feet, and adjusted her hijab. Her eyes moved about the room and settled upon the Yaz above the door. It reminded her of that awful day. The image of Hira shrouding her jida flashed across her mind and tightened her chest. She felt sadness and gratitude at once.

"So, tell me, how have you been?" Hira asked, handing A'isha a steaming cup of mint tea. "And how is Amir?"

"Shukran. I have been well, and so is Amir. He has asked for you."

"Ah, please give him my regards," she said, puckering her lips and blowing into her cup. She patted A'isha's knee. "You look well. I often wonder how you are coming along. I thought of asking my niece to walk with me to your home for a visit, but here you are."

"Is your niece…um…Meena…home from school?"

"Do you mean Nadesh?"

"Yes, yes, Meena is her sister. Nadesh…is she here?" A'isha asked, wide-eyed.

"No, not yet, but she will arrive next week. She's coming with her father to bring me to their home in Asni for a few days."

A'isha moved to the sofa's edge, recalling Nadesh's long lashes and alluring smile.

"I would love to see her. I'd love to talk with her about my college applications and—"

"Well, she will be here next Wednesday. You can come and see her then."

"I will do that," A'isha grinned, lifting the cup to her lips.

"Inshallah," Hira said, amused by A'isha's excitement.

"What time should I—"

"A'isha, tell me," Hira interrupted, furrowing her brow, "how long has it been since we buried your grandmother?"

Her smile faded. "Two months, almost three. My jida died in April."

Yes, that's right." Hira put her cup on the table and turned toward A'isha. "I should tell you that I knew your grandmother."

A'isha gulped a mouthful of tea, scorching her tongue. Her eyelids fluttered. "Huh? What did you say?"

Hira stood up and walked toward the firepit. "Yes, I knew her. How could I have not? Ouirgane is small. Just a tiny village hanging onto the edge of a mountain." She lowered onto a wooden chair near the firepit and continued, "I have lived here all my life. When my husband died, my family wanted me to move into their home, in Asni. But I wanted to stay here. I was much younger and could get around and tend to my home without help.

Well, one day I saw this gentleman, a handsome fellow…tall and lanky with almond eyes. In fact, you resemble him. Anyway, he said he was heading into the forest to gather timber and asked if I needed firewood.

I said yes. He…he returned." She looked at the smoldering embers with a distant gaze. A'isha sipped her tea, staring at her wide-eyed.

She looked at A'isha and continued, "He returned a few hours later with an armful of timber, and I offered him a glass of water. We spent the afternoon talking about this and that, but mostly about his childhood." She raised her eyes to the ceiling and smiled. "So, one thing led to another and before we knew it, he was spending more time with me. I knew he was married and that he and his family lived somewhere nearby, but he…" She shook her head with a sigh and returned to the sofa.

A'isha tightened her grip on the cup.

"Anyway, one day while we were having breakfast he mentioned that one of his daughters was sick and that his wife had become despondent. He said her name was Isir. I remember because it was also my grandmother's name. He used to—"

"*What?*" A'isha winced, placing her cup on the table. She stood up and walked toward the firepit. Squinting at the pile of ashes, she shook her head. "Are you telling me *you're* the woman my grandmother used to talk about?"

Hira raised her brow. "What do you mean?"

A'isha snapped her head toward her. "My grandmother…she once said she wasn't sure if her husband—*my grandfather*—disappeared because he was eaten by a leopard, or because…because he left her for another woman." She eased onto the chair and shook her head. "So, *you're* the mistress who stole my grandmother's husband—*my mother's father? You?*"

"I wouldn't say that I *stole* him from his family. He just enjoyed spending time with me."

"But you knew he was married. How could you?" A'isha looked at her satchel, leaning against the sofa.

"How could I what?" Hira asked, reaching for her cup.

"How could you shroud and bury the woman whose husband you stole? *How could you do that?* And just think, I thought you were a kind old lady. But you…you destroyed my family. You took away my grandmother's husband—*my mother's father*—at a time that they needed him most."

"Why shouldn't I have shrouded your grandmother? What does one thing have to do with the other? Besides, that was many years ago, and I—"

A'isha jumped to her feet, glaring at Hira. "My grandmother spent her life waiting and wondering what happened to her husband. Whenever we harvested near the forest she would look between the trees as if searching for something. She tried to hide it from me, but I knew what she was doing. She was looking for him. Sometimes, I wanted to grab her by the shoulders and tell her, 'he is *never* coming back to you!' And I was right." She clamped her lip between her teeth, eased onto the chair, then asked, "What happened to him? My grandfather…what hap—"

"I didn't steal your grandfather away from his family. No one can force anyone to do anything. He made a choice."

"But if it weren't for you, he wouldn't have had a choice! He would've remained with his family, and my grandmother—my mother and my aunts—wouldn't have suffered."

"If it weren't for *me*? I am not responsible for your grandfather's actions—he was. We're all responsible for our actions. There is no one to blame, not even Allah. And if you think otherwise, you are foolish. And if you blame yourself for the actions of others, then you are beyond foolish, you are ghabi…stupid."

"But you haven't answered my question. Where is my grandfather?"

"I don't know. One day he left and never returned. I have spent many nights wondering what happened to him. I do know that he would go into the forest, often. Just to wander. He used to say that the forest was the only place where he could be free. I know that he loved his family, but when his daughter became ill it was as if he couldn't handle the pain. It was too much for him. Not only his pain but his wife's and daughters' pain. It crippled him. And so, he would disappear into the forest whenever he could. It is where he felt free. Maybe your grandmother was right. Maybe a leopard did put an end to his life."

A'isha shook her head. "But that was so selfish of him. He knew his family needed him. How could he abandon them at a time like that? How could he…what gave him the right!"

"A'isha, maybe he lacked the strength expected of him as a man, as a descendant of the Imazighen. Maybe he wasn't the warrior he was expected to be, so he chose to escape and hide, knowing he could not give his family what they needed. Maybe he was ashamed." Hira raised her eyes to the Yaz and inhaled. "And if that was so, then you must accept him for who he was, and forgive him for what he could not do, including the pain he caused your grandmother."

"And my mother," A'isha whispered.

"Yes, and your mother. I am sure he did not intend to hurt them. I got to know your grandfather well, and I can tell you he was not an uncaring man. He was soft-spoken and kind."

A'isha snapped her head up. "But you…how could you? How could you shroud my grandmother, knowing what you did to her and her family?"

"Please lower your voice, A'isha," Hira said, massaging the ache in her knee. "As for your grandmother, tell me, what did I do to her? Huh? What did I do?"

"You destroyed her! That's what you did."

"I did no such thing. Your grandfather would come here on his own. I never asked him to arrive *or* to leave. We would simply talk and offer each other companionship."

"But the Qur'an…it admonishes such a thing. That's adultery!"

"Is companionship adultery? Your grandfather and I never engaged in anything sexual. We talked and laughed and shared meals. We never even kissed. What is so wrong with that? I don't consider that adultery. Do you?"

"Would Allah? Would *He* consider it wrong? Do you even care what He thinks?"

"Of course, I care. I know the Qur'an talks about sexual matters and adultery, but it does not say you cannot share a meal with a married person."

"Would you have wanted *your* husband to do that with another woman?"

"Perhaps he did. I could not tell you and frankly, I would not have been bothered if he had. Whether he had a mistress or not, he was a wonderful husband to me."

"Then what is marriage for? Why get married if a husband could do what my grandfather did with you, and abandon his family? How is that okay?"

"Your grandfather did not abandon his family because of me—that's if he abandoned them at all. He was not here in my home enough for anyone to say he abandoned them because of me. That is a judgment and accusation I cannot accept."

A'isha raised her eyes toward the Yaz. Her grandmother's proud smile flashed across her mind. She looked at Hira and frowned. "I don't know what to think. I thought you were this sweet old lady, and it turns out that you're the one who caused my grandmother so much grief."

"I was not the source of your grandmother's grief. Perhaps your grandmother spent her life grieving and longing only because she believed she deserved to suffer."

A'isha glared at Hira. "*Excuse me?*"

"Yes, it is as I said. Our lives merely reflect what we believe to be true about ourselves. If we think we deserve to suffer, then we will. And whatever we do to others will be done to us. It is a cycle of life. That's why Allah teaches us to treat others as we would want to be treated. It is all quite simple."

Maybe that's why you're alone, you old prune. A'isha walked toward the sofa and sat as far away from Hira as possible. She grabbed her satchel off the floor and yanked out a wreath. "I brought a gift for you."

"How beautiful," Hira said, placing her cup on the table.

"I made it for you…to thank you for helping me shroud and bury my grandmother." A'isha shoved it at her.

"Shukran. How thoughtful of you."

"You're welcome," A'isha replied, dryly. "I made it out of pinecones, cork and—"

"And fennel, my favorite."

A'isha stood up, clutching her satchel against her chest. "I must leave now."

"I do hope you return. I know that you cannot understand why I was able to follow Allah's command and shroud your grandmother. But you are a smart girl, and I am confident one day you will understand. With time, there is wisdom."

A'isha opened the door. "Salaam."

"Goodbye, my child. If you ever need anything, please come back to me. And remember, Nadesh will be here next week. She would be delighted to see you, as will I."

"Thank you."

A'isha scrambled down the bluff and onto the road leading her into the village. She looked back at Hira's home, obscured by brush and twisted vines. "I am sorry, my jida," she whispered. "I did not know who she was. I will never speak to that woman, ever again." A sudden breeze rustled deadened leaves, and the screech of an Ibis pulled her attention toward the graying sky. "I'm sorry, Jida," she whispered again, watching the Ibis glide onto an outcrop, stretching its wings. Her stomach growled and her mouth watered. She walked off the path, into the forest and pulled two figs off a tree. She wiped off the fuzz on the bib of her yellow jumper and sank her teeth into one. The juice burst into her mouth and soothed her scorched tongue. She walked along the river's edge, listening to shallow water flow upon a bed of stones. She thought about Hira's relationship with her grandfather, and about her father's relationship with Amir. And she thought about Saira.

"A'isha, there you are!" Amir shrieked as she entered the shop. "You are late today."

"I stopped by Hira's home to give her a wreath. It was my way of thanking her for shrouding my jida, but I should have just flung it into the river. What a fool I was."

"Ouch!" Amir yelled, pricking his finger with a needle. He tossed the black-beaded kaftan into a bin near his feet. "Why would you say such a thing?" he asked, sucking his finger.

"Oh, it's nothing. Have I had any customers?"

"Yes, you have. Your money is in the can. And I have even better news!"

A'isha spun around. "What is it? Was my family here?"

"No, they weren't. But my merchant from Marrakesh, al-Majid, came by this morning and saw your wreaths. He thinks they are beautiful, and he wants to talk to you about selling them in the medina." Amir eased off the stool and walked toward A'isha.

"Can you believe it?" he clapped. "Do you know what this could mean for you?"

"I…I…" A'isha gripped the counter and looked around the shop. A surge of anxiety shot through her. She wiped her sweaty palms on her pant leg and turned toward Amir. "Are you *sure?*" she asked.

"Of course, I'm sure!"

"When will he return? Or…or should I go to Marrake—"

"No, no need to travel there. He will return in one month to pick up the abayas I'm beading. And he said that when he returns, he wants to speak with you!"

"I…I…*my wreaths?* He wants to sell my wreaths in the *medina?*" She threw her arms into the air; then hugged Amir and jumped up and down. "Shukran! Oh, Amir, this is good news for sure!"

"You will have to make more—many more! You want to be prepared for his return."

"Yes! I will do that. In one month, you say?"

"Yes, so you have time to stock up." He looked at his watch, tapped it, swung open the door, and hurried onto the road. "Nasim! What time do you have?" he called out. He cupped his mouth, "I said what time do you have? Shukran!" He entered the shop, grinning at A'isha. "I can never trust this stupid watch. But this time, it is correct, and so I must leave."

"Where are you going? I just got here. I thought we would spend the day together. I could help you bead, and then we could get some pastilla and papaya juice for lunch…and celebrate!"

"I would love to do that, but I must visit my doctor today. We can celebrate another day," he smiled.

"Are you well, Amir?"

"Yes, of course. I have an appointment, that's all. I'm glad you arrived before I left. I was so excited to tell you the good news. But I must go now, so you will have the shop to yourself. If anyone comes looking for me, tell them I will return. Inshallah."

"When will that be?"

"Tomorrow morning," he said, placing a jar of beads on a shelf behind the counter.

"It'll be strange to not have you here. I've never been in the shop alone."

He placed his hand on her shoulder. "Well, A'isha, there is a first time for everything, especially if you have the courage to live and not just exist." He walked toward his bundles of fabric, then turned and looked at her. "Did you know that is the meaning of your name?"

"What is?"

"Your name, A'isha…in Arabic it means 'the courage to live.' Did you know that?"

"No, I didn't. The courage to live, you say?"

"Yes, and from the looks of it, your name fits you quite well." He turned off his sewing machine, kissed her on both cheeks, and exited the shop.

She listened to him greet someone at a distance. "As-salamu alaikum!" he shouted, then coughed.

She smiled, delighted that he seemed happier than he had in a long time. Her eyes scanned the room and settled upon her display of wreaths on a shelf behind the counter. "A merchant wants to talk to me about my wreaths…a merchant from Marrakesh!" she said. She reached for her satchel and saw Nasim peering out of his window, watching her with a sinister stare as he had since the day they met. But he never approached her—not until now.

Crossing the road, he pounded his feet into the earth, seething. He entered her shop and slammed the door shut, rattling the windows.

She gasped. "A…Amir is n-not here, Nasim."

"I can *see* he's not here. What do you think, I'm blind?" He swiped his kufi off his head and tossed it onto the counter. "I'm not here to see *him*. It's you I've been waiting to talk to."

Tsewang

This…this hodgepodge…this patchwork of hair and scalp. Perhaps it brings to the fore the conflict that resides within you. Dabir's words echoed in Tsewang's mind and would not leave him alone. He could hear them. They tapped on his shoulder while he prayed and whispered in his ear as he slept. "Is this who you really are?" Dabir had asked him two months ago, the day after he arrived at Dechen Podrang. And whenever he gazed into the shard of mirror, peering at his uneven patches of hair, he searched his soul for an answer. Every day, he would walk the labyrinth and pray to Buddha, asking, "Who am I?" But his question lingered like the smoke and scent of an extinguished candle, and he moved among his fellow monks feeling duplicitous and confused.

Toward them, he spewed words weighed with anger. He was provocative and bitter. Yet, his inner voice and private thoughts were often contrite, a wellspring of Buddhist beliefs that tugged at his attention whenever he was not sparring with his monastic brothers. In their presence, he would pretend their shunning did not matter, did not hurt. But internally, he wished for their acceptance, and he wanted to belong. The self he presented to the outer world contradicted his inner life, the self he kept hidden, and the duality of his existence troubled him more than he would ever admit, even to himself.

At times, his turmoil would pull his eyes toward the high ridge, to its edge. At other times, he would enter the prayer room, light a candle, sit in solitude, and offer Mahakala a quiet gift of gratitude, thanking him for leading him out of the forest. *Maybe I can just let go of one side of me,* he often wondered, but Dabir's words, "Our external life is an expression of the life we live within," would echo from an intuitive place, and deepen his confusion and doubt.

***

"Good morning," Dabir said, stretching and yawning, thankful that the deluge had finally stopped. "That was quite a storm."

"Good morning," Tsewang mumbled. He pulled the quilt over his head and moaned. He had not slept, listening to claps of thunder and watching lightning flash across their room, silently reliving a terrifying night he had spent in the forest.

"Today we are going into town to purchase tools," Dabir said. "Tending to the fields has become impossible." He lit the candle on the table between their mats. The flame flickered wildly in the window's draft and tossed elongated, dancing shadows across their barren room. "We could use an extra hand to help carry them. Do you wish to join us?" he asked, easing his arms into his robe. "Tsewang? Are you awake? Did you hear me?"

"Yes, I hear you. Who's the 'we' that you speak of?"

"What was that?" Dabir asked, gathering his toothpaste and soap. "I would be better able to hear you if you stopped hiding your head under the quilt."

Tsewang yanked the cover from his head, turned over, and asked as he yawned, "I said, who's the 'we'? Who's going with you?"

"I'm not sure, but does that really matter?"

"Yes, it does. You know most of our brothers don't want to be in my company. And so, to avoid punching someone in the face, I need to know who's going with you."

"Ah, Tsewang, why do you insist on making life difficult for yourself?"

Tadashi used to say that to me.

"Perhaps the brothers are simply treating you according to the energy you emit. Why would they want to treat you differently than anyone else?"

"Because of my hair. They treat me—"

"Because of your *hair*? You have been with us for nearly three months. It seems to me that everyone has gotten used to seeing you as such. We have gotten used to who you are. Perhaps it is not they who are uncomfortable with your hair." He opened the door. "I will see you at puja. Do not be late," he warned and hurried to the washroom.

Tsewang stuck his tongue at him. "Perhaps it is not *they* who are uncomfortable with your hair," he mocked. He rolled his eyes, yanked the quilt over his head, and thought of Tadashi, of their walks along the river. "I miss you so," he sighed.

Hushed chatter passed his door, followed by the swoosh of a sweeping broom. He yanked the quilt off his head and sprang to his feet. He moved his hands along his legs. *The pain is gone!* he grinned and slipped on his robe. On his way to the washroom, he passed Dabir. "Yes, I will go with you to Thimphu," he said, bowing with a smile. Dabir knitted his brow and nodded, then entered their room.

Tsewang attended morning puja. It was the first time he arrived at the opening chime. He sat among his brothers and not on the threshold where he was usually found. He closed his eyes during meditation and bowed his head when he prayed. He removed his mala beads from his pocket and advanced them between his fingers as he joined in the mantra for the Second Chakra, Sacral: 'I am the creator of my entire reality.' At the closing chime, he exited the prayer room with his brothers. He did not sit and wait until he was alone. And in the dining hall, he chose a seat among them, not off to the side.

Still, his brothers ignored him. They treated him as if he were invisible, as did Rinpoche. But unlike most mornings, this day he moved about undisturbed by their shunning, untouched by the anger it typically aroused, and he did not know why. Yet, he knew something was different, that a shift occurred within. Something had lifted. He felt unburdened and he felt free. *Perhaps Buddha has answered my prayers,* he thought, as he enjoyed his warm oats, chamomile tea, and yak-buttered bread.

"Ah, there you are, Tsewang," Dabir said as he descended the stairs, lifting his kasaya, and avoiding puddles along the way.

Tsewang watched him, smiling. *He reminds me of Tadashi.*

"And what brings a smile to your face?" Dabir asked, approaching him. "You seem to be in a better mood this morning. I have been watching you. What gives?"

"Oh, I don't know. I…what is *this*?" he gasped. The monk with the birthmark exited the monastery. "Is *he* coming with us?"

Dabir spun around. "Yes, and Uddi will join us, too."

"Who's Uddi?"

The monk with the birthmark approached them.

"Namaste," Tsewang and Dabir said, in unison, bowing at the thin, bespectacled, middle-aged man.

Dabir turned to Tsewang. "Have you two met?"

"No, I don't believe we have," the monk replied, cleaning his eyeglasses with his sash. "My name is Doijin, and yours?"

So, this is Doijin! Rinpoche's assistant. "Namaste. My name is Tsewang."

"Of course, it is. I have heard a lot about you and I have seen you in action."

"Is that so?" Tsewang asked, pursing his lips.

"Yes, it is. And I—"

"Ah, and here is Uddi," Dabir said. "Now, we can leave."

Tsewang snapped his head toward the door. *That's Uddi? Big Nose is Uddi?*

He watched him lumber toward them with a slight bend and hunched shoulders, a gangly man in his early twenties. His head was large, and his limbs were long, but his physical presence was obscured by his timid demeanor, which made him seem diminutive and opaque.

Maybe I should back out of this now. Tsewang tried to craft an excuse, but before he could speak, Dabir clapped, "Brothers, let us leave. We have a long walk ahead of us and must return by midday puja."

"But where is Kasim?" Tsewang asked, staring at the doors, wide-eyed.

"He's working the fields today," Dabir replied over his shoulder. "It'll be just the four of us. You will see Kasim when we return."

They walked the pebbled path in a single file until they arrived at a bend just behind a magnolia tree, where the road widened and was no longer paved with pebbles, but with wind-tossed twigs and deadened leaves atop rain puddles and a soggy earth. On one side, there were jasmine bushes, rhododendron, and brush. Poplar, hemlock, and pine trees lined the other. Dabir and Uddi walked side-by-side, Doijin and Tsewang followed them, steps behind.

"So, I hear you are from Pali Sholing, yes?" Doijin asked, tightening his sash, then clasping his hands behind his back.

"Yes, you've heard correctly," Tsewang snapped. *If he thinks he will use this journey to get into my business, I have a surprise for him!* "And you, Doijin? Where are you from?"

"Me? I've been at Dechen Podrang for forty years! I've been here so long that I have forgotten where I'm from."

"Yes," Dabir said, tilting his head back, "Doijin has seen it all. He's the most senior among us."

Geez! Does anyone here mind their own business? Tsewang wanted to shout, but said, "Oh, so you have known Rinpoche for a long time." *That creepy bastard.*

"Yes, I have. He is Dechen's second Rinpoche—since I've been here, at least. His predecessor was as kind as he is." He looked at Tsewang and searched his face. Tsewang remained expressionless, refusing to even blink.

The muffled chatter between Uddi and Dabir pulled his attention toward them. *Are they talking about me?*

Then he heard Doijin say, "…yes, and his name is Tadashi."

His words sounded as if they were stretching toward him from afar, as if they were bubbling up from underwater. Tsewang snapped his head at Doijin and stopped walking.

"*What?* What did you just say?" he asked, peering at Doijin.

Dabir and Uddi turned around. No one moved.

Doijin looked back at Tsewang, furrowed his brow, and chuckled. "Yes, as I said, I have a nephew at Pali Sholing. His name is Tadashi. He is my sister's son."

Tsewang's knees buckled and his head spun. The sound of Tadashi's name spoken outside of his mind kicked up tangled emotions, mostly guilt. He wanted to vomit.

"Are you feeling ill, my brother?" asked Doijin.

Dabir and Uddi rushed toward him. "Do you need some water?" Uddi asked.

"In the name of Mahakala!" Dabir howled. "We forgot to bring water! How could I be so stupid? What is wrong, Tsewang? What did you say to him, Doijin?"

"Why, nothing. I only mentioned that my nephew, Tadashi, is at Pali Sholing." He placed his hand on Tsewang's shoulder. "Do you know my nephew?"

Tsewang walked toward a boulder just off the path and plopped onto it. Dabir sat next to him. Tsewang looked up at Doijin and slowly nodded, "Yes, I know your nephew. I know him well. He was—I mean, he *is*—my closest, dearest friend."

He looked beyond Doijin, into the forest, and added, "He is the only person in this world who has ever loved me."

Dabir shook his head, "Indeed, the world is small." He looked up at Doijin and asked, "Did you know this?"

Doijin shrugged. "I wasn't certain, but I figured he must've known my nephew. How could he not?"

Tsewang peered at him. "Why did you take so long to tell me that Tadashi is your nephew?"

"Tsewang, you have been too busy fighting with our brothers for me to even introduce myself to you."

Tsewang glanced at Uddi. Uddi lowered his eyes and walked away.

"Have you talked to Tadashi?" Tsewang winced. "Do you know what is happening at Pali Sholing…to the novices? Has he told you?"

Doijin and Dabir looked at each other, then turned to Tsewang. "What do you mean?" Dabir asked. "What is happening at Pali Sholing?"

Tsewang passed his hand across his head, feeling the lines between his uneven patches of hair, and he thought of Tadashi. He could hear him say, *the path of least resistance leads to the end of suffering. Accept what is and suffer no more.* Then he thought about Satya, the precept of truth.

"Tsewang, do you hear me?" Dabir asked. He sprang to his feet and stood next to Doijin. "What is happening to the novices at Pali Sholing?"

"I…I…" Slowly, Tsewang stood up and walked away.

"Come back here!" Dabir shouted.

Tsewang turned, lowered his head, and walked toward them. "I…I…"

"Tell me!" Dabir demanded, grabbing Tsewang's arm. "Why did you run away from Pali Sholing?"

Tsewang's eyes shifted from Dabir to Doijin and down the path toward Uddi. "The Rinpoche…he…he…is abusing the children. He abused me. And…and"—he looked at Doijin, blinking away tears— "he has abused Tadashi."

"Abused you, how?" Dabir hollered, tightening his grip on Tsewang's arm.

"Sexually," Tsewang whispered. "He abused me for years. And not only me."

Dabir tossed his face to the sky. "In the name of Lord Shiva!" he screamed. "Are you speaking truth? Are your words truthful, Tsewang? Do you know what you are saying!?"

"Yes, I am telling the truth."

"Have you told this to Rinpoche? Does he know?"

"Yes, he knows. And he did this to my hair. When I told him, he became enraged and stopped sha—."

"Uddi! Uddi, come back here this instant!" Dabir yelled.

"Sir? Are we not going to the city for tools?"

"We are doing no such thing. We are returning to the monastery at once. I must speak to Rinpoche at once!"

"But…but…" Tsewang begged.

"But what?" Dabir shouted.

"But he will ask me to leave. I am sure. He already thinks I'm a troublemaker."

"He will do no such thing. And if he does, I will take matters into my own hands."

Dabir marched on, pounding his feet into the soggy earth, splattering mud onto the hem of his kasaya. Doijin, Tsewang, and Uddi followed in a single file. Silently, they walked the path back to the monastery.

Dabir stomped up the stairs and swung open the massive red door. "Uddi, you stay outside. Wait right here. Doijin and Tsewang, come with me!"

"Rinpoche!" Dabir called out, storming into the dining hall. "Rinpoche! I must speak with you," he yelled, pounding his muddy, sandaled feet onto the hollow, wooden floor. He charged down the corridor, heading for the prayer room.

"Dabir! Dabir, I am here," Rinpoche said, standing at the doorway to his bedroom at the end of the hallway.

Dabir, Tsewang, and Doijin spun around. A novice scurried out of Rinpoche's room and into the washroom.

"Sir, I must speak with you at once. May we enter?"

"No, no. Meet me in the dining hall. No one is here. Give me a moment."

Dabir yanked a chair, plopped onto it, and drummed his fingers on the splintering table, breathing rapidly. Tsewang and Doijin sat next to him. Doijin closed his eyes and whispered a mantra. Tsewang bit on the interior of his cheek, wringing his hands and shaking his leg.

Rinpoche entered and eased onto a chair at the head of the table. "Now, tell me, what is going on?

Did you run into trouble in Thimpu?"

Dabir flared his nostrils and inhaled. "No, but we ran into trouble on the path." He peered at Rinpoche. "Tsewang shared disturbing information with us. Just disturbing…disgusting!"

Rinpoche glared at Tsewang. "What did he say?"

"Tsewang, do you want to tell him?"

Tsewang stared at Rinpoche. "He already knows what I told you, Dabir."

"And what is that?" Rinpoche seethed.

"As I have told you…that the headmaster at Pali Sholing is abusing the novices. I told you he has abused me." He looked at Doijin. "And he has abused my best friend."

Rinpoche slammed his hand on the table. "That is absurd! I know him and he would never do such a thing—never!"

"But Rinpoche," Dabir begged, "why would Tsewang say this if it is untrue? What would he have to gain?"

"I don't know! I don't know this boy. He is just being vindictive! He could have been *thrown* out of Pali Sholing—the same way his mother threw him away."

Tsewang banged his fist on the table. "You do not know my mother! Take her name out of your filthy mouth before I--"

"Before you what, Tsewang?" Rinpoche hissed.

Doijin intervened, "Please, my brothers. Let us not lose our senses. We must approach this by the precepts. In a way that is pleasing to Lord Buddha."

"Sir, we must listen to Tsewang," Dabir said. "Don't you think we should look into—"

"Into what!" Rinpoche screamed. "Why should we allow this child, this *throwaway*, to come here and disrupt our lives? I owe him nothing!"

Tsewang tilted his head and smirked. "What are you afraid of, Rinpoche?"

"Do not start this with me again! I will throw you out of here!"

"Are you afraid that *your* secret will be revealed, too?"

"Tsewang! What are you saying?" Dabir shrieked.

"He knows exactly what I am saying?" Tsewang replied, staring and smirking at Rinpoche.

"Get out of here, now!" Rinpoche yelled, jumping to his feet, and knocking over his chair.

"I will not," Tsewang said, leaning back. "I will leave this place when I *feel* like leaving. And if you try to throw me out, I will tell everyone the truth about you, too."

Doijin's jaw dropped. Dabir slapped his fingers over his own gaping mouth. They stared at each other. Rinpoche lifted his chair from the floor and lowered onto it, glaring at Tsewang.

"Lord Shiva, please help us," Dabir whispered, shaking his head. He looked at Rinpoche and thought about the novice who had scurried out of his bedroom moments before.

Tsewang rose to his feet. "Are we finished, my brothers? It is getting late." He grinned at Rinpoche. "You *do* have to prepare for midday puja, don't you?"

Dabir, Doijin, and Rinpoche stared at Tsewang, wide-eyed. He nodded at each of them, turned without bowing, and sauntered out of the room, heading for Uddi.

A'isha

"Talk to *me?*" A'isha asked, squeezing out a smile. "About *what?*"

"You know exactly what!" Nasim hissed. "When are you going to stop this? When are you going to leave? You're not welcome here. What girl works in a shop? Especially a mithlia."

A'isha's head snapped back. "*A what?* Who do you think you're talking to?"

She tossed her satchel onto the counter, slid her hands into her pockets to hide their tremble, and calmly walked toward Nasim. "What gives you the right to come in here and speak to me like this? And so, what if I like girls? Who knows," she said, poking her finger into his chest, "maybe you're a homosexual too, but you're just afraid to admit it."

"As afraid as your father?"

A'isha stepped back. "*My father?* What are you saying about my father?"

"Oh, come on. I'm sure you've heard the rumors. Don't act like you don't know."

"Rumors about what?"

"About your father and Amir. Everyone knows and I'm sure you do, too. And if you didn't know, you're more stupid than I thought."

"What…what are they saying?"

"That your father and Amir had, shall we say, more than a work relationship. Everyone knows they're two mukhannath. Two sissies."

A'isha lowered her eyes and leaned against the counter. Nasim watched her, waiting for her to speak, puzzled by a surge of compassion he tried to ignore.

She lifted her eyes to Nasim's. "Please don't call them that."

"What? Sissies? Why not? That's what they are. They're not *real* men."

"How can you say that…that Amir is not a real man? You're disrespecting him, yet you treat him so kindly. Do you mock him with the other men, or do you defend him?"

Nasim huffed and walked toward the door. He folded his arms and peered out the window. "He's an elder, so we try to respect him…to his face, at least."

"But do you defend him?"

"Defend him from what? From the truth? That he's a mukhannath?"

"I said stop calling him that!"

He turned and looked at her. "I…I guess I don't, but I show him respect when he's here."

"Then you're a phony…a hypocrite. And anyway, why do you show him respect and not me?"

"Are you trying to compare yourself to *Amir*? There's no comparison."

"I'm doing no such thing, but why the double stan—"

A woman holding the hand of a solemn child entered the shop. "As-salamu alaikum," she said, greeting Nasim.

"Wa-alaikum salaam," Nasim replied, grabbing his kufi off the counter and covering his head.

"How can I help you?" A'isha asked.

"Is Amir here?" the woman replied, looking at Nasim.

"No," they said in unison and glanced at each other. Nasim raised his brow and smiled. A'isha clenched her teeth. She pushed past the woman and flung open the door. "Nasim, thank you for stopping by. As you can see, I am busy now."

"Bialtabe…of course," he said, and bowed at the woman. He brushed past A'isha and whispered, "I will return." The woman tightened her grip on the child's hand and followed Nasim out the door.

"Sayidati? Did you want something?"

The woman turned around and stared at A'isha, then shook her head slowly and walked away.

A'isha slammed the door and plopped onto a stool at her father's workbench. Nasim's words rattled her mind. "Amir and my baba were *lovers*?" she whispered, then tossed her head back and laughed. "I knew it! I knew it! Wait until I see Amir. And my baba…that hypocrite!" She slammed her hand on her father's workbench, bolted to her feet, and swung open the door.

She stomped onto the road and swept her eyes across the dusty village cloaked in simmering heat. She watched women peruse prickly pears and mustard leaves atop donkey-drawn carts, clinging onto the hands of rambunctious children wanting to break free. She surveyed the men sitting in the doorway of their shops, surrendering to arid air with pushed-back kufis and raised tunics, dangling cigarettes between their lips. She smiled at the absentminded children playing dinifri upon a thirsty earth. "You hypocrites! Who are you to judge us?" she wanted to shout but tossed her face to the sky and released howling laughter. Heads turned toward her with taut frowns and crinkled brows. Nasim gawked at her through his window. She put her hands on her hips and glared at him with pursed lips, then spun on her heels, entered her shop, and slammed the door.

She gathered her father's tools and tins of mink oil and placed them in a bin behind the counter, then lay two wreaths on the workbench. Scanning the shop with smiling eyes, she slung her satchel across her chest, yanked the chain on the dangling bulb, and closed the door.

Amir did not come to the shop the following day, or the day after. So, A'isha decided to go to his home. She walked the road leading her away from the village and toward a backroad, where clay abodes cling onto cliffs and roosters run free. She walked past her family's home and frowned at the empty shell it had become, ignoring the urge to peek through the chicken wire window and pull off creeping, leafless vines.

She trudged up the hill, passing the boulder she and Saira spent many afternoons lounging upon, sharing dreams and making plans. She passed a goat chewing roadside brush and a woman walking downhill, bent beneath a bundle of mustard greens tied to her back.

She turned the bend. "Ya Allah!" she gasped. Her legs locked and her heart pounded at the sight of Saira and her grandmother hanging clothes on slackened twine. Silently, she watched Saira hoist water from the well, pour it into a bowl, and place it in front of her impatient goat. She watched her toss grains into the chicken coop. "She's still so beautiful," A'isha whispered. She inhaled deeply, tightened her hijab, and continued up the hill.

"As-salamu alaikum," she said, softly. Saira and her grandmother spun around. Saira's jaw dropped; her grandmother grunted and wobbled into her home. Grains trickled from Saira's hand until her fingers were free, and A'isha smiled, wiping her sweaty palms on her pant legs.

"A'isha! What are you doing here?" Saira gushed, extending her arms toward her.

"I have missed you so," A'isha whispered, taking Saira's hands into her own. Saira glanced at the house and pulled away.

"Where have you been?" A'isha asked. "Why have you not come to school?"

Tears filled Saira's eyes as she gazed into A'isha's. "My baba sent me to live with his sister in Imlil after…after you went to your jida. Is that where you went? I heard what your father did. That he…well, that night."

A'isha nodded. "Yes, that's where I went. I'm still there, but my jida has died."

"Oh, my sweet girl," she said, pulling A'isha into her arms, and hugging her. "I am so sorry. Taeazi…my condolences."

A'isha placed her hand on Saira's cheek. "There is so much I want to say to you," she whispered. Saira placed her hand atop A'isha's, closed her eyes, and pressed her cheek into A'isha's palm.

"Saira, I miss you so much. Tell me, what are you doing here? Are you here to stay?"

"No, we came just for a visit. My aunt—"

"How long will you be here? Come to my house. I'll make your favorite dessert, apricot biscuits."

"You remember," she blushed. "I—"

"Saira! Ta'al huna!" her grandmother yelled.

"I must go."

"Do you remember how to get to my jida's home?" A'isha asked.

"I think so."

"Saira! Come in here, now!" her grandmother screamed.

"Listen, I am in my father's shop every day. Please come. It's just Amir and me."

Her grandmother pushed open the door, knocking it off a hinge. It dangled on an angle as she waved her cane and yelled, "Get away from that girl, Saira. A'isha, go away! You have caused enough trouble in this family. You are not welcome here. Go away!"

"Bialtabe," A'isha replied, chuckling at the dangling door.

"I said, go away!"

A'isha said, "Ana bahebik! I always have and I always will."

Saira spun around and smiled, then entered her home.

"Ya Allah!" A'isha shrieked, skipping onto the path to Amir's home, singing a nasheed her jida had taught her, The Spirit of Bravery.

"Amir? Hello?" she called out, knocking on the door and peering into a window. She walked toward the rear of their house, but neither he nor his wife was home. She removed tunics and hijabs from the clothesline, then folded and placed them in the shed. She tossed grains into the chicken coop, scattered hay for the goat, and plopped onto a wooden bench. She scanned the tangerine sky, searching for the sunset, listening to the Mu'addin's call for prayer, "Allahu Akbar!" She closed her eyes and bowed her head. "Allah," she whispered, "please let Amir be well. Bring him back to the shop, and please help me get home safely. Inshallah." She tightened her shoelace, tucked strands of hair into her hijab, and began her long walk home.

Amir did not return to the shop the following day, nor the day after, and Nasim did not know why.

"But he hasn't been here for five days," A'isha winced, searching Nasim's face for an answer.

"I told you. Nobody knows where he is. But if I hear of anything, I will let you know."

"Shukran, Nasim. Inshallah."

"I didn't know you speak Arabic," he grinned.

A'isha opened the door. "There's a lot about me that you don't know. Goodbye."

She sat at her father's workbench and put the final touch on a wreath, adjusting pinecones and fennel leaves. "Today, I will make five more," she declared, but was too distracted by her thoughts of Amir. So, she spent the day sorting beads, spools of thread, and rolls of fabric.

Each day, A'isha arrived at the shop at the same hour Amir had for seventeen years, and worked until dusk, *as he would, if he were here,* she often sighed. Some customers stopped by and tersely asked, "Have you heard anything?" Others peered into the window, refusing to enter.

The morning Nadesh was due to arrive at Hira's home, A'isha was fraught with indecision. She wanted to see her, but thoughts of Hira reignited her anger, and she feared that Amir might arrive at the shop and not find her there. Despite her confusion, she yielded to her excitement and traveled to Hira's home, anxious to see Nadesh.

"Salaam, Sayidati," A'isha said, knocking on the door.

"Oh, A'isha! Please, come in," Hira replied, greeting her with a kiss on each cheek. "You have arrived at the right time. Nadesh is here. She's out back. You may go to her. Are you thirsty?"

"No, I am not, thank you."

"You will meet my brother when he returns. He is in the forest, collecting firewood."

"Of course," A'isha said.

"Do you see your wreath?"

"Yes, it looks pretty there, but most people hang them on the outside."

"I love the scent of fennel, so I hang it here."

A'isha raised her eyes to the Yaz just above the wreath. The vision of Hira shrouding her grandmother flashed across her mind.

"Please, go to Nadesh," Hira said. "She will be delighted to see you."

A'isha exited the house and walked to the clearing behind it. She watched Nadesh harvest mint. *She is as beautiful as I remember.*

"Nadesh?"

"A'isha! It's so good to see you. It's been so long." She placed a bundle of mint in a basket, wiped her hands on an apron, and wrapped her arms around A'isha. "You look so…so mature," she gushed. "How long has it been?"

"Over a year, I think. Yes, it's been a long time. How are you?"

"I am well. In September I begin my third year at the university. Do you still plan to leave Ouirgane? My aunt told me about your grandmother's passing. My condolences to you. I know how difficult that kind of loss can be."

"Thank you. Yes, it's still painful. I miss my jida, but I know she's always with me." She slid her hands into her pant pocket and looked at Nadesh, her long eyelashes, her full lips. "And yes, I still plan to leave Ouirgane next year. I wanted to show my college applications to you, but I forgot to bring them."

"That's not a problem. Maybe you can visit me at school and bring them with you." Her smile widened. "And if you do, you'll have a chance to see what a campus is like. Have you ever been to one?"

"No, but I'd love to visit yours."

"That would be wonderful. I would take you around. You could talk with other students. You can even stay with me for a few days if you'd like."

A'isha's skin tingled and her heart raced. She wanted to grab Nadesh and kiss her. "I would love that," she said.

"Wonderful! Let's go inside. I'll write down my address and you can give me yours."

As A'isha entered the house, Hira asked, "So, how is Amir?"

"He's…he is fine, Hira," A'isha replied over her shoulder. "Thank you for asking." She watched Nadesh write her address on a piece of paper. *She's left-handed, like me.*

Nadesh handed her the pen. "Oh, you're left-handed, like me. I wonder what else we have in common."

A'isha looked up at her. "Yes, I wonder, too. Maybe one day we'll find out."

Nadesh glanced at Hira, Hira glanced at A'isha, and A'isha smiled at Nadesh.

"Be sure to write to me, A'isha. And remember, you are welcome to come at any time."

"But how will you travel to Ifrane from here?" Hira asked.

"Ifrane is just seven hours away," Nadesh said.

"Trust me," A'isha interrupted. "I will figure it out. As my grandmother always said, 'Where there's a will, there's a way.'" She turned to Hira, and dryly said, "Goodbye," then kissed Nadesh on both cheeks. "You will hear from me," she smiled.

"I hope so," Nadesh gushed.

A'isha winked at her and closed the door.

"Amir, there you are!" A'isha shrieked. "Where have you been?" She tossed her satchel onto the counter and hugged him tightly. He eased onto his stool, closed his eyes, and wiped his brow with his kufi. "Are you well, Amir? Do you need water?"

"No, A'isha. I am fine, thank you. But I do need to talk to you. Come," he said, patting the stool at her father's workbench. "Come, sit down."

She sat, clenching her teeth onto her lip, startled by his new thinness and the hollow in his eyes. "Amir, what's going on?"

"A'isha, I fell sick last week and traveled to Marrakesh, to my merchant's doctor. I must…" He swept his eyes across the shop and gazed at the bundles of fabric stacked along the back wall. Then he looked at her. "I have been ordered to remain home for a few days. My doctor wants me to rest." He searched her face and continued, "So, you will have to manage things here. I am counting on you to do that."

"But when will you return? What shall I tell the merchant? He will be here in just two weeks."

"I am not sure when I will return, that is up to my doctor. And as for al-Majid, give him the abayas I have completed. They are folded, there on the shelf, wrapped in plastic."

"Yes, I know. And those you have not finished, I—"

"If you wish to bead the remaining abayas, I will be forever grateful. You have learned how to bead, and you are good at it. But it most important that you come to the shop no later than nine o'clock each day. As you know, we have many customers who purchase fabric and—"

"Of course, I will, Amir," A'isha nodded. "I was late today only because I had to go to Hira's home."

"That is fine. Sometimes we must be late. But many of our customers travel a long way, so you must be here when they arrive."

"Yes, I know. You can trust me. I will make you proud."

"Thank you, A'isha," he coughed.

He eased off the stool and walked behind the counter. "Everything you will need is right here, on these two shelves. And if you need any help—any help at all—you must seek Nasim or Abdullah. You know him, he owns the restaurant down the road."

"Amir, they will never—"

"Listen to me, if you *ever* need help, you must go to them. Trust me, they will help you. I have spoken to them. Do you understand?"

"Yes," she nodded. "I will…I promise."

"Very well. I must get ready to leave. Abdullah will be here soon to take me home."

"You're leaving *now?*"

"Yes, I am tired, and I must get some rest."

"I will visit you. I'll make almond biscuits for you; I know they're your favorite," she said, following him out the door.

"That would be nice, A'isha. Thank you." He kissed her on both cheeks and locked his eyes onto hers. "I am proud of the young lady you have become. Your father would be proud of you too."

"Amir…Amir, I know about you and my—"

"Ah, I see Abdullah," he said, waving his arm. He looked at A'isha and coughed. "What was that? What did you say?"

"I…I want to tell you that I am proud of who you are, too. Of you and my baba…I'm proud of you both."

They gazed at one another and smiled. "Thank you, A'isha. One day you will be able to say that to your father. That would be a good thing, don't you think?"

"Yes, it would be. The three of us"—she grinned— "we have more in common than…than he would want me to know."

"Or that he would want to admit," he chuckled. "He just did not know what to do, how to handle it…too afraid of what people might think." He looked over his shoulder at Nabeel's workbench and shook his head. "Such a loss. Such an unnecessary loss," he whispered.

Abdullah opened the car door for Amir, helped him settle in, and nodded at A'isha. She leaned into the car and kissed Amir on his cheek.

"I will see you soon. And don't worry about the shop, I will be here," she said.

"Thank you, A'isha. I know I can count on you."

"Uhibbukaya, Amir," she said, blinking away tears.

He gazed up at her and smiled. "I love you too, A'isha. I always have and I always will."

Tsewang

"Uddi!" Tsewang called out, lifting his kasaya to his knees, and running toward the bluff. "Uddi, wait!" he begged, watching him enter the labyrinth. Tsewang ran up the hill and approached the maze of billowing flags, panting. He tightened his sash and paused, wondering if he should enter or wait for him at the other side. He entered.

"Uddi," he said, softly.

Uddi spun around. "Tsewang, you do know this is a place of silence. We should not speak in here."

"Yes, I know, but I—"

"But what? We were together all morning, and you wait until *now* to speak to me?"

"I need to talk to you…to apologize to you."

"Might you be able to do that without dishonoring our principles? You seem to have difficulty following the path, difficulty with non-resistance."

"Yes, but I—"

"As I said, if you wish to speak with me, you may do so on the other side. I am here for contemplation, not conversation; you should be too. I will meet you on the other side."

"No, please. I will not take too much of your time."

"If you *must* talk at this moment, I will listen," he said, shifting his eyes beyond Tsewang, scanning the rows of prayer flags surrounding them.

"Thank you," Tsewang bowed. "Uddi, I was unkind to you, and I apologize. I should not have called you 'big nose;' and I wonder if you will forgive me."

Uddi pursed his lips, then exhaled. "Yes, Tsewang. I forgive you."

"Thank you. And anyway, your nose isn't so big. I mean, it's *big*, but not that big."

"How kind of you."

"Well, that's all I wanted to say. And if you ever need my help with anything at all, please tell me."

Uddi stared at Tsewang, then nodded slowly and said, "I know you have spent time here, in the labyrinth. I have seen you. It is said that this place, these flags, have the power to transform. One can enter the labyrinth as a certain kind of person and arrive at the other end changed. Now that I have met you, I know it is true."

"Yes, change is difficult, but I suppose people really can change if they want to."

"Change is not difficult. It is our resistance to change that makes it difficult. You must remember that resistance is the root of all suffering."

Tsewang nodded. "Yes, I'm beginning to understand." He looked beyond Uddi, at the path that awaited them, and said, "Please proceed. I will remain here until there is proper distance between us, then I will begin. Perhaps you and I will meet again on the other side."

"Yes, perhaps we will. But as you know, in this life of impermanence, nothing is ever promised, and so it is futile for us to expect. We never quite know what the next moment will bring. So, we must stand firm in what is, free from desire and in total surrender to the unfolding of life." He turned and walked until he arrived at the first bend, then glanced back at Tsewang, bowed, and went to the other side.

Tsewang removed his sandals, sat in lotus position, and closed his eyes. He listened to the silence that cradled him; and remained still until the sun lifted its warmth and shifted shadows of rooted, sentient beings. The trumpeting call of a crane pulled his eyes toward the pristine sky. He stood up, slipped his feet into his sandals, and moved through the labyrinth, feeling lifted and free. When he arrived at the other side, Uddi was not there. Feeling neither relief nor regret, he did not look for him. *Is this what non-resistance feels like?* He brushed his hand across his head, fingering jagged spaces between patches of uneven hair, then returned to the path leading him back to the monastery.

"Dabir?" Tsewang whispered from the threshold of the prayer room. "Dabir, is that you, sir?" He pulled a cushion from the stack and sat beside him. Dabir remained in lotus position, advancing mala beads between his fingers, gazing at the thangka of Mahakala above the shrine. His lips moved without sound.

"Namaste," Tsewang said.

"Namaste," Dabir nodded.

"If I may, sir, I need a favor."

"What can I do for you, Tsewang?"

"Sir, would you please shave my head?"

Dabir looked at Tsewang and frowned. "I would be delighted to, but I have questions for you."

"Yes, sir, what do you wish to know?"

"Tsewang, this morning, when we were on the path, did you speak truth about what is happening at Pali Sholing?"

"Yes, sir, it is the truth. I have always honored Satya. I did not tell a lie."

Dabir eased his eyes away from the thangka of Mahakala and onto the bronze statue of Buddha. "And…and as for Rinpoche, here at Dechen. Do you know something about him that I do not?"

Tsewang lowered his head. "No, sir, I cannot say for certain that I do."

"Then why? Why did you lead Doijin and me to believe that…that he has…that he has abused…" He looked at Tsewang. "Do you know the trouble—the *destruction*—your words could cause for us all?"

"Yes, sir, I do. I just figured if Rinpoche at Pali Sholing is abusing the novices, then…then maybe this Rinpoche is, too. Especially given how he reacted when I told him what had happened to me. And…and when the novice came out of his room, I thought…it reminded me of…of me."

"But was that fair? Could the assumption of truth ever *be* truth? You say you honor Satya, but you do not. Satya *is* truth, not an assumption of truth."

"That was not my intention…to assume. I just—"

"Tsewang, do you recall our conversation, right here in this room, about the importance of releasing fear? That if we do not release fear the moment it is no longer justified, it becomes a filter, a lens, through which we see the world and everyone we meet. Do you remember?"

"Yes, sir, I do."

"Well, this situation you have created here is *exactly* what I was speaking of. You had an experience with one person that produced fear—many emotions—difficult emotions. Feelings that were justified. But the moment you removed yourself from that situation, from that person, you should have released the feelings attached to him—the fear, the rage, the sadness. But you did not. You held onto them and moved into the world. And your perception of the people you have met along the way has been filtered through those emotions. Emotions they did not elicit from you, feelings for which they are not responsible.

Had you released those feelings the moment you left Pali Sholing, had you freed yourself—not only physically, but spiritually and mentally, too—you would have continued your journey with a clear perspective of the truth that lay before you…the truth of your journey. Not as it had been, but as it is. And had you done that, my child, you may have had a vastly different experience here at Dechen Podrang." He inhaled and shook his head. "And now, you have accused this Rinpoche of an atrocity none of us have ever witnessed, have ever experienced at his hands. And that is so unfair to him. It is unfair to us who have been here with him for so many years and, of course, your actions were unfair to you."

Dabir's words were as painful to Tsewang as they were liberating. He wanted to get up and run away as much as he wanted to sit and listen.

Dabir continued, "Indeed, Doijin and I will look into what is happening at Pali Sholing. We owe it to the novices. Lord Buddha teaches us that three things cannot be long hidden: the sun, the moon, and the truth." He lifted his eyes to a prism of light pressing against the circular window and sighed. "So, we will travel to Pali Sholing. That will be our next step." He looked at Tsewang and asked, "What will be yours?"

"What do you mean?"

"Exactly as I said. How are you going to move forward? What will be the next step in your journey?"

"I suppose I can…"

"No. Do not speak it. You must show it."

Dabir grimaced as he stood up, then held Tsewang's eyes with his own. "Be still and sit in silence. Buddha tells us silence is not empty, it is filled with answers. The quieter you become the more you can hear. Listen to your heart, for it is there that your answer lies, your *true* answer to that question: what is the next step in your journey?" Dabir walked to the shrine and bowed with praying hands. "Namaste," he whispered, and exited the room.

Tsewang removed the mala beads from his pocket, closed his eyes, and inhaled the blended scent of candles and myrrh. He turned his attention inward, to the whisper of his heart. He felt the presence of a monk entering the room, easing into lotus position at the threshold, where he once sat. But he did not turn around. He returned his attention to his heart and remained there until the boom of sutra drums and the bellow of dungchen horns echoed across the valley. He closed his eyes to the movement of monks and novices trickling into the room.

Dabir, Kasim, Doijin, and Uddi settled onto prayer pillows next to Tsewang. Rinpoche eased onto a pillow at the dais, and the novices sat in the first row, near his feet. The chime of tingsha bells tangled with the vibrating hum of meditation bowls, as monks and novices released from their core the chant for compassion, "Om mani padme hum." Tsewang moved his hand across his hair and opened his eyes to Rinpoche's gaze. They locked their eyes as their mouths moved to the chant, and they held each other until the end. Rinpoche stood up, turned to the shrine, and led the final prayer. The monks and novices bowed with praying hands, returned their pillows to the stack, and walked the hollow corridor, ready to receive midday meal.

"Dabir," Tsewang said as they approached the dining hall, "will you shave my head today? Perhaps after midday meal?"

Dabir moved his eyes across Tsewang's head, then searched his face. "Yes…yes, Tsewang," he smiled. "I believe you are ready, and I would be delighted to. I will fetch my razor after we eat."

"Thank you. And you do not need to look for the shears. I have them."

Dabir furrowed his brow. *"You have the shears?"*

"Yes," Tsewang said, pulling out a chair for him. "I once thought I might need them, but now I know that was not true."

Kasim, Doijin, and Uddi took their seats across from Tsewang and Dabir. They talked quietly and muffled their laughter as they sipped chamomile tea and smeared yak butter on unleavened bread.

"I have learned so much from each of you," Tsewang said, looking into their eyes. "You have helped me, and I will be forever grateful."

"You speak as if you are leaving us," Kasim said.

"Leaving?" Tsewang grinned, "Perhaps I already have."

As Dabir shaved Tsewang's head, neither spoke. The room was quiet and still. Long and short locks tumbled onto the cloth that covered Tsewang until his head was bare.

"There you are," Dabir said, handing him the rolled cloth filled with his hair. "You may take this and decide what should be done with it."

"Thank you, Dabir," Tsewang said, embracing him tightly. "Thank you for saving my life, and for returning my life to me."

Dabir looked into his eyes and nodded. "Thank you for allowing me."

Dabir left the room and headed for the fields. Tsewang retrieved the shard of mirror from the cubicle and peered into it. He moved his hand across his scalp and smiled at the man he saw. He reached beneath his mat, collected his tangled hair, tucked it into the cloth, and headed for the forest. At the foot of a towering evergreen, he dug a shallow hole and buried his bundled locks; then stood up, bowed, and said, "Lord Buddha and Mahakala, with humility I ask that you continue to protect and guide me. I leave myself in your loving care. Namaste."

He walked away from the forest and past the labyrinth. Before descending the bluff, he looked back at both. He gazed at the ridge he once stood, high above the valley, and thought of Kasim. "Thank you, my friend," he whispered, "for you have saved my life twice." He swept his eyes across the valley below and smiled at the monastery, and at the novices spilling out of the massive red doors, laughing in delight, having completed their monastic studies. He descended the bluff and walked onto the pebbled path that would lead him away from Dechen Podrang and toward the city of Thimphu, in search of his mother and his beloved dog, Nugai.

A'isha

A'isha tended to the shop as she had promised Amir. Each day, she arrived at the Mu'addin's second call for prayer and stayed until the sun seared strokes of scarlet and marmalade onto a darkening sky. Women would enter the shop with children in tow to buy fabric, buttons, and thread, adhering to their husbands' command that the village must patronize Amir's shop as if he were there and nothing had changed. And they came and went and carried on as if A'isha was insignificant and incidental to the wreaths they bought to flavor their homes with aroma and beauty. At times, as she fashioned wreaths at her workbench, she would watch the movement of Ouirgane through the open door and recall the countless times she begged Allah to make her invisible as she walked to school. And now, she wondered if He had. Still, she honored her promise to Amir. She spent her days creating wreaths and beading abayas, restocking shelves and registering sales, crossing off on a calendar the days until the merchant from Marrakesh was due to arrive.

"As-salamu alaikum," al-Majid said, entering the shop. "Are you A'isha?"

"Yes, sir. I am. Wa-alaikum salaam, sayidi," A'isha replied, greeting him with a slight bow. She had never met any of Amir's merchants, but she knew the gentleman who stood at her doorway had to be the one she anxiously awaited. Tall and broad-shouldered, his thick mustache framed a radiant smile, and his large brown eyes sustained a warm-hearted look of surprise. He donned a white tunic, green silk kufi, and blue leather babouche, which distinguished him from the men that lined the road, some lounging on crates in front of their shops, and others selling figs and eucalyptus from their donkey-drawn carts. She knew he was not of the mountains, but a wealthy merchant from Marrakesh, and his presence reignited her excitement about leaving Ouirgane to live in one of Morocco's big cities.

"I received notice from Amir that he would not be here today, and that I should speak with you," he smiled, flashing a gold tooth.

"Yes, I…I have the abayas for you. Fifty in total," she said, hurrying behind the counter and lifting three large plastic-wrapped bundles of carefully folded abayas off the shelf.

"And those," he pointed, "are you the maker of those most creative wreaths?"

"Yes," she blushed.

"Jamila! They are beautiful. May I see one?" he asked, extending his arm. She placed the largest in his hand.

"I make them with cork, fennel, thyme—things I find in the forest. And…and I make them in different sizes."

"How many do you have there?" he asked, turning the wreath this way and that, tugging at the cones and fennel leaves.

"Twenty-five."

"Hmm, how much would you want for each?"

"How much would you sell them for in the medina?"

Al-Majid raised his brow and chuckled, "Smart response. You are a wise young lady." He surveyed her overalls and scuffed, laced-up shoes. "You are not like most girls, I see."

"No, I've never been," A'isha said, wiping her sweaty palms on her pants.

Al-Majid placed the wreath on the counter. "They are well-made…tightly wound. I will pay you two dirhams for each."

"I thought," she quivered, "you might have offered four."

"Ha! Four dirhams? I will sell them for that amount in the medina…maybe five."

A'isha lifted her chin. "Exactly."

Al-Majid wagged his finger. "Oh, you're more than wise, you're a sly one," he chuckled. "Very well, I will give you three dirhams for each. That is my final offer."

A'isha beamed, "Then, sir, you have a deal!"

He extended his hand to her. She looked at it, unsure of what to do, then placed her hand in his and matched the firmness of his shake.

"I have a duffel bag in my car," he said, hurrying out the door. "I will be right back."

A'isha swept her eyes across her wreaths. "Now, I *know* I can leave Ouirgane next year," she whispered. "Inshallah!"

While al-Majid moved the abayas into his car, A'isha packed her wreaths. After his third trip, he swung the door shut and shoved his hand into his pocket. "So, let me pay you for the abayas first," he panted. "I owe Amir seven thousand four hundred dirhams for fifty abayas."

"Has Amir agreed to that price?"

"Yes," he said, raising a brow, "that is our standing price." He pulled a bundle of dirhams bound with a rubber band. "You must know that Amir and I have been in business for many years." He lifted his eyes to A'isha's and frowned. "I would never cheat him."

"Oh, I wasn't suggesting that. I'm sorry. I was just—"

"Being smart? Why would you apologize for being intelligent?"

He snapped off the rubber band, licked his thumb, and counted each note aloud. One by one he placed them on the counter.

"There! Seven thousand four hundred dirhams. Count it, please." He glanced at the workbench and shook his head. "It is a shame Nabeel left this place. He was much better off here."

"Na…*Nabeel?* You know my…my…"

"Of course, I know Nabeel. He is your father, isn't he? If I recall correctly, he used to bring you here when you were a little girl. You would be his little helper." He pulled a handkerchief from his pocket and dabbed his forehead. "There is no better cobbler in these mountains than Nabeel. His shoes are still in great demand in the medina."

A'isha's heart pounded. She looked at the money on the counter, too dazed to count.

"Do…do you know where…where my fam…where Nabeel is?"

"Why, of course I do. They're in Imlil."

"*What?* My family is in *Imlil?*"

"Yes, they are. Did you not know that?"

"N- No. I…I…" She shook her head with furrowed brows. The coincidence that her father moved his family to the same village Saira was sent to made her chuckle.

"You find this funny, eh? Well, I think it's quite sad you did not know where your family is. What kind of father leaves his daughter to fend for herself?"

She leaned against the counter. "Have you seen my father?"

"It's been about a month, but I am traveling to Imlil next week and I'll be stopping by his shop. We still do business, you know."

"You…you *will?*" She wanted to yank her hijab off her head, feeling stifled by the heat. "May I ask, where is his shop?"

Al-Majid fanned himself with his kufi. "Well, it's not quite a shop. Nothing like this," he said, darting his eyes around the room. "It's more like a…a makeshift. A roadside stand. But with the money he is earning, I am sure he will be able to open another shop in no time. The Europeans who travel to Imlil to hike Toubkal are delighted that he's there. He repairs their tents, backpacks—you name it. And of course, he has the business of the locals who bring their shoes and saddles to him for repair." He returned his kufi to his head. "Well, I need to move on. Let's close our deal with the wreaths, shall we?"

My family is in Imlil? She could hear al-Majid counting, "ten…fifteen…thirty…" but he sounded far away, as if his words were bubbling up from underwater. *Could my family be just an hour away?*

"A'isha? Are you listening to me? Please count it. Make sure you agree. That would be two hundred sixty-eight dirhams for twenty-five wreaths."

"Yes, yes…it is correct. Thank you."

"I am certain your wreaths will sell fast," al-Majid said, lifting the duffle bag onto his shoulder. "If you wish to sell another twenty-five to me when I return, I would be delighted. A'isha? Did you hear me?"

"Huh? Oh, yes, sayidi. I will have them," she nodded impatiently. "When will you return?"

"I am not sure. With Amir sick, I don't know if he will have abayas for me. So, I don't—"

"How many does he usually have for you? How many would you want?"

"He usually has anywhere between ten to one hundred. Sometimes he produced like a workhorse, and other times like a turtle."

"When you return, I will have the wreaths and at least twenty abayas beaded for you."

"But will he—"

"Sir, most of the abayas in your car were beaded by me. I am sure you will be pleased with my work. I will have more for you when you return."

"Very well. I will see you one month from today. It has been a pleasure to do business with you, A'isha," he bowed. "Very much so!"

"Thank you. I will see you in one month. Inshallah."

He turned around and looked at her. "Have you ever been to Marrakesh?"

"No, but I'd love to go one day."

"Maybe you will. You are a smart young lady."

She watched him place the duffle bag in his car, shift into gear, and drive away. She entered her shop and closed the door; then swung it open and ran onto the road, waving her arms. "Sayidi! Sayidi!"

Al-Majid peered into the rearview mirror and grounded the car to a halt.

"Sayid—" she panted.

"Yes, what is it? Did I miscount the money?"

"No, you did not. I am sure the money is correct. I wanted to ask you…when you see my father, please tell him that Amir is sick. Tell him my jida has died. Tell him I am working in the shop, and I am well."

Al-Majid furrowed his brow. "Yes, I will be sure to tell him, A'isha."

She returned to the shop, scooped up the dirhams, and stuffed the stack into her pocket; then plopped onto the stool at her workbench, lowered her face into her palms, and wept.

"A'isha? A'isha are you okay?" Nasim asked, entering the shop. "I…I was passing by and noticed you were crying. What's wrong? Is it Amir?"

A'isha wiped her tears, adjusted her hijab, and raised her face to him. "Thank you, Nasim, but I am fine."

"No, you're not. You're crying. What's wrong?" he asked, closing the door.

"I…I miss my family. I'm here in this world all alone. I have no one to turn to. No one to talk to about good news or bad."

"Oh, A'isha, you're never alone. You should know that. Our ancestors are always with us. Your jida has not left your side."

"How do you know about my jida?"

"Amir told me. And…and although Amir is not here in the shop, you still have him to turn to. He loves you very much. And…and…" he said, pushing back his kufi, "you have me."

"*Huh?*" She stood up and walked to the rear of the shop. "But you hate me."

"I don't hate you, A'isha. Maybe…maybe I hate your courage. You're not like most girls I know. You're not like *any* girl I know. But I don't hate you." He removed his kufi and walked toward her. He took her hands in his, parted his lips, and gazed into her eyes.

"Please, Nasim. Don't…"

"Don't what?" he asked and kissed her lips softly.

She placed her hand on his chest and eased him away. "Nasim, you must leave."

"But I…" He kissed her again.

Her knees weakened. She tightened her buttocks to squeeze the flutter between her thighs. "Please, you must go," she begged.

Abdullah pushed open the door and entered the shop. Nasim spun around. "Sayidi!" he exclaimed. He reached for his kufi and slammed it on his head.

Abdullah snapped his head back. "Ma hadha!" he chuckled, patting his paunch. "Did I come at an inconvenient time?"

"N--No," Nasim said. "I was just checking on A'isha, but I am leaving now."

A'isha slid her hands into her pockets to wipe the sweat off her palms. "Thank you for coming, Nasim," she called out as he hurried across the road. She walked behind the counter. "Sayidi, how may I help you?"

He tossed his head back and laughed. "*Me?* I need no help at all. The question is, my dear, how may I help *you?* I saw al-Majid. Amir told me he would arrive today. Did all go well?"

"Yes, he took the abayas. I will bring the profit to Amir on Saturday."

"Very well. And your wreaths, I see they're all gone. Did he purchase them, too?"

"Yes, he did," A'isha blushed.

"That is good news! Well then, I will be on my way. I was just checking on you. I suppose not quite like Nasim"—he grinned— "but I am delighted that the merchant arrived, and all is well."

He walked to the door, placed his hand on the knob, then turned around and locked eyes with A'isha.

"Before I leave, let me give you a word of advice. Never announce to anyone—not even those you trust—when you will be traveling with dirhams. Do you understand?"

A'isha nodded. "Yes, I do. Shukran."

"Let that be the first lesson I will teach you."

"Thank you, Abdullah. I will remember."

"And the second lesson is this: you must never mix business with pleasure."

A'isha shook her head. "I'm sorry?"

"In other words, don't poop where you eat," he winked, then exited the shop and closed the door.

A'isha arrived home just before nightfall. As always, Ali greeted her in the front yard with a loud bleat and nudge of her thigh. She patted his head, walked to the backyard, and stood at her grandmother's grave. "Hi, my jida. I had a good day. I sold all of my wreaths." She patted the bundle of dirhams in her pocket. "And the merchant wants to purchase more."

She knelt and removed wilted leaves from the tin can of wildflowers she kept at the head of her jida's grave, and she straightened the stones that she had laid in the shape of a "J." Ali nudged her neck, tickling her with his whiskers and blowing his hot breath on her cheek with each "maa."

"Okay, Ali. I know you're hungry." She hoisted water from the well and filled his bowl; then fed him a handful of figs and tossed hay into the trough. Yawning, she entered the chicken coop, tossed grains, and gathered the eggs.

"Finally," she whispered, opening the door to her home. She lit the lantern, kicked off her shoes, and slid her hijab off her head. She pulled the stack of dirhams out of her pocket, wrapped it in a chador, and stuffed it in the back of her drawer. She lit a log in the firepit and hung the kettle over it. She undressed, poured a bucket of lukewarm water into the zinc tub, eased into it, and scrubbed her skin. She slipped on her grandmother's kaftan, removed a slice of khobz from the tin box, slathered it with butter, shoved it into her mouth, and then another. She slurped a spoonful of cold lentil soup from the pot before warming it above the fire, closing her eyes to savor its earthy flavor. She opened the door for Ali, and he lay near the firepit, watching her as she moved about until she climbed into bed, leaving her mug of tea and dirty dishes on the table.

"I'm so tired. Good night, Ali," she whispered, blowing on the lantern. She closed her eyes and thought about her day: the merchant's arrival, the sale of her wreaths, learning her family is in Imlil, her message to her father, Nasim's kiss, and Abdullah's warning. "What a day," she whispered, inhaling the scent of cinnamon wafting across the room. "What a day."

Tsewang

From a forested bluff high above, Tsewang beheld the city of Thimphu. He moved his eyes along its paved roads lined with quaint shops of wooden facades painted in chipped yellow and cobalt blue. He gasped at the phallic stencils which adorn each storefront, large ejaculating penises and testicles with prickly hair, and wondered with a chuckle what Buddha might think. He gazed at the movement of men cloaked in knee-length ghos and at the smattering of women wrapped in silk embroidered kiras walking about with an invisible purpose, a stillness in movement. And his eyes followed the women. He smiled at the packs of wild, barking dogs roaming unbothered and free, rummaging dumpsters, and sniffing curbsides for wilted lettuce and discarded gristle.

He squinted at the rusting Toyotas. Some chugging along, others grinding metal spurred by a pumping of pedals and an impatient turn of a key. He recalled the last time he had seen one. The thought of it made him shudder and return to the day he was yanked from his mother's thigh, tossed onto a backseat of cold, cracked leather, and driven to Pali Sholing. The flash of that memory pounded his heart and beaded sweat upon his scalp. He shook it away with a grimace and huff and turned his attention to a car paused for the crossing of a man and his mule. But the memory nagged him—the inner vision of the little boy he used to be. The seven-year-old in the backseat of a black Toyota, pressing his cheek and palms onto its dust-riddled window, screaming for his mother until the man behind the wheel threatened to throw him over the cliff if he did not sit back and shut up.

"Uggh!" Tsewang moaned, tossing his eyes toward the sky. The memory of that day gripped his heart, still. He clenched his teeth and squeezed his eyes, blinking away tears as he watched the women, searching for one with hair streaked in silver. And he swept his eyes across the packs of roaming dogs, looking for one with a patch of white on a curled, brown tail. He inhaled deeply, lifted himself out of the crouch he had eased into absentmindedly, and wiped his eyes. He tightened his sash, brushed soil and deadened leaves off the hem of his kasaya, moved his hand across his shaven head, and descended the bluff.

He stepped onto the paved road, feeling displaced and disoriented. He turned around and raised his face toward the bluff, toward the magnolia, juniper, and evergreen trees that once cradled his life. With purpose, but no direction, he walked, looking at the cement road beneath his sandaled feet. Images of Tadashi, Dabir, Kasim, and Uddi flashed and faded like frothing waves of a resting tide, and he wondered what Dabir might say as he walked this unfamiliar road. *Would he tell me to hold him, and the others close to my heart, or let them go?*

"Kuzuzangpo," said a bespectacled, middle-aged man standing on a corner.

"Namaste," Tsewang replied with a slight bow.

"Namaste?" The man chuckled and coughed. "Did you say '*namaste*'?"

"Why, yes, I did. Have I offended you in some way?"

"No, not at all," the man said, scanning Tsewang's kasaya and shaven head. "From the look of you, you are not from here, but from a monastery, yes?"

"Yes, that would be truth."

"*Truth?*" The man chuckled, removing his eyeglasses and pulling a handkerchief out of his pant pocket. Unlike most other men on the streets of Thimphu, his head was not shaven, and he was not wearing a gho, but a beige button-down shirt with brown trousers and a blue, crooked tie. The oily swirls of his thinning black hair and tobacco-stained teeth lent to the contradiction of his dapper yet disheveled appearance. Tsewang watched him in wide-eyed awe.

"Which one?" the man asked, cleaning his eyeglasses. "There isn't a monastery anywhere near here. Where are you from and how did you arrive?"

"I...I'm from Dechen Podrang. Well, not exactly. I'm actually from Pali Sholing, but—"

"*Pali Sholing?* The monastery in Paro?"

"Yes, that's it," Tsewang nodded. "Are you familiar?"

"I sure am. It's quite a distance from here—clear on the other side of these mountains." He raised his eyes toward the bluff. "How did you get here? You drove?"

"No, I walked from Dechen Podrang. It's not too far from here."

"Yeah, sometimes their boys come here to stock up on stuff. Nice boys. Weird, but nice." He tucked his handkerchief into his pocket and looped his eyeglasses behind his ears. "And so why are *you* here? Shouldn't you be there, praying or lighting candles or something?"

"Well, maybe. I don't know. I'm…" He watched the man remove a brown paper bag from under his arm, pull out a momo, and bite into it.

"Umm," the man moaned, holding the other half close to his mouth as he chewed. He watched Tsewang lick his lips and lower his eyes. "Do you want one?" he asked. "I have another." He reached into the bag and handed it to Tsewang. "Take it, please."

"What is this?" he asked, squeezing it between his fingers, examining it, turning it this way and that.

"It's a dumpling. Have you ever had one? This one is filled with pork. There are other kinds, but the pork ones are my favorite." He tilted his head and grinned, "You've never had a *momo*?"

"No," Tsewang replied, biting into it.

He closed his eyes and exhaled into the burst of flavor, saffron and curry. He put the other half in his mouth and chewed slowly, trying not to swallow.

"Are you hungry, my friend? Come with me." The man sauntered away and turned the corner.

Tsewang hurried to his side, walking with him in lockstep and peering into the windows of sparsely stocked shops. Shelves displayed weatherworn tarp and plumbing tools, motor oil and mufflers. He watched a woman lay beaded bracelets beside thimbles and spools of thread while her neighbor, an elderly man in a cream and burgundy gho, dragged a sack of cardamon between barrels of ginger and sundried chilies that dotted a warped, wooden floor. Outside a shop displaying bundled fleece and embroidered silk, a young man stood behind a table, flicking a band of feathers across an array of large, erect penises molded in clay, and bronze figurines of lovemaking couples contoured in every imaginable position. Tsewang moved his eyes across the table with raised brows and parted lips.

The young merchant lifted the duster and tapped Tsewang's shoulder. "Have you ever seen this before, my friend?"

"I…I…well nnnno," Tsewang blushed.

"What a shame," the boy winked.

Tsewang scanned the figurines wide-eyed, then snapped his head up, winked back at the boy, and hurried toward the man. "Sorry to make you wait," he said.

The man grinned. "No need to apologize, my boy. I can tell this is all new to you." He swung open the door and said, "Please, come in."

The strange aroma of chili peppers, stewed lamb, and boiled potatoes rushed up Tsewang's nose and watered his mouth.

The man pointed to a table. "You may sit there. I will return shortly."

Tsewang eased onto a chair next to a window and peered at the muted movement of Thimphu. *Could I be dreaming?* he smiled. *I have entered another world.* He looked at the six wooden tables surrounded by red-cushioned chairs, listening to muffled voices behind the swinging saloon doors. A blend of aromas wafted along an invisible plane, swirled around his head, and landed in his lap. It produced a craving he had never experienced, even at his hungriest times.

"Well, well," the man said, loosening his tie and lowering onto the chair opposite Tsewang. "Your meal will be out shortly."

"Thank you, sir."

"You are quite welcome. You know, we have yet to introduce ourselves. What is your name, lad?"

"My name is Tsewang, sir."

"Tse *what?*" he replied, shifting his eyes toward a slender young man wrapped in a grease-stained apron, balancing a large tray on the palm of his hand just above his head.

"Kadrin Chhe, Julji," the man said to him in a language Tsewang did not understand.

"Mongse bay jay," he replied, placing platters of dumplings, lamb, red chilies, fiddlehead fern, mullet grain, and datsi on the table. A sudden pop and fizz made Tsewang flinch, and the young man chuckled as he poured the sizzling brown liquid into two glasses from a red tin can.

"Have you ever had a Coca-Cola?" the man asked, slipping a straw into each glass.

"I…I…no, I have not. The only thing I have ever been given to drink is chamomile tea and yak milk. Oh, and water." He turned his head and looked out the window. "But I have not had yak milk since my mother…since I was a child."

The man stared at Tsewang as the server put two sets of utensils on the table, bowed, and walked away. Scooping food from each platter, he filled Tsewang's plate, then his own.

"Thank you," Tsewang said, pulling his mala beads out of his pocket and bowing his head in prayer.

The man gripped his utensils with one brow raised, watching Tsewang until he heard him whisper, "Namaste," and lift his head with a sigh.

"Has Buddha given you permission to eat?" the man asked, stabbing his fork into a chunk of lamb.

"Gratitude is important. It brings forth abundance," Tsewang replied, mimicking the man's handling of his utensils. He gripped the knife with his left hand, then switched it to his right. He switched it back to his left hand and again to his right. He dropped it onto the floor, picked it up and wiped it off, and as he cut into the meat, his fork scraped across the plate and flipped a dumpling onto the table. He grabbed it and shoved it into his mouth with a grin, refusing to let the delicious morsel go to waste.

The man smirked, "Would you rather have chopsticks?"

"Oh, no, these are fine," he replied, easing his fork into the chunk of meat.

"So, tell me again, *what is your name?*"

"My name is Tsewang. My sister once told me that I was named after my great-grandfather. But I don't know who he is, so I don't know if that's true."

"An interesting name," the man said, sitting back. He raised his eyes to the ceiling. "Tsewang, you say? Hmm, familiar, yet unique." He stuffed a chunk of cheese into his mouth. "Well, my name is Chimé. It means immortality."

"Chimé. I like that name. I remember hearing it once, but I don't remember where."

"Well, my lad, Bhutan is a tiny country. It is often said that all Bhutanese are neighbors because it's so small. Even the forests and mountains cannot separate us." He sucked his teeth and lifted his glass. "Do you know that only fifty names exist for Bhutanese women? That's right, only fifty names! So, that means either there aren't too many women here, or they all have the same name. Imagine that! I'm sure many men share my name, too."

Tsewang shrugged his shoulders and bit into another pork-filled momo. "I love these," he gushed.

"And try the datsi. It's cheese made fresh, right here in our kitchen."

"Is this your place?" Tsewang asked, digging his fork into a piece of cheese and popping a red chili into his mouth.

"Yes, I own it. I have for a few years," Chimé replied, scanning the room with a wide grin, and flashing his tar-stained teeth. "I've come a long way, Tsewang. I have had many struggles in my life. I arrived at this restaurant with nothing except the clothes on my back and worked my way up from washing dishes to serving tables, then to owning the place."

"How did that happen?"

"The original owner went away one day and never returned. He just disappeared. He owed me some money, so I kept the business going because I figured he would repay me either with money or with his restaurant. He never returned, so now I call it my own."

"But what if he returns?"

"After all this time? I doubt it. But if he ever did, he would still have to settle his debt with me. As you might know, a debt never remains unpaid." He raised his glass, toasting his words. "Now, what about yourself? You mentioned you were originally from Pali Sholing…from Paro."

"Yes, that is right," Tsewang said, feeling a sudden rumble in his belly.

"And so, what brings you to Thimphu?"

"I…I…uh…" Beads of sweat popped onto his forehead. He dropped his fork into his plate and pushed his chair away from the table.

"What's wrong? Are you ill?" Chimé asked, wiping his mouth.

"I…I need to use the restroom, may I?" he asked, gripping the edge of his seat.

"Sure, it's right back there to your—"

Tsewang jumped up. Feces oozed down his leg as he hurried to the restroom. Just as he entered the tiny, windowless room his belly exploded, and his meal shot out of his rectum like a busted steampipe. Chimé heard the eruption and spun around in his seat. Tsewang locked the door, biting down on his lip as feces puddled in his underpants and slid down his legs. He lifted his soiled kasaya, pulled down his underpants, and sat on the toilet, squeezing into it with a clenched jaw and tightened eyes, the remains of his lunch. Gagging at his stench, he lowered his face into his palms and cried.

Chimé tapped on the door. "Tsewang? Are you sick?"

"Please go away. I am fine."

"I have towels and a bar of soap for you. I will leave them here at the door and wait for you at the table."

"Thank you," Tsewang sniffled. "I am sorry."

"You have nothing to apologize for, my lad. We all shit on ourselves from time to time."

Chimé's words made Tsewang cry and laugh at once. It was the funniest thing he had ever heard. He laughed until new tears welled in his eyes, until he was doubled over on the toilet seat, muffling his laughter and gasping for air. He retrieved the towel and soap just outside the door and filled the sink with sudsy warm water.

"Tsewang?" Chimé knocked. "Here's a plastic bag for you. I also brought a shirt and a pair of trousers, should you need them."

"Thank you, Chimé."

The thangka of Mahakala flashed across his mind, the one he had prayed to for the past three months. "Mahakala," he whispered, "Thank you for leading me to Chimé." He removed his mala beads from his pocket, kissed them, and hung them around his neck. He stuffed his underpants and kasaya into the plastic bag and scrubbed himself clean.

He had never worn anything other than a kasaya, so he felt strange, detached from himself, as he returned to the table wearing black trousers and a white, button-down shirt that fit as if they were made for him.

"I'm sorry I made such a mess," he said to Chimé, dropping the bag onto the floor and easing onto his seat.

"All is well, Tsewang. Like I said, what fun is life if we don't shit on ourselves now and then? I do it all the time!" he winked. "Besides, your body probably isn't used to these spicy foods. This stuff will make anyone's backside erupt."

The server brought out two steaming cups of chamomile tea. "Here, drink this," Chimé said. "It'll settle your stomach. So now, tell me, where are you heading? You never told me why you're here in Thimphu."

"I... I'm here to find my mother."

"*Your mother?* Who is your mother?"

"It's a long story. I would rather not talk about it at this time. I—"

"Alright then, so where are you going to sleep tonight? Do you know?"

"No, I don't," he replied, watching the server seat two men at a table.

"Well, *I* know where you're staying—with me. You can stay at my place tonight. It's not fancy, but it's warm and clean."

"I…I…"

"You what? Know where you're going?"

"No, I guess I don't."

Chimé lowered his voice and leaned toward Tsewang. "Let me tell you, now. Thimphu is not a monastery. It's a city. And as spiritual as this place is *supposed* to be, strange people roam the streets at night, not just dogs. Things aren't always what they appear to be. You should know that."

Tsewang thought of Rinpoche. "Yes, I guess that is truth. But…but we just met. You have given me so much already."

"My lad," Chimé replied, wiping his mouth, "you are old enough to be my son. How could I not help you in your time of need?" He spun around in his chair. "Julji! We are leaving. Say goodbye to Tsewang. Come on, let's get out of here," he said, jumping to his feet. "Zip up your trousers and pick up your bag of shitty clothes. Let's go!"

He removed his spectacles and yanked a handkerchief out of his pocket. A large betel nut popped out, bounced onto the table, and pinged onto the floor. He and Tsewang watched it roll to a stop, then raised their heads and stared at each other with fading smiles.

A'isha

"Salaam, Hakima, how are you?"

"A'isha! I am so happy to see you. It has been much too long. Please, come in," Hakima said. She hugged A'isha and kissed her on each cheek. Her petite frame was draped in a black abaya; her thin lips were chapped, and her eyes were bloodshot and puffy.

"It is good to see you too," A'isha replied. "When did you return from school? Are you home for summer vacation?"

"Well, not quite. The university is closed for the summer, but I work at a textile factory. I would still be in Fez if my father weren't so ill."

A'isha looked around the darkened room, unsure of what to say.

"I...I haven't seen your father in two weeks. I have been told his condition has worsened."

"A'isha, he is very sick. My mother told me you're tending to the shop and have been working with him for several months."

"Yes, I have."

"She also told me about the passing of your jida. I am sorry for your loss. I know how much you loved your grandmother."

"Yes, I miss her, but I often feel she is with me. It's strange that I still feel her presence."

Hakima eased onto the sofa and gazed at the floor, wringing her hands. A'isha sat beside her.

"The doctor has told us that my father does not have much time left on this earth." She looked at A'isha, tears welled in her eyes. "He is dying. My baba is leaving us."

A'isha slid closer to Hakima and held her hand.

"Would you like to see him?" she sniffled, wiping her tears. "He is in his room. My mother is with him, you may go."

A'isha hugged Hakima and walked toward Amir's bedroom, asking Allah for courage.

She knocked on the door. "Amir? It is me, A'isha."

The door swung open. "Salaam, A'isha," his wife said, squeezing past her with a basin of soapy water.

A rancid odor of feces, stale urine, and sour sweat charged at A'isha and grabbed her throat. She recognized the smell. It had hung around her home like an unwanted guest long after she buried her jida. Her jaw dropped as her eyes adjusted to the curtain-drawn dimness in which Amir lay under a thin, white sheet tucked tightly under his armpits. His head was covered with a white silk kufi; his face was freshly shaved.

A'isha remained at the threshold, staring at a cameo of the man who saved her more times than she could count. The man who held her up and kept her from drowning in her father's abandonment. The man who loosened the village's noose around her neck, enabling her to remove it. She looked at the scalloped ridge his toes pitched beneath the sheet and moved her eyes along the rail of his shin bones, onto the knobby mounds of his knees, skeletal and still. The saddle scoop of his hip bones spilled into the hollow of his empty belly and lent to the outline of a man she did not know. His arms languished at his side, robbed of purpose and strength. His fingers, motionless and curled, clenching an invisible agony. Fingers that once tucked her unruly hair into her hijab, wiped away her tears and patted her head as he said, "Go A'isha. Go play dinifri with the boys if you must. Allah will love you just as you are, and one day your baba will show you that he does, too."

And she stood at the threshold, staring at a version of the man who had remained by her side when her father did not. She peered at the dark, circular wells into which his eyes had sunk, eyes closed to the world he once loved, the world he encouraged her to enter. She stood at the threshold and watched the ripple of his ribs beneath the white sheet, its subtle rise with each shallow breath as he lay there, suspended between living and lingering. She gazed at the man who loved her father in ways unspoken yet known and felt. Over the years, she had sensed Amir's longing for a love he was denied, blocked by his lover's fear. A fear that left him abandoned, clinging onto an empty vessel, burdened by the weight of a secret known by all. And she stood at the threshold, remembering his words, "Above all else, A'isha, love Allah with all your heart and love yourself as much."

She eased into the room and stood by his side. She placed her hand on his. "Amir?" she whispered. His chest expanded beneath the sheet. He smiled faintly, then his lungs deflated into the flatness of his new being. "Amir, I am here. I have come to see you. I want you to know that I have been taking care of the shop as I have promised." She lifted her face to the ceiling, clenching her teeth to block her scream. She inhaled deeply and continued, "Al-Majid arrived on Tuesday. He paid for the abayas, all fifty of them." She pulled a stack of dirhams wrapped in cheesecloth out of her pocket. "He will return in one month to purchase more. You do not have to worry. I will sew the beads for you, and they will be pretty. You will be pleased." She looked at the stack of dirhams in her hand, then at his withered fingers. Wincing, she gulped saliva and said, "I will give this money to your wife."

He nodded his head slowly then parted his lips, wanting to speak, and she wrapped her arms around the silence of his words. She squeezed his hand and said, "You are welcome, Amir. It has been my honor." He nodded. "Amir, I want to thank you for everything you have ever done for me. I…I…know you love me very much, and I know how you loved my father. I want you to know your love for him has given me the courage to love without fear, and I want to thank you for that." A tear trickled from the corner of his eye. A'isha wiped her tears, and she wiped his. "You do not have to worry about your shop. I will take care of it until the time has come for me to…to…" He nodded his head. "I will follow my dreams as you have taught me." She clenched her teeth, harnessing her sorrow. "Thank you for all you have done for me, Amir. I will never forget, and I will see you, again. Inshallah." She kissed his cheek and caressed his hand, then returned to the threshold. She looked at him one last time, bowed her head, exited his room, and closed the door.

Hakima and her mother were sitting on opposite ends of the sofa.

"Sayidati, this is for you," A'isha said, extending the stack of dirhams to her.

"Thank you, A'isha. And thank you for tending to the shop. Abdullah has told me you are there every day."

A'isha eased onto a chair furthest from Amir's wife. "Yes, I am. Well, every day except Friday."

"I don't know what will happen to the shop after he passes," Amir's wife said, gripping the stack of dirhams. She glanced at her daughter. "Hakima must return to the madrasa, so she cannot take over. And…and I am much too old to handle it." She looked at A'isha. "I know you will soon leave Ouirgane to study at the university. Anyway, that is what Amir told me a while back. So, I don't know what will happen to the shop."

"Sayidati, I don't know what the future holds for me. But yes, I do intend to leave Ouirgane next year. So, as I have told Amir, I will tend to the shop until I leave. If…if that is what you wish. Of course, I will share the profits with you." She looked at Hakima. "Amir took care of me, so I will take care of his family for as long as I can."

"Inshallah," his wife responded, rising to her feet. "Thank you."

"You're welcome, but it is my promise to Amir that I am honoring."

A'isha stood up, unsure if she should hug her or simply leave. She had always sensed a coldness from Amir's wife, a silent rejection that filtered her smile and imposed a palpable denial of everyone's presence, including Amir's. A'isha resented her for that, for that same stoic reception of life she had witnessed within her own mother, within the myriads of women whose eyes were all she could ever see. And it was more than enough for her to know from when she was a child who she did not want to be.

She hugged Hakima. "Please send word when the time has come. I am sure the village will want to know. Amir is much loved in the village."

"Yes, A'isha, I will send word. Thank you for everything you have done for my father. You have been as much a daughter to him as I."

"And Amir has been more of a father to me than my own. He was a blessing to me, and he saved my life."

She glanced at Amir's wife, said goodbye; then exited the house and closed the door.

Two days later, word of Amir's passing spread across Ouirgane like vines of ivy upon barren stone. His funeral was held in a small mosque on an outcrop high above amber slopes dotted with rosebushes and juniper trees. The Iman bellowed the prayer of Al-Fatiha across the valley. The beg in his voice blended with the screech of a Bald Ibis circling above. A'isha lifted her head toward the gray clouds weighed with the threat of an impatient rain and recalled the smile that filled Amir's eyes when an Ibis swooped across the sky as they walked the ridge the day her grandmother died. And she listened to the Mu'addin's call for prayer, beckoning Allah's forgiveness for the sins of man.

After his burial, most of the villagers walked to Amir's home, but A'isha went to the shop. She knew Amir would understand. *Be who you are*, she could hear him say. And so, she decided to spend the rest of the day beading an abaya she had been working on for nearly a week. "I will finish it today," she whispered and smiled, approaching the shop just as the sky opened, releasing a torrent of rain upon the still and silent village.

She removed her hijab and patted her hair and kaftan with a towel, peering out the window at the tarp-covered carts and row of shops closed in honor of Amir. As she reached for a can of beads on the top shelf, it slipped from her fingers and crashed onto the floor. Beads in sparkling shades of red splattered, clinking like rain on a zinc roof until they rolled to a stop. "Uggh!" A'isha grunted, dropping to her knees to scoop them up. "Uggh!" she repeated, crawling behind the counter, and plopping handfuls of beads into the tin can.

"Ya Ilahi! What is wrong?"

She peeked over the counter. "Nasim! What are you doing here?" she gasped, jumping to her feet and grabbing her hijab. "Why aren't you at Amir's home?"

"Why aren't you?" he grinned, removing his kufi, and dabbing his face and arms with the towel.

A'isha looked down at the imprint of her knees upon her soiled white kaftan. "Uggh!" she grunted, rubbing at the stains and shaking the hem of her dress. "What a day!"

Nasim chuckled. "You are correct! It is quite a day. What are you doing on your knees? I thought girls like you would never be caught in such a position."

"Girls like *me*?" she said, kicking beads out of the way, and placing the can on the shelf.

"Yes, you know…girls like you. Girls who like girls. Although I must say, you do look quite stunning in your kaftan. I saw you at the funeral and I almost didn't recognize you. I don't recall ever seeing you in anything other than those…those overalls you wear."

"Tell me, Nasim, did you skip the gathering so you could come here and critique my attire?"

"No, I came here because I saw you leave and, well…I didn't want you to be alone."

"As you once told me when my jida died, I'm never alone. So, you should have gone with the others. I'm sure you're hungry. You're missing out on the meal."

"Am I? Maybe it's not food that I'm hungry for."

"And maybe it's time for you to leave."

"I have the key to the bakery. Would you like to share a pastilla? Something tells me you're as hungry as I am."

A'isha's stomach growled at the thought. She hadn't eaten anything since last night's bland goat cheese and khobz dinner. She wanted him to leave, the sound of his voice irritated her, but the craving in her stomach spoke louder and made her say, "Yes, I will go."

"I'm delighted! You wait here. I'll get an umbrella from my shop."

Crouching under a tiny umbrella, A'isha held Nasim's elbow with one hand and raised the hem of her kaftan with the other as they walked down the muddy, rain-soaked road, skipping puddles. An empty silence spilled from shuttered windows, and from the sullen donkeys whose heads hung low, while stray dogs curled in doorways, lulled to sleep by the patter of a steady rain.

Nasim slid the key into the lock and opened the door with a quick, firm push. A'isha's mouth watered as she wiped rain off her arm and moved her eyes across the trays stacked with almond briouat, and spirals of mhancha dusted in confectionary sugar. She had not tasted her favorite pastry, sesame cookies with honey, since she celebrated Eid al-Fitr with her family nearly two years ago. She suddenly longed to see them and thought, *I will visit them in Imlil,* as she scanned the mounds of sweetness.

"Wow!" she said, shaking her head, staring wide-eyed at the bottom shelf lined with stacks of sellou. "I have not had sellou since I was a child."

"What would you like?" Nasim asked, gazing at her, smiling. "You can have anything you want."

She stood up and looked at him. "Yes, that is what Amir used to say. Of course, he meant in life—that I could have anything I wanted in life. He didn't mean in a bakery," she chuckled.

"And he was right. But today you can also have anything you want in a bakery." He moved closer to her.

She stepped back, away from the counter, away from him. "I changed my mind. Nothing...I don't want anything," she said, folding her arms.

"Why, of course, you do, A'isha. Stop acting as if I'm your enemy. I want to be your friend. Now that Amir's gone, who do you have to look after you?"

"I have myself." Her anger surged and harshened her tone. "I don't need you or anyone else to care for me. My own family has abandoned me."

"And is that how you want to go through life? Not trusting or depending on anyone? What kind of life is *that*?"

"I have learned that loneliness is easier to deal with than disappointment...abandonment."

"Maybe that is true. But how can you know who will abandon you and who won't? You must trust people until they prove to be untrustworthy. As for me? You can trust me."

"Ha! *You*? You have made fun of me and of the way I dress. Why should I ever trust you? You have disrespected me for who I am."

"What do you mean 'for who you are'? That's ridiculous. Do you even *know* who you are?"

"Yes, I do, Nasim. I know that I am a lesbian. You're right, I *do* like girls." She turned toward the window, folded her arms, and watched raindrops trickle down the pane. "I once loved a girl," she whispered, "and she left me, too."

Nasim waved his hand dismissively. "I *know* that. Everyone knows you like girls. But I still want to be your friend."

"No, you don't. You want to...to kiss me and...and."

"And what? Make love to you?"

A'isha's eyes widened.

"Why do you respond as if you're shocked? Have you ever made love, A'isha? To a boy? Or maybe to a girl?" He chuckled. "I don't care who you have made love to. I won't lie. I want to make love with you."

A'isha wiped her sweaty palms on the bodice of her kaftan. From the corner of her eye, she could see the outline of his penis beneath his white tunic. Hakima once told her that penises have heads that look like mushrooms, or like a crooked kufi. *Is this what she meant?* She forced her eyes to remain locked onto his face but could not resist. Her eyes moved away from his and slid down his neck, to his chest, and to his groin. His penis, long and firm, grew slowly and steadily. He watched her, and she watched it. She could feel that special, private place between her thighs, throbbing. She usually tightens her buttocks and thighs whenever this happens, especially when she bathes herself, but this time she did not resist the feeling. Not this time. She let it happen. She held her eyes on Nasim's groin, his penis. She wanted to touch herself as she watched it rise, pitching his tunic into a taut tent, rising higher and higher—and A'isha thought it was the funniest thing she had ever seen.

She burst out laughing. Covering her mouth with her palms, she looked at Nasim's groin. Holding her belly, she threw her head back, howling with laughter. "It looks like…it looks like…" she said, gulping air, "it looks like the nomads' tents! The ones…the ones on the plateau!" Her hijab slipped onto her shoulders as her head bobbed. She looked at his groin and watched the tent slowly flatten like a deflated balloon. Her eyes widened at the wet spot on his withering erection. She slammed her hand on the counter and burst out laughing. "Did it…did it rain on your *tent*?" She grabbed her belly and bent over, howling with laughter. She lifted her head and looked at his groin. "Was it windy? Where'd…Where'd your tent go?" she said, slamming her hand on the counter and holding her belly, laughing with abandon.

Nasim was speechless. He looked down at his tunic, embarrassed by the huge wet spot. He didn't know what to do or say. He wanted to leave her standing there, but he had to turn off the lights and lock the bakery. He wanted to bring her behind the counter, lay her on the floor, force her legs open, pull her panties aside, and penetrate her with all his might. But he respected her too much to do such a thing. He had done that once before, but not this time. He wanted to blame her homosexuality for her insensitive laughter. He wanted a reason to be angry with it. But he knew her sexuality was not to blame. Her laughter arose from innocence, not malice—he could not be angry with her. And so, he too began to laugh. He laughed at her laughter. He laughed at her childish absurdity of comparing his erection to a nomad's tent. And he laughed because he had not laughed since the age of four, when his mother fell sick with malaria and died. He laughed to prove to himself that he had not died with her, as he believed for so many years. He threw his head back and howled with laughter to prove to his mother and to himself that he had lived, that he had survived, and that he was alive.

"So, A'isha," he said, gasping for air and wiping away tears, "what...what do you want?" He waved his hand across the counter. "Take your pick!"

"Oh my! I do not recall ever laughing like this," she said, tucking her hair into her hijab. She looked down at his groin, chuckled and shook her head, then raised her eyes to his. "Everything, Nasim!" she beamed. "I'll have one of everything!"

"One of everything, you say? How about two? Two of everything!"

"If we may, then why not? Two! Yes, two it is!"

Nasim snapped open two brown bags and wrapped each pastry in wax paper. One by one he placed them in each bag. A'isha watched him work behind the counter, admiring the gentle manner with which he handled each sweet, sticky delight that teased her mouth and tempted her heart. He eased from behind the counter and handed her both bags.

"But isn't one of these yours?"

"No, both are for you."

"But I thought…"

"Please take them." He opened the door and swept his eyes across the sky. "I will walk you home."

"Thank you, but that is not necessary. Anyway, I have to close up the shop."

"Fine. I'll walk with you to your shop, and then walk you home."

A'isha watched him turn off the light and lock the door. She was relieved the rain had stopped, and they did not have to huddle under the umbrella.

From the road, he watched her straighten bundles of fabric along the back wall, tiptoeing between scattered beads until she pulled the chain on the dangling bulb. With her hand on the doorknob, she moved her eyes across the shop and saw a vision of Amir sitting upon a bundle of black organza at the rear of the store. She gasped, exhaled, and smiled. "Rest in peace, my friend and father," she whispered, then closed the door.

"Allahu Akbar…Allahu Akbar…" The Mu'addin's call for prayer echoed across the valley as they walked along the high ridge, marveling at the brushstrokes of plum and tangerine that stretched across the yawning sky. "Allah will forgive me for missing salat today," Nasim said.

They nibbled on sellou, and other sweets A'isha unwrapped with as much care as Nasim had used to wrap them. They reminisced about Amir and the wisdom he had shared with them. They imitated how he would wag his finger when he was angry, and hold his belly when he laughed, and the way he would push back his kufi and scan the sky in search of an answer.

A'isha chuckled. "Remember how he used to say, 'Ya Allah!' whenever he got excited?"

"Yes, of course," Nasim smiled.

They brushed their eyes across the sky in a silent search for Amir, giving each other time to embrace him privately, and to say goodbye.

"What are you going to do, A'isha?" Nasim asked, gazing down at the swiftness of the river's flow.

She wiped her mouth. "What do you mean?"

He looked at her. "You know…with the shop. Are you going to stay?"

"Yes, I promised Amir I would stay until next year; until I leave for the university."

Nasim picked up a pebble and tossed it into the river. He touched her arm and turned her toward him. "I see, but until you leave—*if* you leave—you should know that I will always be here for you. Whatever you need, A'isha. Whether it's help with the shop or even at your home, you can count on me, okay?"

A'isha stared at him, seeing, for the first time, his long lashes and full, bow-shaped lips. "Thank you, Nasim. I will remember." She hugged him and they continued to walk, turning the bend behind the Tamarisk tree. She lifted her eyes and saw a figure standing in front of her home, a slender silhouette.

"Is that your home?"

"Yes, it is," she said.

"It looks like you have a visitor. Do you know who it might be?"

A'isha squinted, recognizing through a swirl of mist and dusk the purple hijab and matching chador she once loved.

Her heart pounded as they got closer, and her eyes no longer squinted—they sparkled. She could see who was awaiting her, who had finally returned. They flashed each other a knowing smile. A'isha approached her with open arms and drew her into a long, tight embrace. "I knew you would return to me one day," A'isha whispered into her ear.

She turned to Nasim with warmth in her eyes and said, "Nasim, please meet Saira."

Tsewang

Chimé tossed another shot of whiskey into his mouth, grimacing at the sting that slid down his throat. He lit a cigarette and a candle and ran his hand through his oily hair; then raised his face toward the ceiling and released a stream of gray smoke into the stale, damp air. "Uggh," he moaned, easing onto a sofa of faded gold, spreading its fray beneath his bony weight. He unbuckled his black faux leather shoes and kicked them off. Caked mud crumbled onto the floor. He slammed his feet upon a grease-stained stool speckled with hardened rice, then crossed his legs, slipped his hand into his pants, and scratched his crotch. "Have a seat," he said, pointing at a flattened cushion on the floor.

Tsewang lowered onto it, clutching the plastic bag stuffed with his soiled kasaya. Curiosity wrinkled his brow as he watched Chimé inhale smoke and blow it out, and his eyes flitted across the dimly lit room. The smell of wet wood reminded him of the attic he and Tadashi would hide in to embrace. He watched his shadow dance with Chimé's in the honey glow of the candle burning at a precarious tilt near a stained mattress shoved into a corner upon a cold, splintered floor. And he wondered who besides Chimé occupies this lonely room.

"You drink?" Chimé asked, sauntering toward a rusty icebox propped atop a gray metal chair next to Tsewang.

"Drink what? What is that?" he asked, looking up at the bronze liquid Chimé poured into a glass.

Chimé chuckled, "It's monkey juice."

"*Monkey juice?*" Tsewang replied, reaching for the glass. He sniffed it and jerked his head away. "No, thank you," he said, curling his lips and handing it back to Chimé.

"Yeah, yeah, I know…you're a good kid," Chimé smirked, snatching the glass from Tsewang and gulping the whiskey. He walked across the room with his glass filled to the brim and giggled when he tripped over a tattered red rug that looked like it was once a bed for a dog. "Uggh!" he growled, plopping onto the sofa, looking at Tsewang and sipping his drink. Tsewang clutched his soiled kasaya and moved his eyes around the hollow room, dodging the weight of Chimé's gaze and the edginess of his silence.

"So, Swang Tee. I mean, I mean Toesung…*Tangso?*" Chimé slapped his thigh and threw his head back, howling with laughter. "Wh…what's your name, again?"

"It's Tsewang."

"That's right. Sweatang," he replied, bobbing his head up and down. "You know, I think I can trust you. You're one of those good boys. I think you can keep a secret. You can, right?" He paused, waiting for Tsewang's reply. "Right!?"

"Y-yes, I can."

"I thought so. Lemme tell you sumthin.' You know that restaurant we were at earlier? You 'member?"

"Yes, I do."

"Well, it's not *really* mine. I mean, I told you it is, but it…well, it is, and it isn't." He paused and looked at the half-empty glass in his hand.

Tsewang shook his head. "Sir, I don't understand."

"What I'm saying is I don't *own* it, but I help keep it going. You know? It's called bankrolling."

"Bankroll?"

"Yes. Lemme 'splain it to you. If anyone needs money–not just here in Bhutan, I work with a lot of people…here in this country and other countries. Anyway, *what was I saying?* Oh, yeah, that's right. If anyone needs money, I lend it to them—with interest, of course. A few years back, the owner of that restaurant needed money, and I lent it to him. But he made the mistake of not paying it back, so now the restaurant is mine. You know what I mean?"

Tsewang looked around the room. *How could he be rich enough to lend people money and live like this?*

"I know what you're thinking. If I have so much money, why am I living here, right? RIGHT?" he yelled, jumping to his feet.

"N--no, I wasn't thinking th--that."

Chimé chuckled. "Of course you were, and it's alright. As I told you earlier, things aren't always as they appear." He lit another cigarette, tossed the expired matchstick onto the stool, and continued, "I lend people money, but I'm also in the international trade. I sell what people need, and what they need is produced here, in Bhutan."

"And what's that?" Tsewang asked, sliding the plastic bag off his lap and onto the floor.

Chimé sucked smoke into his lungs; a long trail of ash fell between his feet. He stared at Tsewang, glassy-eyed, and tossed whiskey into his mouth, emptying the glass. "Arrgh!" he grimaced, tightening his lips onto his teeth. "What's your question?" he snapped.

"I said, what do you sell?"

"Betel nuts. I sell betel nuts. You know, the thing that slipped out my pocket when we were in the restaurant."

So that's what they are. He recalled the clusters he had picked and stuffed into the sack he left behind in the forest. He thought about the months he spent scurrying up trees to gather them. His skin tingled, his heart pounded, and his palms sweat as he relived the sensation, his addiction to them. He recalled what his sister, Takuma, used to say, "Father is in the forest looking for betel nuts. They are more important to him than we are." He squeezed his eyes shut and shook his head; then looked at Chimé.

"Who…who do you sell them to?"

"To whoever wants them," Chimé shrugged. "I sell them here in Thimphu, in Paro, even to people in other countries— India, China, Morocco…wherever."

"But how do you get to those countries?"

Chimé frowned. "I walk. How else do you think I get to them? I fly, of course!"

"Do you *really* go to those places?" Tsewang gawked. During his monastic studies, he learned about different countries, especially Hindu and Buddhist countries. He had read of a place called India but had never met anyone who had been there. His fascination with Chimé returned. He sat up and crossed his legs as if in prayer.

"What is it like there? In India. Is it true that they worship cows?"

"They practice Hinduism," Chimé shrugged. "And yeah, I think they believe the cows are holy, or some shit like that."

"Wow, I would love to go there."

"Would you?"

"Yes, I have read about it…about a river there. I cannot remember the name. It's the—"

"The Ganges?"

"Yes! Yes, that's it. It's considered a holy place. They cremate people along the riverbank and pray…and…and I would like to go there."

"Well, maybe one day you will."

Tsewang smiled, "Maybe one day I can go with you."

"Or maybe you will go alone. I have a boy or two who travel there for me. They deliver the betel nuts to my friend. They do a decent job, but I could always use the extra help." He stumbled to his feet and walked to the tiny bathroom hidden behind a shredded swath of red damask. He shoved it aside and yanked the chain next to a dangling bulb. Tsewang could hear him urinating. "Would you want to do that?" Chimé called out.

Me? Go to India? Alone? What's in that monkey juice? This man is crazy!

"Did you hear me?" Chimé asked, running his wet fingers through his dampened hair. "Would you want to go?"

He filled two glasses with water from the bathroom faucet, handed one to Tsewang, and returned to the sofa.

"I…I never thought of it. I never thought I would leave the monastery, or even come to Thimphu. So, no…I never—"

"I didn't ask if you ever *thought* of going to India. I'm asking if you would *want* to go."

Tsewang inhaled deeply and sighed. "Chimé, when we were in the restaurant you asked why I was here, in Thimphu. I…I ran away from Pali Sholing six months ago to find my mother. I spent three months lost in the forest and three months at Dechen Podrang. It's been a long journey, but I am finally here." He lifted his chin. "I came to Thimphu to find my mother, not to go to India. If I ever leave Bhutan, first I would have to know where my mother is."

"And what makes you think she's here?"

"Because, if I recall correctly," Tsewang replied, shifting his eyes toward the candle's flame, "we used to live in the countryside, just outside this city. I was a young boy when I was taken from my mother. I was just…I was just seven years old. And I have not seen her since that day." He pulled his knees to his chest and wrapped his arms around his legs. The flame tossed dancing shadows upon his face.

Chimé sat up. "Who took you away from her?"

"A State official, I guess. He never told me who he was. He never spoke to me, but I remember his sunglasses. I remember…"

"But why did he take you away? Do you know?"

"I don't know. I've wondered about that all my life. Sometimes, when I was younger, I used to cry myself to sleep, wondering if I was being punished for something I did. I would ask myself, over and over, did I wet the bed? Did I forget to collect the eggs? Did I eat too much?" Tsewang lowered his head onto his knees.

Chimé leaned back. "I can't imagine your mother would send you away for any of those reasons. What kind of mother would do something like that?"

Tsewang lifted his head and looked at Chimé. "That is exactly what I want to ask her. Why did you send me away?" A tear rolled down his cheek. He shifted his eyes toward the flame. "There is so much I want to ask my mother. I want to ask her what happened to my father. And where is my…" He looked at Chimé and sighed. "Anyway, that is why I am here, to find my mother."

"But until you do, where are you going to live? Did you think about that when you ran away? How are you going to eat?"

"I ran away from my first monastery, the one in Paro. But I walked away from the second one. I did not run. And no, I didn't think of any of that—where I'm going to live or how I am going to eat. I just knew that it was time for me to leave and I trusted that Mahakala would—"

"Mahaka *who*?" Chimé giggled.

"Mahakala, the Deity of Protection. I trusted that he would take care of me. He always has."

"And you believe that he will help you find a place to live…help you find your mother?"

"Yes, I believe I will be guided in the right direction because of him, and because of my karma."

"Your Karma," Chimé said, dryly. "You monks kill me with that karma shit. My life is proof that it's nonsense."

Tsewang's jaw dropped. *Buddha, please forgive this man! He's a fool!* He jumped to his feet, scooped up his kasaya, hurried to the door, and grabbed the knob.

"Where are you going? Come back here," Chimé waved. "Sit down. I didn't mean to upset you. I'm just telling you what I believe. We're all entitled to our own beliefs, right?"

Tsewang released the doorknob.

"Are you hungry?" Chimé asked, walking to the icebox. He removed a brown bag, pulled out two momos, and handed one to Tsewang.

Tsewang's mouth watered. He looked at his bundled kasaya under his arm, then at the dumpling. He shrugged and said, "Thank you," then popped it into his mouth.

Chimé handed him another. "Don't leave. Come sit."

"So, you are correct, Chimé," Tsewang sighed, plopping onto the cushion. "I don't know what I'm going to do. But I do know one thing, tomorrow morning I will start looking for my mother."

Chimé watched Tsewang as he spoke, and he thought of his own son, the infant he had abandoned many years ago. *They must be about the same age.* He leaned forward and peered at Tsewang. "How old are you?" he asked.

"I am…I am *sixteen*…wait…*am I?*" he said, knitting his brow. He stared at the floor, then lifted his head. "Yes, I am sixteen years old. I will be seventeen in December. On December seventh, to be exact.”

Hmm…my boy would be around that age, Chime mused. He gulped his glass of water and jumped to his feet. “Would you like another momo?”

“No, thank you. But I would like to use the restroom if I may.”

“Of course, you know where it is. But you’re not gonna shit yourself again, are you?”

“No, not this time.”

When he returned to the room, Chimé was covering the sofa with a quilt. He fluffed a flattened pillow and tossed it to Tsewang.

“There,” Chimé said, “you should be comfortable. I’ve slept on this couch many nights when I was too drunk to walk to my mattress. I’ve had some good sex on it, too, but that’s another story.”

“Thank you, sir.”

“You are welcome, my boy.” He put his hand on Tsewang’s shoulder. “In the morning, you can come with me to the restaurant. I will introduce you to the crew. You can work there until you find your mother, or…or whatever your next step will be. Either way, you’re going to need money.” He looked around the room. “It’s not a palace, but you’re welcome to stay here for as long as you want.”

“Sir, thank you. Your kindness will be repaid.”

“Don’t thank me,” Chimé said, plopping onto the mattress, “thank Mahakala. *He* is your protector, not I.” He yawned and blew out the candle.

Tsewang removed his sandals and shirt and pulled the quilt to his chin. The room eased into stillness; its silence competed with Chimé's grating snore. Tsewang lay awake until he heard a rooster crow from afar. *There are no roosters in the forest.* He sighed. Clutching his mala beads, he closed his eyes and whispered, "Thank you, Mahakala, for protecting me every step of the way." Then he slipped into a dream. In it, he lifted his kasaya to cross a river with clear water. When he got to the other side, he saw upon a bluff a woman with long silver braids, waving at him and smiling. A dog was at her side, wagging his tail. He stretched his arms toward the woman as he ran up the hill, and when he approached her, he could see she had no eyes.

"Tsewang, wake up!" Chimé whispered, shaking him.

He opened his eyes, startled and whimpering.

"You were having a bad dream. Are you okay?"

He stared at Chimé, wide-eyed.

"You were grunting and moving your legs as if you were running. At one point, you sounded as if you were crying. Wait here, I'll get some water for you."

Tsewang looked around the room. Daylight pressed against the drafty window, dulled by a swath of yellow damask slung on twine. He took the glass of water and drank until it was empty. "Thank you," he gasped and lay down.

"Rest for a minute, but don't get too comfortable, my boy. We have to go to the restaurant. I want you to get there in time to help prepare the food. I want you to meet the crew."

Tsewang sat up and rubbed his eyes.

"Take a shower," he continued, tossing a towel at Tsewang. "The staff wear black slacks and a white shirt. Yours are still clean, right?"

Yawning, Tsewang nodded.

"Good." He tore off a strip of brown paper bag and handed it to Tsewang. "Sprinkle some salt on this to scrub your teeth. The salt is in the bathroom. And remember to bring your kasaya so we can drop it off at the laundry. You might want to wear it again one day."

They walked along the main road in the city's center.

"Meet Tsewang!" Chimé said to the laundress, and to the vendors who lined the road with tables, selling everything from clay penises to dried chilies.

"Tashi Delek! Welcome!" the men replied, arranging their wares, dressed in knee-length socks and colorful, silk ghos.

"Namaste," Tsewang said, nodding and bowing to each of them with praying hands.

Chimé laughed. "You keep that up and you're gonna have a backache by the time we get to the restaurant."

Tsewang continued to bow at the vendors, blushing at the stencils of large, ejaculating penises that adorn the buildings' façades. *What would Buddha say about this?* he giggled, thinking of Tadashi and wishing he were there to see this spectacle and unholy practice.

"Chimé?" he whispered.

"Yes, Tsewang?"

"Why are penises painted on all of the buildings?"

"I was waiting for you to ask. It's for good fortune."

Tsewang clutched his mala beads. "I'm sorry?"

"The Bhutanese believe—well, *they* believe, not me— that an ejaculating penis wards off evil spirits. And so, they paint this shit all over the buildings. And as you can see," he said, pointing at the vendors' tables, "they also sell these dicks as good luck charms. It's all a bit hypocritical if you ask me. Because if you pulled out your penis right now and ejaculated on that building, everyone here will curse you and call you crazy."

Tsewang giggled and followed him into the restaurant.

"Julji! Takum!" Chimé shouted, "Come, I want you to meet a new member of the crew."

Two men in their early twenties, pushed through the swinging saloon doors, wiping their hands on clean, white aprons tied around their slender waists. Their butterscotch complexions were radiant and flawless, revealing the hours they spent at home giving each other facials with the olive oil and lard they would steal from the restaurant whenever Chimé was not around.

"Tashi Delek!" they said in unison, taking turns to kiss Chimé on both cheeks.

"Tashi Delek," Chimé replied. "This is Tsewang. Julji, you met him yesterday, remember? He had shit on himself, but he won't be doing that again."

Julji and Takum giggled.

"Anyway, he's going to work here. We can use the help, and he can use the money."

"Sure! Of course," Takum said, batting his long eyelashes.

"Good! You both can show him what needs to be done, you know, introduce him to the place, to the people. Make him feel welcome. Give him an apron and something to do." Chimé turned to Tsewang and put his hand on his shoulder. "I will return later today. I have business to take care of." He nodded at Julji and Takum, then walked out the door.

Takum hurried into the kitchen and grabbed a clean apron off a hook. "Here, you can use this one," he said, sashaying toward Tsewang.

"Thank you," Tsewang replied, and wrapped it around his waist.

He did whatever they told him to do. He washed dishes, peeled potatoes, cleared tables, and secretly slipped a momo into his mouth whenever he could. Patrons came and went. Some acknowledged him with a nod and a smile, but most did not.

"Your bald head and mala beads are confusing people," Takum whispered in his ear.

"Why would it matter?" Tsewang asked, stacking dirty dishes onto a tray.

"Because you look like an imposter, like a monk in hiding. You're wearing slacks and a shirt with mala beads and a shaven head. And you greet the customers by saying, 'namaste,' when you should be saying, 'Tashi Delek.'"

"Well, maybe I *am* an imposter," Tsewang winked. He raised his hand to his neck and touched his mala beads. "Or maybe there are two sides to me and you're seeing both at the same time— lucky you."

"Two sides? Ha! We all have many sides, but there's just one real side. The other sides? They're just masks we wear until we figure out who we really are. And once we do that, we can toss our masks into the river. It's all quite simple." He put his hand on his hip and smiled, "Don't you think?"

Tsewang brushed his hand across his scalp, feeling the fuzz of new hair. "I never looked at it that way, but I think you have a point."

"Of course, I do. And we should talk more about it. What are you doing tonight?"

"Tonight? I'm returning to Chimé's home, I suppose. Why do you ask?"

"Because, silly, if you have no plans, you're welcome to come by our place. Julji and I live together, with other boys." He lifted his tray, walked toward the kitchen, then turned and looked at Tsewang. "It's sort of like a monastery. You know, a group of boys living together, but without a Rinpoche. You should come." He puckered his lips, blew a kiss, and backed his way through the swinging doors.

Tsewang spun around wide-eyed and gazed out the window. *Did he say, 'like a monastery without a Rinpoche'? What must that be like? And did he really blow a kiss at me?* He bit his bottom lip and dabbed beads of sweat off his brow with the wet rag, leaving a piece of lettuce stuck to his forehead.

Takum returned with a broom and dustpan. "Are you saving that for later?" he asked, pointing at Tsewang's forehead.

"What? What are you—"

"Your forehead…you have a piece of lettuce stuck." He threw his head back and laughed, sweeping the floor with long, graceful strokes. "Are you a monk?"

Tsewang shook his head, "No, I'm not a monk, but I'm close to becoming one. I'm not ordained yet, although I have spent my entire life in monasteries."

Takum splayed his hand on his chest. "Really? *Your whole life?* So, do you mean you have never…"

"Never what?"

Takum chuckled and waved his hand. "Forget it, forget it," he said, and leaned the broom against the wall. He pushed through the swinging doors. "Julji! Julji," he shouted, "Come here!"

Tsewang listened to them whisper and burst into laughter.

For the rest of the day, he was silent. He did whatever he was told to do and spoke only when spoken to. During intermittent lulls between customers, he gazed out the window and watched Thimphu move to the beat of its own rhythm, far from the dungchen horns and tingsha bells that once defined the rhythm of his own life. He watched the sun shift across the sky as motion slowed and patrons dwindled.

"Well, the day is done," Julji yawned. "And I must say, Tsewang, you did a good job."

"Thank you," he replied, removing the apron and handing it to Takum.

"Will you return?" Julji asked.

"That is Chimé's decision, I suppose."

"Well, I hope you do. I think the three of us work well together. Do you agree?"

Tsewang looked at both men, feeling as if he were seeing them for the first time. He moved his eyes from one face to the other, noticing their resemblance to Kasim and Doijin. He stared at Julji's long nose and remembered how he had once teased Uddi by calling him "big nose," and he remembered Doijin's silent admonishment. He suddenly longed to see them—Uddi, Doijin, Dabir, and Kasim—and wondered if he should return to Dechen Podrang, at once.

"Tsewang, did you hear me?" Julji asked.

"Oh, yes," he replied, rubbing his eye. "Yes, I suppose we do work well together, but Mahaka—I mean Chimé—will decide if I should return."

Tsewang opened the door and stepped onto the barren road. The vendors were gone, and the streets were silent. He walked away from the restaurant, passing shuttered shops and wild dogs roaming. He walked to the end of the road; to where it intersects the path which leads to the forested bluff he had descended the day before. He lifted his eyes toward the hilltop and watched the sun slip behind the trees, casting a turquoise outline to a jagged silhouette. And he remained there, longing to hear the voices of the men he had left behind. *Are they looking for me? Did I matter?* He returned to the restaurant, sat on the curb, and waited for Chimé.

"So, are you *sure* you don't want to come home with us?" Takum gushed as he locked the door.

"No. But thank you for inviting me. Chimé will be here soon."

They waved goodbye to Tsewang and walked to where the road meets the path. Just before they turned the corner, Takum shouted, "Tsewang! If you change your mind or if he does not show up, you can come to our place. We live just four blocks this way, and one block to the right."

"I will remember. Thank you."

He watched them turn the corner. "Tomorrow, I will go to the countryside and find my mother," he whispered. He pulled his knees to his chest and lowered his head onto his arms, then closed his eyes and fell asleep.

"Tangso! What are you doing there?" Chimé slurred, clutching a bottle of monkey juice.

Tsewang lifted his head and watched Chimé walk with an unsteady gait. He raised his hand above his eyes to block the blinding halo a streetlight tossed upon Chimé's head.

"What are you doing, sitting out here by yourself? I told you these streets aren't safe."

"I was waiting for you," Tsewang frowned.

"Well, here I am, my boy!" he swayed, wiping drool off his chin. "Let's go home."

Tsewang shook his head and sighed, then rose to his feet and clutched Chimé's arm to help him stand on his own.

A'isha

"Marhaba, Saira. I'm delighted to meet you," Nasim replied with a fading smile. "I've heard a lot about you."

Saira folded her arms across her chest. "Is that so?" she quipped and turned to A'isha. "Have you told—"

A'isha shook her head. "No, I have never discussed—"

"That is true," Nasim said. "A'isha has not spoken of you. It is also true that you and I have not met, but I have seen you around. And yes," he chuckled, "I have heard a lot about you."

Saira nodded. "I suppose you have. These mountains are filled with nosy gossipers, and the men are worse than the women."

Nasim snapped his head back. "Excuse me? I'm not so sure about that. The women—"

"Maaa!" Ali bleated, trotting toward them.

"Ali!" A'isha shrieked, thankful for the interruption. She petted his head with vigor, wiping her sweaty palm. "Shall...shall we go inside?" she asked, darting her eyes from Saira to Nasim. "Will...will you join us?"

"No, I must return home," he said. "It's a long walk, and I'd like to get most of it behind me before nightfall. But thank you for the invitation."

A'isha extended a bag of the remaining pastries to him. "Here, take these. You can nibble while you walk."

"Keep them. It was my gift to you. Remember," he said, glancing at Saira, "you wanted two of everything, and now you have it."

"Well, thank you, Nasim," she blushed. "You have been kind."

"You are most welcome. And do not forget my offer."

Their eyes locked. She walked toward him, kissed him on both cheeks and whispered into his ear, "Yes, I will remember," then watched him walk away.

"He seems to be a nice young man—nice to you, that is," Saira scoffed.

"I'm sure he treats me the same as everyone else. Shall we go inside?"

"Yes, I will follow you."

A'isha smiled. "Do you know how long I have waited to hear you say that?"

She lit the lantern and the charred logs in the firepit, then hurried toward her messy bed and straightened the quilt. "I was in a bit of a rush this morning," she blushed. "I usually clean up before I leave."

"It's quite alright. I do recall you to be the carefree spirit among us," Saira said, sweeping her eyes across the room.

"Please, sit. Are you hungry? I can prepare a meal for us. I…I just need to tend to Ali and the chickens. I will return in a minute."

"May I join you?"

"Sure, you may." A'isha wiped her sweaty hands on the bodice of her kaftan, then held the door open for Saira. She walked to her grandmother's grave; Saira watched her from afar, petting Ali.

"Marhaba, my jida. I am here," she whispered, glancing over her shoulder. "Today, we buried Amir. So now I have two people watching over me from heaven." She closed her eyes and inhaled deeply. The events of the day flashed across her mind: Amir's funeral, the bakery, Nasim, his erection, their walk along the ridge. "Jida, I've had an interesting day, and it's still not finished." She glanced over her shoulder and lowered her voice. "You once told me things happen so we can learn a lesson, and…and that the lesson will be presented to us over and over until we learn what we must." She kneeled and straightened the can of wilted wildflowers. "Well, Jida, I think I'm about to learn a lesson. I'll let you know what it is when I figure it out. Laylat saeidat ya jadati. Good night, my grandmother." She blew her jida a kiss, then walked toward Saira.

"Oh, my dear girl," Saira said, extending her arms. "I remember when you told me your grandmother passed away." She hugged A'isha tightly. "I know how much she meant to you."

"Thank you," A'isha replied, pulling away from her. She looked at her grandmother's grave. "I miss her so much, but I still feel her presence. It's quite odd. I talk to her every day."

"There's nothing odd about it. You know our ancestors remain with us after they have passed on."

"Yes, there was a time I didn't believe that, but now I know it's true." She looked at the chicken coop and sighed. "This won't take long."

She tossed grains at her chickens and placed their eggs into a basket, whispering "thank you," as she closed the gate. "Come, Ali, it's your turn," she said, walking toward the shed. She scattered hay, then drew water from the well and filled Ali's bowl, the can of wildflowers, and two large jugs. She placed the jugs in the shed and picked up the basket of eggs. "There! my job is done. And now," she said, walking toward Saira, "I can take care of us." She brushed her hand along Saira's arm and whispered, "There is so much I want to say to you."

The room was cozy, warmed by the slow burn of flickering, honey-glow flames. A'isha placed the basket of eggs into the tin box, washed her hands, poured water into the kettle, and then hung it above the firepit. She prepared a plate of sliced goat cheese, a bowl of olives, khobz with butter, and three koftas she had made the Sunday before. She arranged two place settings, stuffed two mugs with fresh mint, and poured steaming water from the kettle into each. She removed her hijab, loosened her hair so it draped over her shoulders and down her back, then held Saira with her eyes before asking, "Are you hungry?"

"Yes, I am. It all looks so delicious."

They clasped hands as A'isha prayed, thanking Allah for the meal and His guidance. And just before she raised her head, she silently asked Him to forgive her lustful thoughts.

"Well, A'isha, you surely have changed," Saira said, raising the mug to her lips.

"How so?" A'isha asked, cutting into the kofta, releasing the blended aromas of lentil, paprika, and cumin.

"*How so?* Just look at you. For starters, you've prepared this wonderful meal. I remember how your father would scream because you showed no interest in learning how to cook. Do you remember?"

"Of course, I do," A'isha replied, shifting her eyes toward the firepit. "It was the cause of so many arguments in that house."

"And now, look," Saira gushed, passing her hand over the table as if it were a showcase. "You have prepared this delicious meal. Not just a slab of cheese, but an actual meal!"

"I'm no longer the little girl you once knew. A lot has happened this past year. So, yes, I suppose I have changed. But the question is," she continued, blowing into her mug with a hiss, cooling her tea the way her mother used to, "how have *you* changed? What brings you here, Saira?" A'isha leaned back, circling the rim of her mug with her finger. The crackling flames tossed dancing shadows across their faces.

Saira licked her lips, placed the fork on her plate, and leaned forward, reaching for A'isha's hand. "I've never seen you in a kaftan, especially a white one. You look so pretty. You used to wear those overalls every—"

"We buried Amir today."

Saira pulled her hand away. "Oh, I'm so sorry. I didn't know. What *happened?*"

"It's alright, you have nothing to apologize for. He was sick for quite some time. Your grandmother knew about his death; she was at the funeral. I'm surprised you didn't know. But please," she said, shifting in her seat, "don't change the subject. I'd like an answer. What brings you here? Do you know how much—*how long*—I have looked for you?" Her anger welled, tightening her words. "You just disappeared without telling me where—"

"I *did* tell you where I was, the day we saw each other at my grandmother's house. Don't you remember? I told you my father sent me to live with my aunt in Imlil."

"Yes, I remember, but why didn't you—"

"I could ask you the same question. Why didn't *you* look for me?"

"In *Imlil?* How am I supposed to know where you are in a whole different village? It would have been easier for you to find me, obviously. You knew where I would be. When I saw you that day, I told you I was at the shop every day, and not once did you appear."

"I'm sorry, A'isha. I apologize, but I could not—"

"Could not what?" A'isha asked, leaning forward. "Could not have the decency to tell me…to look for me? We loved—"

"Yes, we loved each other. But after the blow-up between your father and Amir, the entire village learned of our relationship." She stood, walked toward the door, and peered across the road. "And when my parents found out, they…they sent me to live with my aunt in Imlil. I haven't attended school since that day." She spun around. "I will *never* be able to complete my education. My family has practically disowned me. I…I have not seen my siblings. My relationship with you has ruined my life."

"*Excuse me?*" A'isha squinted, rising slowly. "What did you just say?"

"Yes, that's right," Saira nodded, "My relationship with you has ruined my life. I was sent away because of it—away from my family, away from my friends, my education. Away from…from you."

"And whose fault is that? *Mine?*"

"No, it's not *your* fault, it's our relationship's fault."

"How dare you say such a thing, Saira? I loved you! When my father learned about us, I wasn't sent to live anywhere. I was thrown out of my house in the middle of the night. But I never blamed you or my relationship with you."

"Then who do you blame?"

"I don't blame anyone for how my life has turned out. But if I were to blame someone for the pain and…and the *shame* I have felt, it would be my father. Him and his hypocrisy, that's who. I would—"

"A'isha, I'm not saying it's your fault. I'm—"

"Yes, you are! If you blame your relationship with me for what has happened to you, then you're also saying it's my fault. And I will not accept that. I have nothing to do with how your father or my father has chosen to respond to us…to who we are."

"What do you mean 'who we are'? I'm not a—"

"Ha! You're not a lesbian? Is that what you were going to say? Then how do you explain the things we used to do with each other in the forest…or have you forgotten?"

"I was just—"

"You were just what?"

"I was just doing what you wanted me to do."

"How dare you!" A'isha screamed, walking toward her. Ali bleated, nudging at the door. "You did nothing of the sort! Everything we have ever done—in the forest, in my bedroom, in yours—we did because we *both* wanted to. Don't try to deny who you are by saying you did it for me. How dare you!"

"I…I…am sorry," Saira whispered. She wrapped her arms around A'isha and leaned her head on her shoulder. "I just don't…I don't have the courage that you have. I…" She lifted her head and kissed A'isha on her lips. She kissed her again.

A'isha squeezed together her buttocks and thighs, and parted her lips, easing her tongue into Saira's warm mouth. She kissed her softly, then pulled away long enough to remove Saira's hijab and chador. Looking into her eyes, moving her fingers through her thick, waist-length hair, she whispered, "You are stunning."

She touched Saira's lips with her own and kissed her long and deeply until Saira moaned. A'isha held her hand and led her to the bed, where they lay. Moving to a silent rhythm, syncopated bodies pressing, hands caressing, searching. Breasts touching in a slow writhe. A'isha eased on top, and they moved like the rise and fall of the ocean's waves. Connected from within by a rising heat radiating from their innermost selves. A guttural moan and release, privately and together. Energy unleashed, but not desire. Bodies arched and taut with gasping pants, until their moan returned with another release, and the warmth of their breath spilled through parted lips onto tingled skin. Their movement slowed to a rhythmic writhe, and the pound of their hearts eased with subtle breath. Wrapped in arms and kaftans, they slipped into a dreamless sleep. And there they remained until the embers died and the rooster crowed, welcoming the glimmer of a new day rising behind the jagged edges of silhouette trees.

"Good morning, A'isha."

"Oh my! What time is it? I must be at the shop by nine o'clock!"

"It's…it's a little after eight," Saira said, squinting at her watch.

A'isha kiss Saira's cheek, jumped out of bed, tossed a log into the firepit, and lit it. She poured water into the zinc basin and turned to see if Saira was watching her as she removed her kaftan. *This is ridiculous,* she thought, covering her breasts. *After what we did last night, why should I care if she sees me naked?* She washed her body and slipped into her blue overalls. She brushed her teeth, combed her hair, covered her head with a clean hijab, and ran outside to feed Ali and the chickens.

Easing the door open, tiptoeing into the house, she whispered, "Saira, are you awake?"

"Yes, I am," she replied, turning toward A'isha, brushing hair away from her eyes.

"I must leave now."

"But have you eaten? I can make—"

"No, I'll take a pastry with me and buy a cup of tea when I get to the village. Will you be here when I return?"

Saira yawned, pulling the quilt under her chin. "Do you want me to be here?"

"I think you know the answer to that question."

"Then, I will be here."

"Wonderful! Please make yourself at home. I will see you this evening."

"Thank you. I'll have dinner prepared."

"And when I return," A'isha said, opening the door, "you can tell me why you are here. You have yet to answer that question."

She arrived at the shop a little after nine o'clock, sweating and panting. The village was abuzz with activity--shopkeepers sweeping doorways, vendors stacking mustard greens, prickly pears, and figs onto rickety carts while their thirsty donkeys lapped water from leaky buckets. And the women, whose eyes were all that could be seen, meandered through the village, in and out of shops, cradling babies and clinging onto restless children.

"Marhaba, A'isha," the butcher called out as she jiggled the key into the lock. "I am delighted you will look after Amir's shop." A pungent odor of blood and raw meat trailed him.

A'isha gagged as she opened the door and watched him saunter down the road. His comment irritated her. *What makes him think this is my goal in life?*

"Zubair," she called out. "Zubair!"

He spun around, flashing a wide smile and tobacco-stained teeth. "Yes, A'isha?"

She put her hand on her hip. "What makes you think this is my…" She shook her head and waved her hand. "Forget it," she grunted. "Atamana lak naharan sa'eedan."

"Ah, you have a lovely day as well, A'isha!"

She rolled her eyes, entered the shop, slammed the door shut, and left the "Closed" sign facing the street. She did not want to be bothered. *These people annoy me!* Without turning on the light, she grabbed the broom, swept the remaining beads into a pile, and scooped them into the can. She retrieved the kaftan she had been beading and pulled the low stool behind the counter where she could not be seen. She tried to concentrate on her work. *Al-Majid will be here in just one week. I have so much to do.* She looked up at the bare shelf that once displayed her wreaths, then she looked at the kaftan on her lap. "I would rather make my wreaths!" she huffed.

By noon, her work was complete. She laid the garment on the counter and smiled at her accomplishment. "Well done," she whispered, then turned on the light and opened the door. She was ready to receive customers. She peered into Nasim's shop and noticed he had not arrived. *Hmm, that's odd,* she thought, rubbing her belly. It ached with hunger and her throat was parched, so she walked down the road to Abdullah's shop for a cup of tea and a slice of khobz. Beneath the din of activity, the village was sullen with its mourning of Amir, weighed by a permeating silence that lingers after death and lifts without notice.

"Marhaba, Abdullah," she said, less buoyantly than usual.

"A'isha, it is good to see you," he replied, drying his hands. "How are you feeling?"

"I'm coming along, I suppose. How are you?"

"I thank Allah for this day, but my heart aches with the loss of my dear friend."

"Yes, I understand. I miss him too. Amir was like a father to me."

"Yes, he was. He was like a father to us all, even to those who were his age." He poured water from a kettle into two mugs. "Tell me, does your father know that Amir has died?"

"Abdullah, I have not spoken to my family in almost two years. I don't—"

"*Two years*?" he grimaced, handing her a steaming cup of mint tea. "How could that be?"

"What do you mean? I'm sure you know what happened…why I went to live with my jida."

"Of course, I know what happened, but I wasn't aware that you have not spoken to your family since then. Amir never mentioned that to me." He slathered butter on a large slice of khobz and handed it to her.

"Shukran," she nodded. "I'm not surprised Amir didn't tell you. That's what I loved about him, he wasn't a gossiper, unlike the other men in this village. People gossiped about him, but he never—"

"I…I don't know what you're talking about," Abdullah said, wiping his brow. "Who gossiped about him? What was the gossip?"

"Abdullah, *please* be honest. You know what I'm talking about. The rumors…the rumors about him and my—"

"That's enough, A'isha. I don't want to hear anymore. All I know is Amir was my friend, and I loved him. Your father was my friend too, but he has been away for so long. He hurt Amir, so I don't—"

"Hurt *Amir*?" she asked, feigning confusion. "In what way?"

"In so many ways…and for so many years." He walked to the door, lit a cigarette, and gazed at the dusty, amber road. "Yes, A'isha, we all knew about their relationship. But theirs was no different from many others. Amir and I never spoke about it, but we knew—we *all* knew. He was an elder and we had to respect him. So, what could we do other than leave judgment in Allah's hands?" He turned and looked at A'isha. "Who are we to judge a man for who he is? Or a girl, for that matter?"

His words made A'isha drift back to the night her father threw her out of the house, the night her grandmother said, "Who am I to judge you for who you are, A'isha? My blood runs in your veins." She returned her attention to Abdullah.

"…so, I loved Amir. And that is all that matters, isn't it?"

"But what about my father?"

"What do you mean? What about him?"

"Do you love him? What if he came back? How would he be treated? After all, that shop is his, too."

"As I said, I am angry with Nabeel for hurting Amir. He abandoned him. But, if he returned to the village I believe everyone would welcome him. You must remember, he too was an elder."

"Do you know where my father is?" A'isha asked, regretting the plea in her voice.

"Yes, I do," Abdullah nodded. "Al-Majid sees him quite often in Imlil. That is where your family lives."

"Yes, I know. He has told me." She sipped her tea quietly, then asked, "Will you take me to them?"

"To *Imlil?* You want to see your family?"

"Yes, I do. I will pay for the gasoline if you drive me to them."

"But what if they don't want to see you? How will you handle that? Remember, your father has not been here in nearly two years. That should tell you something."

"As Amir once told me, the only behavior I am responsible for is my own. How they choose to receive me is beyond my control."

"You are a smart young lady," he nodded, "and yes, I will take you to your family. When would you like to go? Imlil is an hour's drive from here."

"Al-Majid will be here next Tuesday. He'll pay me for the abayas I'm beading, so I will have money for gasoline." She rubbed her chin. "Let's see…how about next Thursday? I'll ask al-Majid for directions to my father's shop."

"Next Thursday, it is. I can ask Tayseer's son to work for me that day. We will need an early start, so let's leave at nine o'clock."

A'isha shoved the last piece of khobz into her mouth and hugged him. "Thank you, Abdullah. Your kindness will be repaid."

"Inshallah!" he exclaimed.

"Yes, Inshallah," she replied, and closed the door.

On the way to her shop, she peeked into Nasim's window. *Where could he be?*

She sat at her workbench, thinking about her family while beading a chador. She was determined to complete twenty-five garments before al-Majid's arrival. As she hummed her grandmother's favorite nasheed, Saira flashed across her mind.

She relived their intimacy and smiled, squeezing together her buttocks and thighs. She recalled their conversation and wondered why Saira had returned. *She never answered that question,* she thought, and was suddenly overcome with anxiety and unease. "I left all that money in my drawer," she gasped, then spun around and looked at the clock. Shaking her head, she chuckled. *I'm being silly. Saira wouldn't do such a thing.* As she rethreaded her needle, the scent of cinnamon wafted across the shop, and a familiar voice whispered into her ear, "Go home, A'isha," it said. "Go home now." She eased to her feet and placed the chador in a bin, then turned off the light, locked the door, and headed home.

Tsewang

"Who's using the bathroom first, you or me?" Tsewang asked, stretching his arms and yawning. He lay, awaiting Chimé's response, then jumped up, folded his quilt, and placed it, along with his pillow, on the side of the sofa Chimé never sits. Having lived with Chimé for the past two months, he learned three things about him: he likes his monkey juice, he likes things done his way, and when he doesn't get his way, he seeks revenge.

"Chimé, did you hear—"

"I'm not deaf, I heard you," he grumbled. "You can use it. I'm gonna lay here a little longer." He turned over, curled into a fetal position, and pulled the tattered quilt over his head. "Listen to that rain; it's pouring out there," he grunted.

"Yes, it is, and I don't have a raincoat. I left mine at the monastery."

"I'll get one for you," Chimé replied beneath the quilt. "It'll be here when you get home."

"Thank you," Tsewang replied, sprinkling salt onto a strip of brown paper bag and slapping it onto his teeth.

He twisted the leaky knob in the shower stall, releasing a dribble of lukewarm water. Shivering, he scrubbed his skin with a coarse rag and wondered with a grin if Julji and Takum were planning another party. He grabbed a towel from the hook, no longer caring if Chimé had used it, and dried his lean body while humming Takum's favorite song. He slipped on the black slacks and white shirt Chimé brought home from the laundress, and lifted his shirtsleeve to his nose, sniffing the lavender scent with closed eyes. Brushing his hair with his fingers, he smiled at his reflection in the cracked mirror above the brown-stained sink, then snatched off a hook the red silk tie Chimé had given him. He slipped it over his head. Tightening the knot how Chimé had taught him, he recalled the night he arrived home with it.

"If you're gonna stay with me, Swetang," he had slurred, "you have to dress the part—none of that monk shit around here."

He had tossed the tie onto Tsewang's lap, then bent over, wrapped his arms around his belly, and released a guttural moan. He lifted his head and frowned at Tsewang, then shot out from his rectum a blow of gas that sounded like a foghorn guiding ships. Beads of sweat popped onto his face. Tsewang stared at him, wide-eyed, pinching his nose. *Why won't this nasty man go to the toilet?*

"Uggh," Chimé had moaned, shooting out another blow of gas, then hurling a gelatinous mix of monkey juice, phlegm, and bits of pink fetid pork onto the tattered red rug, splattering Tsewang's feet.

"Eww!" Tsewang shrieked, pinching his nose tighter, running to the bathroom with splayed toes. Retching with watery eyes, he washed his feet until his skin was red and raw. When he returned to the room, he found Chimé slumped on the sofa, snoring. Tsewang rolled up the rug and vomit, shoved it into a plastic bag, and placed it outside their door. For days, the rancid stench moved around the room like an invisible pest, despite Tsewang's repeated attempts to wash it away.

His face twisted at the memory of that night as he tiptoed out of the bathroom and slipped his feet into his new black leather shoes, listening to Chimé's raspy snore as he buckled the straps. He inhaled deeply, slapped his hands onto his knees, and looked at Chimé. "Goodbye, sir," he whispered, then grabbed his key off the stool and tiptoed out the door.

The wind howled and the rain whipped around Tsewang as he walked to the restaurant. He leaned into it with chattering teeth, jumping over puddles, ducking under storefront eaves. *I hope Chimé has my coat when I get home,* he thought, no longer appealing to Mahakala to provide for his needs.

"Tashi Delek," he mumbled, rushing past shopkeepers jamming their keys into locks, pushing into drafty confines where they would spend the day with a comingling chill, peering out of windowpanes with folded arms and a forced smile, hoping to earn enough ngultrum to deem their effort worthwhile.

By the time Tsewang arrived at the restaurant, the rain had plastered his clothes onto his bony body and was dripping off his hair and hem. He pulled the door open against the force of the wind and cringed at the tinny tingle of the bell Julji had recently hung. "Tashi Delek," he muttered, rubbing his hands and scanning the room.

"Tashi Delek!" Takum beamed. He dropped a basket of utensils onto a table, sashayed toward Tsewang, and kissed him on both cheeks. "Poor baby, I'll get a towel and dry you off."

"Uh, you can just get me a towel. I'll dry myself off," Tsewang winked.

Julji glanced at them and rolled his eyes as he swept the floor. Tsewang walked toward him with outstretched arms and kissed him on the cheek.

"You're such a hypocrite," Julji huffed, wiping his face with the back of his hand without lifting his eyes.

"Aw, Julji," Tsewang said, shaking his head, taking the towel from Takum, "you're as cold as the wind, why is that?"

Julji glanced at him and frowned, "You're just not who I thought you were."

"Huh?" Tsewang replied, patting his hair and clothes. "Why would you say—"

"Boys, please, let's not argue," Takum begged. "Try to be kind to one another today, yes? The rain is much too beautiful. Let's enjoy it."

"He asked me a question," Julji said, tossing the dustpan onto the floor, "so I answered him."

Takum clapped, "We have not had a rainstorm like this in such a long time, but I welcome it! It's cuddling weather. There's nothing better than passing a storm in the arms of the one you love. Isn't that so, Julji?"

"Of course," he replied dryly, "but that's if you have someone to love."

Takum grabbed the broom out of his hand, hugged it, and said, "Broom, will you love me?" then tossed his head back and laughed. Julji rolled his eyes, yanked the broom away from him, and continued to sweep.

"I can see the kind of day we're going to have," Tsewang said, handing the towel to Takum. "Where's my apron?" he asked, pushing through the saloon doors.

He lowered the fire beneath a pot of boiling water, lifted the lids of three large pots, and smiled at the stewed lamb Takum had said he would prepare, "Only for you, my darling." Tsewang no longer blushed at Takum's unbridled affection; he had begun to enjoy it. He wrapped his apron around his waist and piled scrambled eggs and diced red chilies onto a plate. Biting into a biscuit, he pushed through the doors and sat at a table. He bowed his head to pray but snapped it up and shoved a forkful of eggs into his mouth instead, watching Takum and Julji flit around, wiping tables and arranging place settings just so. Takum slid open the green lace curtains, then spun around and looked at Tsewang. "You look stunning in that red tie," he gushed, "You should wear it *every* day."

"And you know how to make a man feel good about himself."

"Only the men I like," he winked. Tsewang and Julji glanced at each other.

"Now," Takum continued, strutting toward Tsewang, "may I get a cup of coffee for you?"

"Coffee?" Tsewang said, leaning back and wiping his mouth. "You know I—"

"Of course, darling, I meant tea. I will bring you a cup of chamomile tea with a dash of sugar."

"That's better," Tsewang said. "Thank you."

Julji watched Takum push through the doors, then rushed to Tsewang, dragging the broom behind him. He slammed himself into a chair. "So, tell me, what's the deal with you and Takum?" he glared.

Tsewang pushed his plate aside. "What do you mean?"

"Oh, c'mon, you know what I'm talking about," Julji hissed. "I saw you two hugging at the party. I see how you look at each other. You act as if you're lovers."

"So, what if we are? What business is it of yours?"

Julji's nostrils flared. "*Excuse me?* It may be no business of mine, but if Chimé ever finds out he'll—"

"He'll do what?" Takum snarled, standing behind Julji, gripping Tsewang's cup of tea.

Julji jumped to his feet. Tsewang tilted his head and grinned, "Please, Julji, tell us…what will Chimé do?"

Takum placed the teacup in front of Tsewang and sat next to him.

"Oh, c'mon," Julji snarled. "You know *exactly* how Chimé feels about us."

"No," Tsewang replied, lifting the teacup to his lips. "I don't know how he feels. Why don't you tell me." He blew into the cup, sipped his tea, and returned it to the saucer.

"Takum, tell him!" Julji demanded. "Tell him how Chimé always calls us fags and sissies and makes fun of the way we walk."

Before Takum could respond, Julji turned to Tsewang. "If he *ever* found out about you and Takum, he'll toss your ass onto the street. You'll be without a home *and* a job."

"Is that so? What makes you so sure?" Tsewang snickered, easing his clammy hands onto his lap. His heart pounded. He knew Chimé could be ruthless. He witnessed that side of him the night he screamed into his cellphone, telling one of the boys who worked for him that he would not send him money to return home from India and that he was on his own.

Takum sprung to his feet. "Why are you starting trouble?" he hollered, wagging his finger at Julji. "You're just jealous that…"

"*Jealous?* Me? All I ever want is for you to be happy, Takum, you know that. We've been friends for many years. Why would I be jealous of you and…" he looked at Tsewang and scowled, "*and him?*"

Tsewang frowned. "You look at me as if I'm gum on your shoe. Why is that? What have I ever done to you?"

"Don't act like you don't want him, Julji," Takum hissed. "You told me so the first night you met him."

"What? The day he shit on himself? Ha! I only felt sorry for him. I didn't—"

"That's a lie," Takum yelled. "You told me! You—"

"Listen, boys, listen to me," Tsewang said, standing up. "Stop arguing, there's no need. Julji, I—"

"You *what?*" he snarled, slamming his hand onto his hip.

"I just want to know if it's true. Do you *really* think Chimé would…would do as you said?"

"Of course, he would! He *hates* fags. The only reason he has kept Takum and me here is because he needs us. The *only* reason Chimé keeps anyone around is to use them—everyone knows that."

"But he's not using me for anything."

"How do *you* know?" Julji said. "You don't know what he has up his sleeve. Why do you think he's letting you stay at his home—especially knowing you're a fag? Trust me, he has *plans* for you, my friend."

"But I'm not a fag," Tsewang winced. "Just because I—"

"Ha! Say what you like, but I know a fag when I see one."

"Would you *stop* using that word? It's so…"

"It's so what? So true?" Julji quipped, grabbing the broom off the floor.

Tsewang walked to the window and ran his fingers through his damp hair. Watching rain trickle against the pane, he said, "He may know who you two are. It's *obvious* that you both are sissies—just by the way you walk." He turned toward them and chuckled, "But I…I don't walk like that."

"Tsewang," Julji said, leaning the broom against the wall, "who are you to label someone, to judge someone by the way they look…or walk, for that matter? I have not seen you in that kasaya you arrived in months ago, and I can't remember the last time you bowed your head and prayed before you ate. Am I supposed to believe that you're no longer a Buddhist? That you no longer believe in the principles you used to speak of? You don't even wear those beads anymore. When you arrived, you were bald like Buddha. Now, your hair is almost touching your shoulders. Does that mean you are no longer who you were? Have *you* changed, or just the appearance of you? Who are you to label us—to judge us by the way we walk, or by how we look? You don't know me."

"I wasn't judging you," Tsewang hollered. "I was just—"

The door swung open, ringing the bell. They spun around and stared at the two men who barged in with a gust of wind.

"Tashi Delek," the bearded man grunted, rubbing his chapped hands.

Tsewang, Julji, and Takum looked at each other, silently wrangling over who would tend to the first customers of the day. Takum dropped his shoulders and sighed, then turned toward the men and gushed, "Tashi Delek!"

They each moved into their respective jobs, daily tasks tacitly assigned and assumed without protest. Tsewang peeled potatoes, diced chilies, marinated batches of fiddle fern, and washed dishes. Julji seasoned chunks of pork and lamb and cooked the meals to an exquisite taste. And Takum did what he does best—greeted customers with batting eyes, wanting them to feel at home. During the lull between customers, they moved about in silence, burdened by thoughts of Chimé, repressing fear. Each time Tsewang's hair fell into his eyes he pushed it away with a huff and then touched his chest, seeking the feel of his mala beads, missing their weight around his neck.

When Tsewang arrived home Chimé was not there, but his new coat was. He tossed into the icebox the bag of momos he had brought home for Chimé, and with wide eyes and a broad smile he beamed at the ankle-length, royal-blue coat carefully placed upon the sofa. He picked it up and held it high above his head, then lowered it onto his chest and hugged it tightly. He eased his arms into it and moved his hands across its blend of wool and fleece. It fit as if it were made for him only. He pulled the hood onto his head and slipped his hands into its deep pockets. He exhaled into its warmth, knowing it would protect him from the harsh Himalayan winter heading their way. It was not the raincoat he needed, but he didn't care—no one had ever bought anything for him, especially something that would provide him warmth. "Thank you, Mahak—" he whispered, then shook his head. "I mean, thank you, Chimé. I know not even a deity can make you do anything you do not wish to do."

He tightened the sash and sat on the sofa. His tired eyes fluttered and gave way to a deep and dreamless sleep. And in the early morning hour, as a muted sun pressed against an obsidian sky, he was awakened by a rooster's crow, still wearing his coat, and covered with his quilt. Chimé was sleeping soundly on his mattress, buried beneath his blanket.

Daylight filtered through the yellow damask slung across the window, and as Tsewang rubbed his eyes and wiggled his toes, he recalled that it was Thursday, his day off. He exhaled, relieved he did not have to see Julji or Takum. Their exchange had left him feeling uneasy and confused. And although he liked them—especially Takum—their constant chatter and flitting about exhausted him at times and made him want to return to the forest.

He removed his coat and gently laid it on the side of the sofa Chimé never sits. He folded his quilt and placed it, and his pillow, beneath his coat. He wanted to be able to look at it, and each time he did, he inhaled and grinned. He cleaned his teeth, showered, dressed, and turned on the hotplate to boil water. Sitting on the sofa and sipping a cup of tea, he had the urge to place his mala beads around his neck but did not dare. He watched Chimé stretch and yawn with a growl, then open his eyes and squint at him.

"So, you finally took off your coat. You must have been burning up in it," he said. "I know it's too warm to wear now, but Yeshi didn't have any raincoats. He had that one though, so I bought it for you because winter will be here quicker than we can rob a mule."

"Chimé, I don't know how to thank you. I love my new coat." He placed his teacup on the stool and rubbed his eyes.

"Don't get all emotional on me now," Chimé said, easing off his mattress and hurrying to the bathroom.

Tsewang wiped his eyes and lifted the cup to his lips, listening to Chimé urinate and then splash water onto his face.

"Today's your day off, right?" Chimé asked, running his fingers through his dampened hair.

"Yes, it is."

"And how do you intend to spend it? Not with those two fags, I hope."

He had never heard Chimé refer to them in that manner; he recalled Julji's claim just the day before. His heart pounded and his hands began to sweat. He gulped his tea and replied, "I don't know what you're talking about. They're my friends and I—"

"I know they're your friends," Chimé grunted, pouring hot water into a cup. "I'm not saying you shouldn't be friends with them. All I'm saying is to be careful. Those two will drop their drawers for you quicker than you can ask them to." He eased onto his mattress, propped himself against the wall, and covered his legs with the quilt.

Tsewang placed his cup on the stool, stood up, and paced the room, unsure of what he should say or do. He glanced at the icebox, bounded toward it, and pulled two momos out of the bag. He stuffed one into his mouth and gave Chimé the other, then plopped onto the sofa and sighed.

"What's wrong? Did I hurt your feelings by calling your friends fags?"

"Well, Chimé, I was taught long ago that we must treat others as we wish to be treated. I wouldn't want anyone to speak badly of me, so I don't speak badly of anyone."

"I'm not speaking badly of them. I'm speaking the truth— they *are* fags!"

"But you hurt their feelings whenever you call them—"

"I *used* to call them that, but not anymore. Not since you've been there," he said, reaching for his cigarettes. "So, you three have been talking about me, huh? What else have—"

"N-no, we haven't been talking about you," Tsewang replied, gasping at the lie he told. His thoughts shifted to Dabir, and in his mind, he could hear his voice, "You must always tell the truth, Tsewang. You must honor Satya." His eyes filled with tears.

"Are you alright?" Chimé asked.

Tsewang pressed his hands against his eyes, then ran his fingers through his hair. "I'm sorry, Chimé, please…what were you saying?"

"Oh, forget it," he said, waving his hand. He lit a cigarette. "I don't understand you sometimes. It's as if you're here physically, but your mind is always somewhere else. It's like…like you're never fully present."

"I don't mean to be rude, but I have so much on my mind."

"Like what?"

"Like…like." He glanced at his coat. "Why are you being so kind to me? You have given me so much. What do you expect in return? What do you want from me?"

Goodness, kid! Can't someone just be *nice*? Why do you think I want anything from you? You've been here for almost three months. Have I ever asked you for anything?"

"No, but…but Julji said—"

"*Julji?*" Chimé grimaced. "What did he say to you?"

"Nothing. He said nothing. I mean—"

"You're not telling the truth, Tsewang. I know those two. Look, when we met, you had nowhere to go, and you were hungry. So, I took you in and I fed you. What crime did I commit? Unlike what most people think of me, I *do* have a heart. Anyway, for all I know"—he huffed, bounding to his feet— "you could be my son."

"Your *what?*"

"That's right, my son," he said, grabbing the bottle of monkey juice and a glass. He held them, glanced over his shoulder at Tsewang, and returned both to the shelf above the icebox. He lit another cigarette and plopped onto his mattress.

Tsewang grimaced, "What makes you think I could be your…your *son?*"

Chimé put the cigarette to his lips, tilted his head back, and blew a gray stream of smoke into the stale air. "I don't know," he shrugged. "When I left my family, my son was a little boy. He should be your age by now." He shook his head and sighed. "At first, I used to come and go. Like a lot of men—like my own father—I would leave my family for stretches of time, until one day I left and never went back. I used to think, what good am I? I had nothing to offer my wife and children. We were poor, cold, and hungry. And so, I just stayed away."

He reached for the ashtray and rubbed out his cigarette; then sipped his tea, leaned his head against the wall, and gazed at the ceiling. "I know I have a son somewhere, maybe even two. I remember his mother wanted to name him after her father. It was a weird-sounding name that I didn't like, sort of like your name." He closed his eyes and shook his head. "I was so addicted to alcohol and betel nuts that I don't remember much about my life, other than I was just a shameful fuck-up. I abandoned my family. I have children I don't know. Children from different women. I…I…" He looked at Tsewang. "Sometimes, I just wish I could start my life over again. There were times that I…"

Chimé's voice became a distant din to Tsewang, as if his words were bubbling up from underwater. Staring at him with narrowed eyes, he thought, *this man is a fool, thinking I might be his son. You are not my father, Chimé. A snow leopard ate my father many years ago, and he is dead.*

"Anyway," Chimé said, shrugging his shoulders, "I can tell you're not listening to me. Like I said, you're always someplace else."

"I'm sorry Chimé, it's all so confusing," Tsewang sighed. "I have so much on my mind."

"Like *what?* What's on your mind? You told me you like working at the restaurant. So, what is it?" He eyed Tsewang, waiting for him to respond, then gulped his tea and said, "I notice you haven't mentioned your mother lately."

Tsewang sprang to his feet. "Would you like another cup? I can make—"

"No, I want you to sit down and answer my question. Your mother…how come you don't talk about her anymore? Do you still want to find her?"

Tsewang inhaled deeply, lowered onto the sofa, and frowned. "Of course, I want to find her. I think about my mother all the time. I think about her…my siblings…and I think about Nugai."

"*Really?*" Chimé chuckled, "Do you *really* think that dog is still alive?"

Tsewang glared at him. "You know, Chimé, sometimes you can be so heartless. I loved that dog. Of course, I don't know if he's alive. I don't even know if my mother is still alive, but I want to find out." He stood up, walked to the window, and pushed back the damask, allowing shadows of gray, shiftless clouds to enter their damp and darkened room.

"Would you close that?" Chimé snapped. "You're letting in the draft."

Tsewang ignored him and gazed at the rainfall whipping about in a restless wind. He locked his eyes onto a trickle of rain against the pane and watched it slither until it disappeared into the splintered frame. Then he raised his eyes to the top of the window, isolated another raindrop, and watched it trickle until it disappeared—just as he used to do with snowflakes when he was a child awaiting his father's return. Standing at the forest edge, he would raise his face to the sky, isolate a flake, and watch it fall until it disappeared into a blanket of snow. And he would do this until his feet were numb and his lips were blue.

"Tsewang," Chimé said in a voice softer than he had ever heard him speak.

He turned and looked at him. "Yes, Chimé?"

"Do you want to look for your mother today? I can take the day off. And I have the car. We can go find her—and Nugai."

"Thank you, Chimé. I…I would be forever grateful."

"Very well. I'll get dressed."

While Chimé showered, Tsewang pulled from beneath the sofa his kasaya wrapped in plastic. He removed his mala beads and pressed them against his lips with closed eyes, then slipped them over his head. When he heard Chimé turn off the water, he removed them from around his neck and placed them in his pant pocket.

Chimé returned to the room fully dressed, as he always had. He picked up Tsewang's coat and held it open. Tsewang eased his arms into the sleeves, then tied the sash and sighed.

"What's with the sigh?" Chimé asked, buttoning his coat, "You should be happy." He swung open the door. "After all, how long have you waited for this day?"

"All my life," Tsewang replied, lifting his face toward the falling rain. "I have waited for this day all of my life."

"Then let's get in the car," Chimé smiled, "This day has finally arrived."

A'isha

"Saira wouldn't do that to me," A'isha mumbled, hastening her pace with elongated strides. "How could I be so stupid," she panted, leaving kicked-up swirls of arid soil in her wake. *What was I thinking? I hope she hasn't run off with my money. I don't know who she is anymore.*

When A'isha arrived at the bend, she stood behind the Tamarisk tree and peered at her home at the top of the hill, wiping sweat off her brow and tightening her hijab. "Walk with me, my jida," she whispered as she approached her home, wringing her sweaty hands. She tiptoed to the rear of the house and swept her eyes across the yard. Ali was asleep at the foot of Isir's grave, the chickens were nestled in their coop, and the back door to the house was open, as she had left it.

Peeking through the screen door, she scanned the room. The bedquilt was folded with precision and the pillows were fluffed. Their untouched dinner from the night before was removed from the table and replaced with a fresh setting for two. Her mouth watered at the blended aromas of rosemary, lentil, and mint that simmered in a pot hanging above crackling embers. And her eyes stopped at Saira, kneeling at a basin, washing dishes. A ray of honeysuckle sun had settled upon her back. *Of course, she's still here,* A'isha smiled, wishing she had picked wildflowers along the way.

"Hello, beautiful," she said in a voice weighed with desire and relief.

Saira turned her head toward the door, her face partially hidden by her hair. "Ah, you're home earlier than I expected," she said, rising to her feet and drying her hands. A'isha pressed her lips onto the screen door as she watched her walk across the room. When Saira arrived at the door, she pressed her lips onto A'isha's until they tossed their heads back and laughed. A'isha swung open the door. As she entered the room she smelled the scent of cinnamon and recalled the voice that had told her, "Go home, A'isha. Go home now."

"Why are you here so early?" Saira asked. "You said you would return this evening."

"I…I…business was slow," she replied, darting her eyes from Saira to her dresser. "So, I thought I would just come home."

"What's wrong?" Saira asked, knitting her brow.

"W--what do you mean?"

"You look like you saw a ghost."

"Me? Oh, no, nothing's wrong. I…I…what are you preparing there?"

"It's a surprise." She grabbed the ladle and lifted the lid. "Well, I guess it can't be much of a surprise given that it's *your* food."

"Just having you here *is* a surprise," A'isha quipped, easing toward her dresser. She glanced over her shoulder, removed her hijab, dropped it in the drawer, and shoved her hand to the rear of it, groping for her money wrapped in a chador. She grinned at her feel of the stack and spun around to hug Saira, but she watched her stoke the fire, instead. A rumble of relief and sadness arose in her heart, causing it to flutter.

"I…I need to feed Ali and the chickens," she muttered. "I'll be back."

"Sure," Saira said, over her shoulder. "Are you hungry?"

"For what?" A'isha replied, forcing a smile.

Saira wagged her finger, "Ah, you're a naughty girl."

When A'isha returned from the yard, the table was adorned with the bowl of olives and plate of crumbled goat cheese she had served the night before. From the pot above the firepit, Saira filled two bowls of harira infused with rosemary and mint, and plated slices of khobz for dipping.

She plopped into A'isha's favorite chair and asked, "Are you ready to eat?"

A'isha frowned, "That's my—"

"Huh? What's yours?"

"Oh, nothing…it's nothing. Yes, I'm ready. I just need to wash up."

"But your soup, it's going to get cold. Can't you—"

"I can't eat without washing my hands."

"Well, I'll start," Saira huffed, grabbing her spoon. "I don't like cold soup."

"I don't know anyone who does."

As A'isha dried her hands, she watched Saira hover over her bowl, scooping soup into her mouth and biting into a slice of khobz.

"See? I didn't take too long," she said, easing into the chair she had not sat in since her grandmother's death. She recalled her promise to her in prayer, "From now on, my jida, I will sit in your chair to keep it warm." Glaring at Saira, she bowed her head to thank Allah for the meal, and to ask for His forgiveness and guidance.

"The soup smells delicious," she said, placing olives onto her plate. "Thank you for preparing it."

"No, thank *you*. After all, it's your food."

A'isha frowned and shook her head. "Won't you just accept my appreciation? I have not had anyone cook for me since my grandmother died. It's nice to be fed."

Saira hung her head over her bowl, scooping soup into her mouth. A'isha looked at her, awaiting a reply, then shrugged her shoulders and ate as if she were alone.

"Yes, it *is* nice to be fed," Saira said, piercing the silence. "I haven't had a home-cooked meal in a long time, either. Not since I was sent to live with my aunt. She's not the homemaker type…always working, never home. But why should I expect anything different? She was never home for her own children."

"Maybe she thinks you're old enough to cook for yourself."

"*Cook for myself?* There was never any food in the house *for* me to cook."

A'isha watched Saira mop her bowl with a slice of khobz. "Speaking of home," she said, "last night I asked why you are here and you've yet to answer that question. I want to know, Saira, after all this time, what made you come to me? Why now?"

Saira darted her eyes around the room.

A'isha leaned forward. "What's wrong? Did you not hear my question?"

"Yes, yes I heard you," she snapped. "I see you're still impatient."

"*Excuse me?* I've been trying to get a response to that question since you arrived. I'm not being impatient, just persistent."

"I…I missed you, that's all."

"*Missed me?* After all this time?"

"Yes, have you not missed me?"

"Well, of course I have. But to tell you the truth, not so much anymore. I guess I've accepted your absence and, well…I've moved on."

"*Moved on?* What do you mean?"

"I mean just that—I've moved on. You know…making plans, setting goals, working toward them."

"But what about us? What about the plans you and I used to have? Remember? We used to talk about running away together and building our own house, and—"

"Saira, those were childhood dreams. As I said last night, I'm not the little girl you once knew. I have had to fend for myself. Sure, my grandmother helped me when I was thrown out of my house. She gave me a safe place to live. But she's been dead for nearly a year, and I've been taking care of myself since. I'm working and making money. It's not much, but it's enough for me to buy food…the things I need." She leaned back in her seat. "And I'm applying to universities. I'm leaving Ouirgane. I've always said I would. You know that."

"Yes, and you said you would take me with you. Has that changed?"

A'isha looked at her with parted lips, then stood up and grabbed the poker. Stoking the fire, she gazed at the persimmon embers that arose from the pit with each jab and returned to it ashen gray.

"Saira," she said, leaning the poker against the wall, then easing into her chair.

"Yes, what is it?" She bit into a chunk of goat cheese and placed on her plate the last piece of chebakia Nasim had given A'isha.

"What are your plans? I don't mean your plans with me, but for yourself?"

"I *told* you. I don't know."

"Do you intend to finish your education?"

"Don't you remember what I told you last night? I haven't been to school since I left the village. When I arrived at my aunt's house, I didn't know what to do and she wasn't around to help me. So, I—"

"*So, you just stopped going to school?* What did you do all day?"

"I…I cleaned. You know…I earned my stay. That was their agreement, my aunt and my father. She let me live in her house, but I had to work for it."

"And now what are you going to do?"

"I'm not sure. Since her daughter returned from the madrasa things have changed. She has taken over and we don't get along. She told me I must figure out what I will do with my life. I don't think she wants me there anymore."

"So, *that's* why you're here," A'isha nodded. "*Now* I understand."

"What are you saying? Do you think I'm here because I can't live in my aunt's house?"

"You tell me. Are you?"

"Oh, silly girl," Saira said, reaching for A'isha's hand. "You know I'm also here for you. You must have known I would return to you someday."

"But I never thought it would be for this reason." She shoved away from the table. "I'll be back," she said, pushing the screen door open and releasing it for the first time with a slam.

Ali trotted toward her as she walked to her grandmother's grave. She could hear Saira tossing utensils onto emptied plates.

A'isha knelt at her grandmother's grave and adjusted the can of wilting wildflowers.

"Marhaban, my jida. I hope you are resting peacefully in Allah's arms. My grandmother, as I'm sure you know, Saira has returned. I don't—" She lifted her face toward the sky, pressed her fingers against her eyes, against the sting of her tears, and continued, "It's strange how someone I have loved for so long could make me feel so vulnerable." She shook her head. "The girl I declared my love for—to my father, to everyone I know—is here to use me, and it hurts to know that. She wants me to do for her what she has not done for herself. I still love her, my jida, but I don't know if I'm willing to take care of her. I'm still learning how to take care of myself." She sighed. "Yesterday, I told you I think I'm about to learn a lesson. Well, this might be it. I guess it's a lesson about love. How can I love someone else and still love myself?"

"A'isha, are you okay?" Saira called out.

"Yes, I am," A'isha hollered. "Go inside. I'll be there soon." She placed her hand on her grandmother's grave. "My jida, I must go. Thank you for listening to me. I love you."

She walked toward the house, then turned away and lingered in the yard, pulling dandelions and tossing hay in the chicken coop. She straightened the "J" upon her jida's grave; then plopped next to it and caressed Ali's nose. She got up and walked to the door but turned away again and looked for something else to do. She thought about the shop. *I'm sure I've lost a sale or two.* And she thought of Nasim.

She returned to her door, inhaled deeply, and entered her home. Saira was lying on her bed with closed eyes. Silently, A'isha retrieved the bundle of money from her dresser drawer, stuffed it into her pocket, and walked out the front door. An echoing grunt lifted her eyes toward the powder blue sky and onto a Bald Ibis swooping and circling among the white clouds.

She crossed the arid, chestnut road and stood at the forest's edge, peering between the trees the way her grandmother used to whenever she searched for her husband. *At least she knew what she was looking for.* She kicked a pinecone, turned away, and wandered until she arrived at the river. She sat upon a boulder, staring into the water, listening to its gurgle against a bed of stones. Images of Saira formed in her mind, images of the girl she once knew, and of the version that returned. She jumped to her feet and threw stones into the river with all her might, trying to release what her mind knew, but her heart denied. And her resistance to an intuitive truth made her sit down and cry.

"Saira," she said, entering her home.

"Where have you been, A'isha? I was worried about you."

"No need to worry. This is my home, I am never—"

"I know this is your house," she sneered. "You don't have to tell me that."

"That's not what I meant. I was going to say that when I am home, I am never afraid or in danger. I am protected."

"I know, I know. Your grandmother is here. That's what you mean, right?"

"Yes, she is present. After all, this was her home before it became mine."

"So, what are you telling me?" Saira asked, plopping into a chair and lifting a cup to her lips.

A'isha sat on the edge of her bed. "What I am telling you is I'm not sure why you have returned, but given what you have said, I don't think you're here just for a visit."

"I *told* you—"

"Wait, Saira, allow me to finish. Whatever your reason is, it's not important to me. As much as I love you, I cannot allow you to stay here. In the morning, you—"

"A'isha, please! You can't."

"I can't what?"

You can't just let me leave. I don't want…I *cannot* go back to my aunt's house. Her daughter doesn't want me there. I have nowhere else to go."

"I'm sorry Saira, but I am not responsible for your situation. I'm trying to take care of myself and…and I have plans that you…that you will not—"

"That I will not what? Go ahead, say it! That I will not be able to have for my own, right? And why not? I'll tell you why. Because of you, that's why! If it weren't for *you*, I would have been able to finish my education. And now that I have nowhere to go *because* of you, you want to—"

A'isha rose to her feet. "That's enough, Saira. You must stop yelling in my home."

"I can yell all I want! You have some nerve, turning me away when you're the one who made a mess out of my life."

"I was going to let you stay until tomorrow morning, but I think you should leave now."

"But where will I go?"

"I don't know. I'll walk you to the village if you…" A'isha peered at her. "I don't even know how you got here. How--"

"How do you *think* I got here? My aunt's daughter drove me."

"Well, I don't have a telephone, so we can't call her. How are you…wait, your grandmother. She still lives in the village. I'll walk you to her house if you'd like."

Saira lunged at A'isha, wrapped her arms around her, and nuzzled her face into her neck. "Please," she begged. "I don't want to live with my grandmother. Please let me stay here with you. I'll cook and clean. I'll lay with you if that's what you want."

"There you go again," A'isha said, prying Saira's arms from around her waist.

"What do you mean?"

"You're saying you'll sleep with me if that's what I want. Would you *really* sleep with someone just because they…" She shook her head. "So, tell me, do you want me to walk with you to your grandmother's home, or not?"

Saira snatched her hijab off the bed and wrapped it around her head so tightly that A'isha wondered if she was going to choke herself with it.

"No, it's quite alright! I know how to get to my grandmother's house from here. Don't forget," she said, shoving her feet into her shoes, "you and I took this walk many times when we were younger."

"Yes, I remember."

Saira stomped toward the door, turned toward A'isha, and glared at her. "You just watch yourself. You may think you have it all now, but remember, those who climb highest fall the farthest."

"Yes Saira, that is true. But that happens only when they do something foolish, like allow someone in their life who *wants* them to fall." She opened the door. "Goodbye, Saira."

"Goodbye? If I stay with my grandmother I'll see you in the village. And you *did* say you work at your father's shop, didn't you?"

"Yes, I do. But let me warn you now, you are not welcome there."

"Is that so? Are you *threatening* me?"

"No, just informing you."

She walked toward A'isha, pressed her finger into her chest, and said, "You won't get away with this. I will see you again."

A'isha watched Saira pound her feet into the earth until she could no longer be seen behind the wisp of the Tamarisk tree.

"Goodbye, Saira," she whispered, wiping her tears. "I have always loved you, and I always will."

Tsewang

"C'mon baby!" Chimé said, shoving a key into the ignition of his rusting blue Toyota. Pumping the gas pedal, he continued, "She's cranky in the morning like most women, but once she warms up, she's a gem." He turned the key once, twice, and on the third try, he flashed a wide grin at the sound of grinding metal and a plume of charcoal smoke that shot out of the tailpipe. "That's my girl!" he said, patting the dashboard. He lit a cigarette and asked, "Are you ready to find your mother?"

Tsewang slowly nodded, "Yes, I am."

"Well, let's go!" Chimé said, skidding onto the main road, tooting his horn at dogs sniffing curbs with an aimless trot. He waved at shopkeepers positioning barrels beneath the edge of eaves to gather rainwater, and when he saw Lathi, the barber, he rolled down his window and yelled, "Where's my money?"

They drove through the village until he arrived at its only stop sign, at the intersection where he and Tsewang had first met. "Since I'm not returning you to the monastery, we'll go this way," he quipped, making a sharp right onto a steep, winding road.

Tsewang listened to the car chug its way up the mountainside; the grinding churn of metal made him cringe. *That car made the same noise*, he thought, recalling the last time he rode in one. He looked down at the growing distance between himself and the village that became his home three months ago and wondered if he would ever see Takum and Julji, again.

Chimé increased the speed of the wipers. "I sure hope this doesn't go on all day," he said, peering at the sway of the balsam and hemlock trees that framed the road. "This old lady doesn't do too well on wet roads. She needs new tires." Glancing at Tsewang, he continued, "But if we do get stuck out here, at least you'll be warm."

"Thanks to you, I am," Tsewang said, his face partially hidden by his hood.

"Thanks to *me*? What about Mahakala? No thanks to him? What's come over you? When we first met, he was all you talked about—Mahakala this, Mahakala that—what happened? You don't believe in him anymore?"

Tsewang stared at the rain rushing toward him in a funneled chase, pelting against the foggy windshield.

"Did you hear me?" Chimé asked. "You don't believe in him anymore? Oh, I see. You're just ignoring me," he said, pressing his foot on the gas pedal and swerving around a sharp bend.

"No, I'm not ignoring you, Chimé. I've listened to everything you have ever said to me. I just don't have much to say right now."

"Why? Are you nervous about seeing your mother?" he asked, shifting his eyes between Tsewang and the road. "I mean, that's *if* we find her, right? I figure we can start with this village, and if she's not there then we can go to the next, okay?"

"I guess so, but how do you know about this village? Have you ever been there?"

"Yes," Chimé nodded. "A long time ago."

Tsewang slid his hands into his coat pockets. He wanted to ask Chimé what brought him to that village, whom he might know there, but a stillness had begun to settle between them, and he preferred the sound of silence rather than Chimé's restless chatter.

They eased into their private thoughts. Chimé mapped out his next delivery of betel nuts to his friend in India, and Tsewang thought about his life with Chimé. At times he felt a blossoming love for him, grateful for all he had provided. But whenever he thought of Julji's remark, "the only reason Chimé is taking care of you is because he has plans for you," he would become wary of Chimé and wonder, *is it possible to love someone you do not trust?*

His thoughts moved away from Chimé and onto all the men who had ever taken care of him—Takum, Dabir, Kasim, and Tadashi. His heart ached as their faces flashed across his mind; he wanted to see them once again. He thought of how they each had helped him survive, and he could hear Dabir's voice from within, "If you live a life of good karma, people will appear on your path to help you along the way." *I guess he was right, but I wish my father had taken care of me, too.*

"Did you hear me?" Chimé asked, clearing his throat and gulping phlegm. "I said we're almost there." His voice was deep and foreboding; it made Tsewang's heart pound. Rubbing his eyes, he sat up.

"Were you asleep? The rain is finally giving us a break."

"No, I wasn't asleep," Tsewang replied, shaking off his hood. He leaned his head against the window and moved his eyes across the sky. In a gray, low-lying cloud, he saw his mother's face. He gasped and spun toward Chimé, wondering if he had seen it too, then shot his eyes back toward the cloud, which was now abstract and oblique. He peered at it, searching for his mother's image. *Mother, I miss you,* he said within. *Do you remember me?* He clasped his hands, closed his eyes, and bowed his head. "Mahakala," he silently prayed, "It has been a long time since I have approached you, but please listen to me. If it is your will that I see my mother today, I thank you with humility. But if it is not meant to be, then help me surrender in acceptance. Namaste." He opened his eyes and squinted at the sky.

"Wow! I can't remember the last time I've seen you do *that*," Chimé chuckled, then returned to making a mental list of the people he needed to call.

They worked their way up the mountain, driving in silence until Tsewang said, "My mother threw me away."

Chimé furrowed his brow. "What did you say?"

Tsewang looked at him. "I said my mother threw me away, and I don't know if I can ever forgive her."

Chimé pulled onto the side of the road, thankful they had reached level ground. He turned off the ignition and faced Tsewang. "Why do you say that…that she threw you—"

"What kind of mother sends her child away?" he winced.

"Aww, Tsewang," Chimé replied, shaking his head, "maybe she thought she was doing what was best for you. Maybe she thought the monastery would provide you with the things she could not."

"But did she ever think about what that would do to me…her throwing me away? Did she ever think that what I needed most was to be with my family? How could she…" His eyes brimmed with tears.

Chimé blinked away his own and placed his hand on Tsewang's shoulder. "Parents don't always know how to deal with their problems. And when they—when *we*—don't handle them the right way, we burden our children. We dump our pain onto them. I know it's not fair, but it's just one of those crazy things that happen in life. It happens to all of us in one way or another."

Chimé looked beyond Tsewang, at the jagged edges of windswept trees, and among them, he saw a silhouette of his own children. Slowly, he nodded, "You must learn to forgive your mother. You must trust that she sent you away–not to punish you, or because she didn't love you–but because it was the only thing she knew how to do. And although it scarred you and caused you pain, you must remember that she did the best she could." A tear escaped from the corner of his eye. He sighed and looked at Tsewang. "And so, you must forgive her."

"But I don't understand. How could she—"

"Maybe you don't understand at this moment, but one day you will. In the meantime, look for the lesson in your mother's actions. What can you learn from her? Maybe it's a lesson in forgiveness. Do you understand?"

Tsewang nodded, "I do. At the monastery, I had a mentor. His name is Dabir."

"Yes, you've spoken about him."

"He often talked about the importance of forgiveness."

"And now you're hearing it from me, an alcoholic who doesn't even believe in Buddha."

"But you're smart and I...I love you," Tsewang blushed, wiping his tears.

"Oh, don't get all mushy with me," Chimé huffed. He pulled out his pack of cigarettes and lit one. "We're just outside the village," he said, rolling down the window. "Do you want to continue, or should we turn back?"

"No...no, we're here. We might as well see if my mother is, too." He shoved his hand into his pant pocket, eased out his mala beads, slipped them over his head, and looked at Chimé. Chimé nodded with a wink.

They drove for another mile and stopped at a crest dotted with shanties fashioned out of poplar and birch. Each was tucked between soaring evergreen trees that shielded them from sudden gales and cloaked them in a stillness that rendered movement intrusive and voices beyond a whisper unwelcome.

"Where *is* everybody?" Tsewang asked.

"In their houses, I guess. The rain is down to a drizzle, but it's enough to keep people indoors. And it's still early."

They drove into the village, searching for life. "Look!" Chimé said, pointing at a swirl of blackened smoke rising from somewhere beyond the bend. He slammed his foot on the gas pedal. The tires whizzed as the car fishtailed around the curve, spewing gravel and clumps of rain-soaked soil over the edge.

Tsewang clutched his mala beads and yelped, "Mahakala, protect us! This man is going kill me!"

Chimé tossed his head back and laughed. "Oh, so *now* you call on Mahakala. See? You haven't changed. That long hair of yours doesn't fool me. You're still the same kid I met three months ago." He slowed to a stop in front of a tilted one-room abode of warped wood held together by loose nails. "Let's see who's here."

As they approached the shanty, an echoing screech pulled their attention toward the sky, to an eagle circling and swooping high above. Tsewang gawked at it as he walked closely behind Chimé, bumping into him and causing him to lunge forward.

Chimé spun around and hissed, "Be careful, would you!" Glaring at Tsewang, he lifted his hand to knock, but the door swung open.

"Oh!" Chimé exclaimed. He bowed at the elderly man. "Hello, sir. I mean, Kuzu zangpo la."

"Kuzu zangpo la," the man replied, gripping with stiffened fingers, the lapels of his faded crimson gho. Leaning his bony frame upon a cane of crooked oak, he pulled a cloth out of his sleeve and wiped the brow of his bronzed face, deeply carved by the toil of life.

"Kuzu zangpo la. Nga gimi ng Chimé in," Chimé said, with an angular grin.

Tsewang's jaw dropped as he stared at Chimé.

"Nga gimi ng. Khey rang kyopa'i du la bed sa."

"I am pleased to meet you, too," Chimé replied. He shook his head. "I mean, Khey rang kyo—"

"It is quite alright," the man chuckled. "I also speak English."

Chimé clapped his hands together. "Thank goodness! This conversation would have been long and difficult."

"Do you want to come inside?"

"No, thank you, sir. We are looking for someone." Chimé turned to Tsewang, "Tell me your mother's name."

"I…I don't know her name. I only knew her as 'Mother.'"

Chimé turned toward the man. "Sir, there is a family that might live in this village, a woman and her—"

"Five children," Tsewang said, stepping forward. "Their names are Takuma, Deki, Lhamo, Jigme, and Tandin."

He clenched his lip between his teeth; it had been many years since he spoke their names.

The old man rubbed his chin, watching the eagle swoop and circle high above. He looked at Tsewang and shook his head. "No…no, I don't know those names. I know of a woman who had many children, they lived down the road but moved away a long time ago."

"Do you know where they went?" Tsewang asked.

"No," he said, shifting his weight upon his cane. "I think they moved to the next village. People are always moving around in these mountains. It's not like it used to be. Everyone wants to be near the big towns—Paro, Thimphu. But not me," he grinned, flashing a lone, red-stained tooth. "I've been here all my life, and this is where I will die."

"Very well," Chimé nodded, eyeballing his tooth. "Sir, may I speak with you for a moment?"

"Come in," the old man said, stepping aside.

Chimé turned to Tsewang. "Go wait for me in the car. I'll be right back."

"But what—"

"I *said* wait for me in the car."

Tsewang's lips quivered. He bowed at the old man with praying hands and said, "Namaste."

The old man chuckled and closed the door.

Leaning against the car, Tsewang searched for the eagle. When he spotted it, their eyes locked as it perched upon a branch. A soothing warmth arose in Tsewang, like the feel of barley soup filling an empty belly, and he was overcome with a sense of safety and love he had never felt before. He smiled at the eagle and asked aloud, "Mother, is that you?" Images of his siblings flashed across his mind as he gazed at the eagle. He could see them running down the mountainside, hungry, barefoot, and free. Skipping over wildflowers with Nugai in the chase, kissed by a tender sun. And he saw his siblings huddling beneath yak skin and sheep's wool with him tucked in between, listening with a touch of fear to the sudden snap of branches blown away in the howl of harsh winter nights. He squeezed his eyes tightly then opened them, and as he gazed at the eagle he heard Dabir's voice say, "Forgive and be free. Forget that you have forgiven and be freer."

The creak of the old man's door pulled his attention away from the eagle. He watched Chimé bow and heard him say,

"Kadrin chhe la," then saunter away counting ngultrum until he plopped in the car and slammed the door shut.

"Did he give you that money?" Tsewang asked, climbing into the car.

"That's none of your business," Chimé snapped. He lit a cigarette and sighed. "If you *must* know, it *was* his money, but now it's mine."

"But why would you take his—"

"Why would I *what?*"

"Oh, forget it," Tsewang huffed. He closed his door and turned to Chimé with a furrowed brow. "I didn't know you speak, uh—"

"Dzongkha?"

"Yes, that's it. Dzongkha."

"I keep telling you, kid, I'm not just a drunken drug dealer. There's more to me than you know." He shoved the key into the ignition. "So, where to, now?"

Tsewang pulled his hood onto his head and slid his fingers along his mala beads. "Home," he said. "Let's go home."

"Are you sure? We can go to the next village if you'd like. I mean, we're already up here and…"

Chimé's words faded into the engine's grind as Tsewang leaned forward, peering through the windshield, watching the eagle take flight. *Mother,* he said within. *I will try to forgive you. I promise I will.* He watched the eagle soar above the clouds, then he sat back in his seat and exhaled.

"As usual," Chimé grunted, shaking his head.

Tsewang looked at him. "What do you mean?"

"You know *exactly* what I mean. As usual, your mind is somewhere else and you're not listening to me."

"Sure I am. I mean…no, you're right. I was not listening to you, but I am now. You have my full attention, sir!" he said, mocking a salute.

"Oh, so now you want to be silly," Chimé grinned, pumping the brakes down the steep mountainside. "But I'm not playing games with you. I'm serious."

Tsewang tilted his head and chuckled. "What do you mean? You're serious about what?"

"About you going on a run to India for me. Still interested?"

A'isha

"Twenty-three, twenty-four…" A'isha counted each garment with a radiant smile, "and twenty-five!" Her eyes glistened as she scanned the chadors and abayas she had spent the past month beading, often staying at the shop well into the night, determined to complete "just one more abaya." She was so busy that she hardly had time to simmer in her anger with Saira, though there were moments she hoped she would appear at her door. She passed her hand across her beadwork. "They are beautiful!" she declared aloud. "Amir, I hope you are pleased with my work."

She glanced at the clock. "He should be here soon," she gasped, grabbing the broom to sweep shavings of fabric and thread into a dustpan. She returned the cans of beads to a shelf, straightened rolls of fabric against the back wall, moved her eyes across the shop, and then plopped onto a stool at her workbench. Her stomach growled, but she dared not leave the shop for her daily walk to Abdullah for tea and khobz. Today she would ask al-Majid for directions to her father's shop, and she did not want to miss his arrival.

The thought of seeing her father made her heart pound. She jumped to her feet and wiped her sweaty hands on the bib of her overalls. *Why do I even want to see him?* She walked to the rear of the shop. *What would I say to him? To my mother? To Basha?* She sat on a roll of black organza, tears welled in her eyes as her sister's face flashed across her mind. She longed to see Basha and decided that an embrace from her sister would make the trip worthwhile, that Basha would be her reason for traveling to Imlil.

"As-salamu alaikum!" al-Majid said, pushing the door wide open.

A'isha leapt to her feet. "Wa-alaikumu as-salaam."

He walked toward her with his arms extended and placed his hands on her shoulders. He kissed her on both cheeks. "Let me start by offering my condolence. I know Amir was like a father to you. His death is a tremendous loss for us all, and I will miss him until it is *my* turn to meet our Maker." He pushed back his kufi. "So, how have you been?" he asked, darting his eyes across the garments spread out on the counter. "Each time I see you, you look more mature. Your parents should be proud of you."

A'isha frowned, "I suppose they would be."

"And if they're not, well…that's their loss," he said, raising an abaya, holding it close to the dangling bulb, turning it this way and that. He laid it on the counter. "Very nice!" He brushed his hand across the beadwork, squinting at it with a wide grin. "Tightly sewn, exquisite design…beautiful!" A'isha lifted her chin and pushed back her shoulders, nodding and smiling.

"And what about the wreaths?" he asked, unzipping the garment bag. "Did we not agree that you would have some for me to purchase along with the abayas? You know, I sold all of them in less than a week—all of them! Much quicker than my popular copper items. I've never seen anything like it! You must make more."

"I know we agreed, but I haven't had time to do both—make wreaths *and* bead. As you know, beading takes a lot of time, especially if you want to do a good job."

"Yes," he replied, placing the abayas into the bag, "and you have done a magnificent job. But I don't see why you can't do both. You're still on summer vacation and you have a month until you return to school, eh? You should be able to have twenty-five garments and twenty-five wreaths when I return next month, yes?"

"That's easy for you to say, but I will see what I can do." She watched him press down on the abayas, yanking on the zipper. "How about fifteen each?" she asked. "Would you agree to fifteen garments and fifteen wreaths? I might be able to manage that."

Al-Majid lifted his face to the ceiling and rubbed his chin. "Very well, if that's the best you can do," he said, extending his hand toward her, "I will agree to that. At the same price, of course."

She put her hand in his and shook it as firmly as he shook hers. "Yes, at the same price. But if you want me to apply more intricate beadwork—and I can—then my price will have to increase."

Al-Majid wagged his finger at her, "Ah, A'isha! You're a quick study. Not as bashful as you used to be, eh? I will surely keep your offer in mind." He shoved his hand into his pocket and pulled out a stack of dirhams. "Let's see, I owe you two thousand two hundred and forty-one dirhams, yes?"

"Yes, that is correct."

He laid each bill on the garment bag as he counted, "…thirty-nine, forty, and forty-one," then scooped up the pile of money and placed it in her hand.

"Thank you, sir," she said, shoving the money into her pocket. "But before you leave, would you tell me how to get to my father's shop?"

"*Your father's shop?* Who? *Nabeel?*"

She furrowed her brow. "Yes, he *is* my father."

"I know he's your father, but why would you…well, I suppose that is none of my business." He plopped the garment bag on the counter. "Do you think he would want to…I mean…I…I suppose he would not mind if I told you where he is."

"If that is your concern, then I won't tell him you gave me the directions. Would that make you feel better?"

"No, no…I guess it's alright. Anyway, he needs me just as much as I need him." He leaned against the counter. "He is no longer on the outskirts of the village, in that silly little shack. Finally, he has an actual shop right in the heart of Imlil. Just follow the main road until you reach the center of the village. His shop is next to the basket weaver; you can't miss it. It's quite simple."

"Shukran," A'isha nodded. "And don't worry. I won't tell him I received the directions from you."

He hoisted the garment bag onto his shoulder. "You know, Imlil is quite a distance from here. How are you going to…" He waved his hand and opened the door. "Never mind. That's none of my business, either. My wife tells me I'm nosy, and I guess she's right." He turned and looked at A'isha with a fading smile. "But I will say this: for whatever reason you want to see your father, just take care of yourself. And remember, you are not responsible for his actions. Go forward with a pure heart. Speak your truth and Allah will handle the rest. I will see you one month from today. Inshallah."

"Thank you so much, sir. And yes, I will see you in one month."

A'isha waved goodbye as he drove away, then peered into Nasim's shop. He was shifting carpets along slackened twine while an elderly couple flipped through a stack of prayer rugs. She waited for them to leave, then hurried across the road, entered his shop, and closed the door. He glanced at her over his shoulder. An unusual sadness occupied his eyes.

"What's wrong?" she asked softly.

"What could be wrong? You're here," he replied, brushing fibers off his hands. "It's good to see you. How have you been?"

"I've been well, I guess. I…I noticed you weren't here for two days last week. Are you okay?"

"My father was ill. So, how was your visit with Saira, or should I not ask?"

"You may, but there's really nothing to say."

"Is that so?"

She leaned against the counter, next to him. "Saira was different. She was not who I expected her to be."

"What do you mean?"

"She just wanted to use me. That's the only reason she came back."

A'isha walked to the door, slid her hands into the pockets of her yellow jumper, and watched the mid-morning heat shimmy off the arid road. Nasim moved his eyes down the length of her.

"She blamed…she blamed me for her situation. She said it was my fault she was sent to live with her aunt. She…I…I love her but…" A'isha spun around and frowned. "Oh, Nasim, I don't know why I'm telling you all of this. I just—"

"Need someone to talk to? We all do."

Their eyes locked. He moved his tongue between his lips; she clenched her lips between her teeth.

"A'isha, I want you to know that you can talk to me whenever you need to."

She nodded, wringing her hands. "Thank you. And…and you can do the same." The image of the wet tent his erection pitched flashed across her mind. She pursed her lips to stifle her laughter.

"What is it?" he asked, walking toward her. "You look like you want to laugh." He placed his hands on her shoulders. "May I hug you?"

"Uh-huh."

He pulled her close and wrapped his arms around her. She didn't know if she wanted to rest her head on his shoulder or burst out laughing.

"I…I should get back to the shop," she said, pulling away. "I'm glad to see you, and I hope your father feels better soon."

"Thank you. I'm glad to see you, too. Maybe one day you will invite me to your home for a meal. I'll bring pastries."

"Yes, maybe one day I will."

He watched her cross the road and enter her shop. They waved at each other, closed their doors, and resumed their daily tasks. He slung prayer rugs on twine, thinking about A'isha; and she plopped spools of thread into tin cans, separating them by color, hoping Abdullah hadn't forgotten about their trip to Imlil. *In just two days*, she thought, placing the cans on a shelf. *Maybe I should remind him. Besides, it's time for lunch.* Rubbing her growling belly, she flipped the "Closed" sign to face the road and sauntered downhill to Abdullah.

***

"Well, well…this day has finally arrived. Are you nervous about seeing your father?" Abdullah asked, plopping into his car. He handed A'isha a brown paper bag. "Here, this is for you. You can eat it on the way."

"Shukran," she nodded, slamming the car door shut. She opened the bag and smiled at the huge slice of khobz smeared with butter.

He pressed his foot on the gas pedal and revved the engine as he winded his watch. Then, gripping the gear handle, he turned to her and asked, "Are you ready?"

"Yes," she said, staring ahead with a faint smile, "I am ready."

They drove away from Ouirgane in a silence interrupted by occasional, random commentaries about the sweltering heat and

341

shallowing river. Abdullah talked briefly about the chasm Amir's death had carved into the village, and A'isha nodded in recognition, wishing he would be quiet. She wanted to be left alone with her thoughts. An awkward silence crept between them as they drove across a plateau of amber earth high above a valley of rippling ridges freckled with wild berries upon juniper. Abdullah shifted in his seat with an intermittent, restless sigh until he blurted out, "So, you're not going to stay in Ouirgane?"

A'isha looked at him with raised brows. *Has he been talking to Nasim?* "No, I am not. Next year, I'm leaving for the university. Why would you ask me such a—"

"But who will mind Amir's shop?" He flipped on the wipers, clearing away road dust. "Who will make the abayas? Who will bead the chadors for our women? You have done an excellent job with it all."

"Abdullah, I don't know what will happen to the shop. Maybe…maybe my father will return and take over. After all, it's his shop too."

"Oh, so that is the reason for this trip? You will talk to him about coming back?"

"I don't know why I want to see my father—my family—especially after all this time. I just know that I need to see them, but I don't know why." She unwrapped the slice of khobz. "Would you like some?"

He shook his head, hugging a curve, swiping past a grazing mule. He rotated the window crank and released the heat that had wrapped itself around their necks, then cleared his throat and said, "A'isha, it's okay that you don't know why you need to see your family. In time, you will understand. Just be patient with yourself.

Sometimes a journey's purpose is made clear only after we take the journey. Perhaps you need to be in your family's presence to understand why you must see them."

When they arrived in Imlil the main road was abuzz with wary shoppers perusing carts and merchants tugging on ropes, leading mules saddled with peaches and cherries. Bare-chested Europeans, oblivious to the natives who toil the land, flitted about the foothills, rolling tents and tying bootlaces in anxious anticipation of their imposition and conquest of Toubkal.

A'isha scooted to the edge of her seat. "Al-Majid said his shop is near…the basket…there it is!" she exclaimed, rolling her eyes as Abdullah drove down the road and parked the car several shops away.

He looked at her sheepishly. "I don't know if I am ready to speak to your father just yet."

"Yes, I understand," she said, and opened the door.

"Very well, take your time. Do not feel rushed. It has been several years since I've come to Imlil. I'm going to visit the butcher. I want to see what his cuts of meat look like. We can meet back here, in the car."

"Thank you," A'isha replied, adjusting her hijab. She closed the door, inhaled deeply, and headed to her father's shop.

With his back to the door, Nabeel was hunched over, gripping a babouche, tapping a nail into it. A'isha watched him, silently moving her eyes along his frame, searching for his presence. The anxiety and apprehension that wracked her mind and body all morning slowly morphed into a palpable grief that attaches itself to loss. For the man that stood before her was not the father she had remembered, but a frail and diminutive version of the man she once knew. The little girl within, the one with dimpled fingers and wild hair, wanted to run to him, wrap her arms around his thighs, and embrace the man she needed him to be. Instead, the young woman she had become cleared her throat and spoke.

"Baba, I am here."

Nabeel's body flinched as if an electrical charge shot up his spine and locked his hand and hammer in mid-swing. A gasp escaped his lips, but he did not turn to face her.

"Baba, did you hear me? It's me, A'isha."

Wringing her hands, she entered the tiny, windowless room that was more akin to a nomad's hut than a cobbler's shop. Its zinc roof and lantern-lit, plywood walls did not measure up to the wooden floor, glass counter, and dangling lightbulb he had left behind.

"Baba?"

"Yes, A'isha, I heard you," he grumbled. Lifting his head slowly, he turned to face her. "What is it?" he asked, tossing the hammer onto the splintering counter, knocking a can of mink oil to the edge. "What do want from me?"

"Baba, I came to see you."

"Obviously, you are here. Now what do you want?"

A'isha peered at him. "Why are you speaking to me like this?"

"And how is that?"

"So…so," she darted her eyes around the room, searching for the words she needed to say. "So coldly. I haven't seen you in nearly two years. What have I done to deserve this treatment? I thought you would be happy to see me."

"I am glad you are well, but I have known that you are."

"How could you know? You haven't—"

"I have my ways."

"And now I'm here, and you act as if you'd prefer that I disappear." She stretched her arms out to him. "You…you offer me no embrace. Not even a smile."

"What is there to smile about, A'isha? Tell me. What do I have to smile about?"

Baba, I could ask the same. Why do you hate me so? What have I done? When I was a little girl we were close, like friends, and then you changed. Why?"

"No, A'isha, I didn't change. You did. And you brought disgrace to our family—to the whole village. You should be ashamed of yourself."

"Why? Because of my friendship with Saira? I brought—"

"Let's not play games. The entire world knows that you and Saira were not just friends."

"And whose business is that? Who cares if we were more than friends? What right does anyone have to judge me? What right does anyone have to judge you?"

Nabeel's eyes widened. "What do you mean by that?"

"I think you know, Baba," she replied, lowering her eyes. She pressed her hand against her chest to calm her pounding heart, then raised her chin and locked her eyes onto his.

"If you came here to start trouble, then I think you should leave now," he snapped, pulling a cigarette out of the breast pocket of his dingy, gray tunic. He lit it and sucked smoke into his lungs.

"*Start trouble*? Why would I travel all this way to start trouble?"

"Then please tell me, why are you here?"

A surge of grief propelled her into a deeper truth, forcing her to relinquish an unrelenting fear of ever being perceived as weak and needy. She stepped closer to her father. "I…I am here because I…because I needed to see you, Baba. I want to see my mother and my sister. I…I miss my family. I miss you." She paused, choking back tears, waiting, hoping he would tell her he had missed her, too. Instead, he tossed her a blank stare.

"Don't you want to say something to me, Baba? Haven't you missed me, too?"

His silence and steady gaze grew heavier and slithered about the room until it crawled up her back and settled upon her shoulders like the cloak he wore. The one he had unearthed long before she was born and had used all these years to conceal his shame, secrecy, and self-reproach. As he glared at her, an awareness arose from the core of her being, and she understood how her father had conveniently used her as a whipping post for the part of himself he had denied but saw within her. The part of himself he had lacked the courage to claim as his own while his daughter attested to it, boldly. As he glared at her, silently punishing her for reminding him of his own truth, she listened to the clock tick, filling the gaps between her own breath. And in that moment, she understood that she was there to return to him the shame, denial, and fear he had shoved down her throat. She narrowed her eyes and brushed her palms together, dusting off, releasing, wiping away the burden her father had placed into her open hands so long ago.

"Baba, although I have declared who I am, and I have walked the roads of Ouirgane with my head held high, secretly, I have been ashamed. I believed that I deserved the shunning I have endured from the village, and from you. But now I know that the shame I have carried in my heart is not my own—it is yours. And I—"

"What do you mean, *mine*?"

"Exactly as I have said. I know about your relationship with Amir. I know that you and he were, shall we say, more than friends."

Nabeel's eyes widened. He stepped toward her, balling his fists. "You are—"

"I want to respect you, Baba. But if you hit me, I will defend myself and swing back. I am not the little girl you once knew, and you will not silence me—not this time."

She closed the door and stepped closer to him. "I know that you and Amir were lovers—the whole village knows. And just think, you had the nerve to punish me, to throw me away, to take my mother and sister away from me simply because I had the courage to declare who I am and who I love. You say that I brought dishonor to the family and that I should be ashamed of myself, but the truth is *you* should be ashamed of your hypocrisy. You should be ashamed for punishing me because I have the courage you lack. You abandoned Amir and denounced him in front of the entire village just to uphold an image of yourself that only you believe. Amir was a good friend to you, just as I was a good daughter. And you denied us both. Not because of who *we* are, but because we remind you of who *you* are. Father, I am giving back to you the shame you dumped onto my lap. It is not my burden; it is your own. And although I love you, I will no longer carry in my heart *anything* that does not belong to me. If you ever want to have a relationship with me, you will have to accept me for who I am, even if you cannot accept yourself for who you are." She turned and opened the door.

"Wait, A'isha. Do not leave."

"What is it, Father?"

"Who…who told you this?"

She looked at him over her shoulder. "Told me what? About your relationship with Amir?"

"Yes," he said, lowering his eyes, "who told you?"

"Why does that matter?"

He lit a cigarette and gazed out the door, locking his eyes onto something beyond her, something only he could see. He sucked smoke into his lungs and released it through his nostrils, then pushed back his kufi and frowned at her. "I…I have nothing more to say."

"Do you know that Amir is dead?"

"Yes, I am aware of that."

"And my jida?"

"Yes, I am aware of that, too."

"And you didn't even come to check on me. You didn't even go to Amir's funeral…to my jida's funeral."

"A'isha, I don't think there is anything more for us to discuss."

"Where are my mother and sister?"

"They're home, of course."

"I want to see them. Where do you live?"

"Turn right at the end of this road," he replied, rubbing his cigarette into a scrap of tin. "It's the first house on the left."

"Father, thank you. Thank you for everything you have done for me, and to me—including throwing me out of your house." She crossed the threshold and glared at him. "One last thing. I promised Amir I would keep the shop open until I leave for the university. That will be one year from now. If you want to return to your shop when I leave, or even before, of course, you may. After all,"—she shrugged—"it's your shop." She paused, waiting for him to look at her, but he did not. "And Baba," she said, softening her voice, "if you ever return to Ouirgane, I can assure you that the village will welcome you. Just as they have welcomed me."

He raised his eyes, looked at her and nodded, then picked up his hammer and the blue babouche.

A'isha walked down the road, listening to her father tap on a nail until she entered Abdullah's car, and could hear him no more.

When they arrived at the thatched roof, one-room abode, Aaminah was on her knees, pulling weeds from a thirsty patch of earth that defined their home.

"Mother?" A'isha said softly as she opened the car door. Aaminah raised her head but did not turn toward her daughter's voice. She remained on her knees. A'isha walked to her and placed her hand on her mother's shoulder. "Mother, it's me."

Aaminah bowed her head and whimpered, then looked up at her daughter. Tears trickled out the corner of her eyes, and onto the edge of her burgundy hijab. "Oh, my A'isha," she whispered, "my dear child."

A'isha held her mother's arm and helped her to her feet. She was startled by her frailty and saddened by the extent she had aged—the hollow in her cheeks, the gray hair that escaped her hijab. They looked at each other. Their eyes moved about, searching for what they had lost, unsure of what that might be. A'isha wrapped her arms around her mother, laid her head on her shoulder, and wept, "Oh Mother, I have missed you so."

Aaminah placed her hand on the back of A'isha's head and gently swayed from side to side, comforting herself and her child. "Let us go inside," she whispered, wiping away A'isha's tears, and her own.

"A'isha!" Basha shrieked, running toward her sister. They wrapped their arms around each other. Basha jumped up and down until her hijab fell off and draped her shoulders.

"Look at how tall you are!" A'isha exclaimed, stepping away from her sister, clenching her hands, then pulling her close and embracing her again. "I missed you so much," she cried.

Aaminah watched her daughters with a glint and muted smile.

Basha grabbed her sister's hand and led her into their home. A'isha followed her, scanning the low ceiling and cement walls painted in a lifeless beige. Unlike their home in Ouirgane, framed photos were not on display, and curtains were not hung. The gray, cement floor was bare, and the scent of stale tobacco and boiled turnips filled the air.

"Come," Aaminah said, patting a stool and easing onto a frayed brown chair. "Come sit here. Are you thirsty? Hungry? "Basha, bring us something to drink," she said, smiling at A'isha and rubbing her aching knees.

"No, I am fine. Basha, I don't need anything to drink. Come sit with us."

Basha glanced at Aaminah with an anxious grin, then sat on a stool next to her sister.

"So, tell me, how have you been? I want to know everything," Aaminah said, reaching for her daughter's hand. A'isha leaned forward, gripped her mother's fingertips, and quickly pulled away.

"I have been well. So much has happened since…since you left me." She shifted her eyes from her mother to her sister, then back to her mother. "Do you know that our jida has died?"

Aaminah winced. Her eyes tightened, revealing more shame than grief. "Yes, I know that my mother is dead. I am sure she is resting in Allah's arms." She stood up. "You must be thirsty. I will get us something to drink. You came at a good time. I have your favorite—papaya juice."

A'isha watched her mother walk away, then turned to her sister. "So, tell me, how is school?"

"Okay, I guess. It's different from Ouirgane's."

"How so?"

"The teachers here are more strict. They're quick to punish you if you don't have your homework, or if you talk in class. And the boys—" She gasped, slapping her hand onto her mouth.

"It's alright, Basha, you always talked to me about the boys. You can still—"

"Nonsense!" Aaminah hollered, entering the room with a tray of mugs. "You can talk to your sister about that nonsense some other time." She handed a mug to each of her daughters, then eased into the armchair.

They sipped in silence, dodging each other's eyes, until Aaminah leaned forward and said, "I know it was you, you and Amir, who buried your jida. You have always been such a courageous child."

A'isha furrowed her brow. "Courageous? No, I don't think burying my jida was an act of courage." She glanced at her sister, then scowled at her mother. "I had no choice. There was no one around. You weren't there, so I *had* to do it on my own. With Amir's help, of course."

Aaminah sighed, "Well, I—"

"You what, Mother? What can you possibly say?" The anger that shot through her at her father's shop resurfaced with a jolt as she flashed back to the night she buried her grandmother—to the countless nights she begged her mother to intervene and protect her from her father's assault. Her heart pounded. "I'm waiting, Mother. What do you want to say?"

"A'isha, I wanted to go. But your father refused to take me to Ouirgane, and I had no way of getting there."

"You have two feet!" She gasped, "Mother, I am sorry. I…I don't mean to disrespect you."

"I understand, A'isha…your disappointment, your frustration with me. We have had this conversation. I know I have not been there for you when you needed me most." She looked at Basha, "Nor you."

"Mother, that is not true," Basha said. "You have been the best moth—"

"Basha, stop it! No, I have not. In many ways, I have been the kind of mother to you girls that my mother was to me."

Aaminah looked at her daughters, then shifted her gaze beyond them. "When I was a little girl, my father ran away with another woman. Her name was Hira. I will never forget that name. It caused so much problem in our home. Anyway, within months of his leaving, one of my sisters died of typhoid fever. Her death, and my father's abandonment, destroyed my family. We *all* died, especially my mother. She was never the same after that."

Aaminah eased to her feet, darted her eyes around the room as if seeking an escape, then sat down. A'isha and Basha glanced at each other, wide-eyed. She continued, "My mother was never there. I mean she was physically present, but mentally? emotionally? No…no," she said, shaking her head, "she was never there for me or my sisters. We pretty much raised ourselves."

A'isha leaned forward, listening to her mother, to the missing pieces that completed the story. And as she listened, compassion arose from deep within and chiseled at the anger she had harbored toward her mother since she was a child.

"Anyway, I don't know why I'm telling you girls this. What difference does it make?"

"It makes a world of difference to me," A'isha said, softly. "It all makes sense now. I see the connect—"

"Who is there?" Aaminah called out. "Who is knocking?" she asked, walking to the door.

"Marhaban, Aaminah," Abdullah bowed.

"*Abdullah?* What are you doing here? Please, come in."

A'isha gulped her papaya juice and hurried to the door. "Mother, he drove me here. I'm sorry to keep you waiting, Abdullah."

"It is quite alright, A'isha. Your time here has been good for me, too. I visited the baker and the butcher. He has very nice cuts of lamb," he said, yanking a piece of paper out of his pocket. "And now I have his merchant's information!"

"Please, come in," Aaminah said.

"Shukran, but I have come to tell A'isha that we must be on our way. I promised Josiah I would return to the shop in time for him to tend to his own business."

"Of course," A'isha said, glancing at her mother and sister.

"Very well. I will meet you in the car." He bowed at Aaminah, "It is good to see you."

"Thank you. It is good to see you, too. It has been a long time," she replied.

A'isha and Basha followed their mother out to the front yard. Aaminah spun around, grabbed A'isha, and hugged her tightly. Basha wrapped her arms around them both.

"Come now," she said, pulling away. "A'isha must leave. You live in your grandmother's home, yes?"

A'isha nodded as she wiped her eyes and held her sister's hand. Basha yanked her hand away, threw her arms around A'isha, and laid her head on her shoulder. "I don't want you to leave me here," she cried.

"You know where to find me," A'isha whispered.

"Come, Basha, let your sister go. It is time for her to leave." Aaminah placed her finger under A'isha's chin and lifted her head. "My child, now you know where we live. You can come here at any time. We don't have a telephone, but you can write to us." She turned to Basha. "Go write down our address for your sister."

"Take care of my child," Aaminah called out to Abdullah.

"Of course, sayadati," he replied. "*Someone* has to."

Basha shoved the piece of paper into A'isha's hand and hugged her. "Don't stay away. Please come back."

"Ana ahibuk amy," A'isha waved.

"*You speak Arabic?*" her mother asked. "Since when?"

"Since you left Ouirgane," A'isha frowned. "Since you left me." She entered the car and closed the door.

Abdullah moved his eyes about her expressionless face as he shifted the car into gear. "Are you ready?" he asked.

"Yes," she nodded, looking ahead. "I am ready."

Tsewang

"I am afraid."

"Afraid of what? Don't be a fag. What's there to be afraid of? I told you—"

"But what if I get caught? I could go to prison for a long time."

"You're *not* going to get caught. Like I said, my boys have been taking these trips for years and not one has ever been locked up—not one!"

"Yeah, but there's always a first time and it could be me."

"I told you a dozen times. I know the people in the airport; if they stop you, you will mention my name. Tell them you are my son, and they will leave you alone. It's that simple. Besides," Chimé said, scanning Tsewang from head to toe, "no one will ever think you're doing something illegal. You look like the perfect monk. I knew that kasaya of yours would come in handy one day."

Tsewang brushed his hand across his shaven head and winced, "I don't know, Chimé, I'm really concerned about this. Why can't one of the other boys go, and I can just return to the restaurant?"

"Because you can't, that's why! Everything's arranged already. I went through all that trouble to get a passport for you, and *your* name is on the ticket. When you arrive in India my people will be looking for you, not for some other boy. Now get your bag and let's go. Your flight leaves in just two hours."

"But I didn't even have a chance to say goodbye to Takum and Julji. And I wanted to visit Dabir and Kasim before I left."

"You can see them when you get back. It's not like I'm gonna abandon you there, am I?" He stepped toward Tsewang, softening his voice. "And remember, it'll be like a vacation. I told you that my friend will take you to the Ganges. Remember when we first met you said you always wanted to see the Indians pray at the Ganges? Well, this is your chance, so don't fuck it up. Let's go."

"But how will he—"

"I *said* let's go. You can't miss this flight."

Chimé drove to the airport in brooding silence, and Tsewang kept his hand pressed against the mala beads around his neck. He begged Buddha to forgive him for wearing his kasaya and shaved head as a "clever disguise," as Chimé had insisted. And to Mahakala, he silently prayed, "Please be with me because I am afraid. If you bring me home safely, I will return to my life at the monastery. I understand this is not who I am."

Chimé slowed to a stop at the airport's lone terminal. "We're here," he said, turning toward Tsewang. "Remember, all you have to do is hand them your passport and ticket. Do not check your suitcase. You will carry it onto the plane and put it in the overhead bin above your seat. Do you understand?"

Tsewang nodded.

"Good, now let's go."

Chimé sprung out of the car, grabbed the suitcase off the backseat, and dropped it onto the ground, swiping Tsewang's toe.

"Ow! Ow! Ow!" he yelled, hopping on one foot.

"Oh, would you stop overreacting!"

"But you dropped it on my toe. It hurts!"

"And I think you've been spending too much time with Takum and Julji."

"Why would you say—"

Chimé waved his hand dismissively. "Listen, my friend will be at the airport when you arrive. Everything is set."

"But how will I know who he is?"

"Don't worry about that. He'll know who *you* are, and that's all that matters." He placed his hand on Tsewang's shoulder. "Everything will work out. Trust me. I've done this hundreds of times." He hurried to the car, swung open the door, and said, "Enjoy your flight," then slammed it shut and sped away.

Tsewang picked up the suitcase and then dropped it with a thud. It was much heavier than the night before. "What else did he put in here?" he grumbled, dragging it toward a door manned by a stoic officer. "Namaste," Tsewang said, forcing a smile. The officer stared at him, nodded slowly, and held the door open until Tsewang crossed the threshold.

Wiping his brow with the sleeve of his kasaya, he swept his eyes across the windowless, white-washed room. He watched the smattering of hushed travelers move about—women wrapped in colorful saris, cradling babies, and men dressed in dhotis with matching turbans. Excitement fluttered his belly and morphed his frown into a muted smile as he dragged the suitcase to the end of a short line. *What will it feel like to fly?*

"Next!" an official called out, impatiently snapping his fingers at Tsewang. "Passport and ticket."

"Namaste," Tsewang bowed, handing him the documents.

"Right…sure. What's in the luggage?"

Tsewang flitted his eyes around the terminal.

"Did you hear me?" the official asked, stamping the passport. "I said, what's in your luggage?"

"Oh, nothing. Just some clothes and things I'm taking to my…to my mother."

"*Things?* What kind of things?"

"I'm not sure, exactly. My father, *CHIMÉ!*" he bellowed, "packed this suitcase and told me to take it to her."

"Your father? And he didn't tell you what he's sending to your mother?"

Tsewang rubbed his fingers along his mala beads. "No…no, he did not."

"Ha! We all know of a so-called father who sends things to his wife almost every week." He tossed his pen onto the counter and sat back. "And I suppose you're a brother to the other boys, eh?"

"I…I…don't know what you're talking about."

"Suuure, you don't," the official mocked. He shoved the passport and ticket into Tsewang's hand. "Go on…go! Your mother is waiting. And tell your father we will do him the favor and not scan your suitcase. We love him that much," he said dryly.

Tsewang nodded eagerly, spun around, and hurried away clutching his beads.

"Hey, you forgot your luggage!" the official hollered.

Tsewang paused, looked at the door, then at the luggage, then at the door, and rushed back to the counter. Dragging the suitcase off the scale, he frowned and said, "Thank you," then bowed deeply and bellowed, "Naamaasteee!"

"Get out of here!" the official snarled.

During the entire two-and-a-half-hour flight, Tsewang gagged and heaved, lurching forward and holding a waxed paper bag to his mouth, then easing back with closed eyes. With a wave of his hand, he politely rejected the suggestion of a matronly woman wrapped in a purple sari.

"If you drink the tea, you will feel better," she said, patting his knee. "But if you don't drink it and vomit on me, I will become quite distressed, and I will slap you."

"I promise…I won't…vomit…on…you," he replied into the paper bag.

He sat back and gawked at the clouds from the corner of his eye, and when he became more curious than fearful, he gripped the armrests, sat erect, and looked around at his fellow passengers reclined in their seats, mostly asleep. *Maybe they're dead*, he thought. *Who could sleep at a time like this?*

"Madam," he called out to a passing attendant, "How much more time do we have to fly?"

"Ten minutes less than the last time you asked."

"Very well, thank you," he said, clenching an armrest with one hand and his mala beads with the other. And when he heard the tires screech and the pilot announce, "Welcome to India!" he threw both arms into the air and yelled, "Thank you, Mahakala!"

***

As Chimé had promised, a slender middle-aged man dressed in a burgundy dhoti and matching turban was there to greet him. He was holding a sign with his name, TSEWANG, written in bold red letters above a throng of people clustered at the terminal's door.

Tsewang pushed through the crushing crowd, dragging the suitcase with a furrowed brow, and waving at the man holding the sign.

"Goodness!" he huffed, adjusting his kasaya. He bowed and smiled, "Namaste. I am Tsewang."

The man tossed a cigarette onto the ground and extinguished it with a quick twist of his foot. "Chimé's boy?" he asked.

Tsewang pushed back his shoulders and lifted his chin. "Chimé's *boy*? No, not exactly. But, he has sent me here."

"Then I'm right"—the man snorted— "you *are* Chimé's boy."

Tsewang glared at him. *I don't like this man. He is an abrasion to my spirit.* Then, he heard Dabir's voice from within, "You know the truth by how it feels." He lifted the suitcase and held it out to the man.

361

"Well, if to you I'm Chimé's boy, then this is Chimé's luggage. You may take it. I've carried it long enough."

The man grabbed the suitcase. "Come with me!"

They pushed their way through the swarm of men and women. Some waved cardboard signs, and some waved their arms yelling, "Taxi! Taxi!" while others held arriving relatives in a tight, cheek-kissing embrace. The high-pitched cacophony melded with the sweltering heat, and as Tsewang wrestled with both, his prickling dislike for the man he followed rumbled in his gut like thunder before a storm.

They drove in silence. Tsewang's eyes brimmed with awe and sadness as he witnessed along the streets of New Delhi the imprint of man, where spirit and flesh intersect and manifest in the inconsistency of behavior and belief. He watched women light frankincense and myrrh at makeshift shrines, amid brown-stained diapers tossed without care, mingling among mounds of human excrement and crumpled newspapers of rain-smeared ink. He listened to the screeching tires of motorbikes honking, crisscrossing, and dodging cars patiently stalled by sacred cows moving against traffic with a slow and pensive gait. And he dabbed his eyes at the sight of toddlers squatting near their mother's hem, picking scabs, swatting flies, and slapping at the sting on their neck. Stretching their soiled hands toward a piece of naan dipped in curry, given to them in an absentminded way. And he watched them devour it, then reach for more until numbness set in. As the turbaned man drove through the din of New Delhi, compassion seized Tsewang's breath and watered his eyes as he witnessed a suffering that extended beyond his own, a story untold to him about a world he had not lived.

"You look like you've seen a ghost. Don't tell me you have Delhi-Belly already," the man said, swinging open the car door. "C'mon, let's go. We're here."

He grabbed the suitcase off the back seat, slammed the door, and strutted across the street toward a redbrick, three-story building tucked between two storefronts. One had a yellow banner announcing, "Custom-Made Silk Suits in Just One Hour," and the other had a blue banner, "Low-Fare, Same-Day Flights to Nepal, Bhutan, and Everest Basecamp." Tsewang followed the man into the building and up two flights of stairs wondering, *what is Delhi-Belly?*

The room was small and musty, like the one he shared with Chimé. But this place had two beds with lumpy, water-stained mattresses separated by a nightstand that could be mistaken for a stool. Although these were beds and not mats, the arrangement resembled the rooms he once shared with Dabir and Tadashi, and the thought of them made his heart ache.

The man tossed the suitcase onto the bed closest to the tar-stained window, pulled down the shade, and said, "Let's see what you have here."

He unzipped the suitcase, and in it were hundreds of betel nuts bundled in cheesecloth. The sight of them cramped Tsewang's stomach and made him sweat. He wrapped his arms around his torso, eased onto the edge of the bed, and in his mind, he returned to the forest, seeing himself scurry up tree trunks, twirl in delirium, and crouch in fear. *That was so long ago. Who was that boy and where did he go?*

The man's pounding dial on his phone pulled Tsewang back into the room.

"Yeah, it's me," he heard him say. "Yeah, he's here and so is the stuff. No, no, I haven't counted them yet, but it looks about right. Of course, I will…yeah, what we agreed to. Four… yes, that's it. On Tuesday. Yes, I know. Do you want to talk to him? Okay, fine. I will. I'll let him know."

Tsewang looked up at him. "Was that Chimé? Did he not want to speak to me?"

"No, not really. But he did say that I should hold on to your ticket and passport until you leave so you don't, uh, lose them."

"What makes him think I'll lose them? I'm more respon—"

"You can ask him that when you see him. C'mon," he said, shoving his hand toward Tsewang, "Give them to me."

Tsewang eased his passport and airline ticket out of his pocket and placed them into the man's hand. And again, he could hear Dabir say, "You know the truth by how it feels."

"I'll be back in three days to take you to the airport," the man said, zipping the suitcase. "I'll be here at—"

"*In three days*? But aren't you taking me to the Ganges River to see the Indians pray? Chimé said that you—"

"I don't care what Chimé told you. Do I look like a tour guide to you?"

"But what about money? How am I going to eat?"

The man huffed and shoved his hand into his pocket. He pulled out a stack of rupees and peeled off five bills. "Here, this should be enough," he said, tossing the money onto the bed. "And here's the key to this room. Just remember, I'll be back on Tuesday. Be ready when I get here because I won't wait for you," he warned, then picked up the suitcase and walked out the door.

Tsewang sat on the bed, unsure of what to do or where to go. He scooped up the key and money and went into the bathroom. "Uggh!" he screamed, cringing at a winged cockroach crawling up the wall. Gritting his teeth, he knocked it onto the floor and stomped on it, gagging at the squish and splatter of the yogurt-like mush on the edge of his sandal. Heaving as he picked it up, he recalled how he used to shudder at the sound of rats within the monastery's walls. "I'd rather deal with that, than with this nastiness," he mumbled. He urinated and splashed water on his face, then headed for the bustling streets of New Delhi.

Wandering through alleyways of ramshackle shanties, he moved through a thickness of people coexisting in choreographed chaos confined to a space bursting at its seams. The growl in his stomach reminded him that he had not eaten since the day before, so he stopped at a cart displaying chunks of meat skewered on a stick.

"One please," he said, holding up a finger and handing the man a bill.

The man snatched his money and gave him the stick of meat. As Tsewang walked away, a woman hurried toward him, grabbed his hand, and returned him to the cart. She yelled at the vendor in a language Tsewang did not understand and waited until the vendor shoved three coins into Tsewang's hand. She looked up at Tsewang, tightening a lace shawl around her chubby arms and large bosom.

"You must be careful!" she said. "Pay attention or you will be robbed of everything you have. That man owed you change. You gave him too much money."

"Thank you, madam. I did not know."

"I was watching you. I could see you did not know and that is why I came to help you. Where are you from?"

"The Kingdom of Bhutan."

"And how long will you be here in New Delhi?"

"For three days."

"Well, enjoy your visit, but remember, you must be careful. If you buy something and do not know how much it costs, just act like you know."

"And how do I do that?"

"It's easy. At the end of every purchase put your hand out and say, 'My change, please.' They will know what you're saying and will think *you* know what you're talking about. If you have paid too much, they'll give you your change. And if you haven't given them enough money, they will let you know that, too. Do you understand?"

Tsewang nodded, "Yes, madam, I do."

The woman gripped his forearm, looked into his eyes, and said, "Pay attention!"

"Thank you, madam," he bowed, "I will."

He watched the woman walk away, then lifted his eyes toward the sky. "Thank you, Mahakala," he whispered, and bit into the skewered meat.

By the time he ate the last chunk, his belly was rumbling as if it were going to explode. He hurried back to the hostel, but instead of running up the two flights of stairs, he rushed into the tailor shop next door.

"Please, sir," he begged, wide-eyed, "I need to use the bathroom."

The old man giggled. "You foreigners always get the Delhi-Belly. Go on, it's behind those curtains."

Tsewang plopped onto the toilet and moaned. He returned to the room drying his hands and thanked the old man, now sitting behind a desk.

"Where are you from?" he asked, eyeing Tsewang over the rim of his glasses.

"Sir, I live in Bhutan."

"Ah! And you're here for business?"

"I…I guess so."

"You *guess* so?"

"What I mean is… To tell you the truth, I don't know. I don't know why I'm here."

"What kind of thing is that? How can you be in a foreign country and not know why? Are you a fool?"

"No sir, I'm not a fool. Well, maybe I am. I'm a fool for believing…for trusting." He lowered his head. "He told me I would see the Ganges."

"*What?* Who told you that?"

"The person who has sent me here. I thought he cared for me, but…"

"But what?" The old man smirked. He leaned back in his chair and clasped his fingers across his belly.

"But now I know he doesn't care. He lied to me," Tsewang said. He eased into a chair in front of the old man's desk. "He said I would see the Indians pray, but that was not the truth. He told me that just to get me here." Anger seeped into his deadening eyes. *Julji was right. He took care of me only to use me.*

"Well, maybe you have been used—it happens to us all. But you know lad," the old man continued, wagging his finger, "things aren't always as they appear to be."

Tsewang lifted his head. "He often said that to me."

"Who?"

"The man who sent me here."

"Yes, but what *I* am saying is, okay, so he used you as his mule, I'm sure."

"As his *what?*"

"His mule. You know, someone who transports drugs."

Tsewang jumped to his feet. "I…I have done no such thing!"

"Please, sit down. Relax. I'm not accusing you of anything. I'm just saying that I have seen this happen too many times. Young boys sent here…transporting drugs in suitcases, sometimes even in their rectum." He shifted his eyes to the window and shook his head. "They believe in false promises, and like fools they do as they are told, only to be abandoned here with no way to return home."

Tsewang winced, recalling the night Chimé yelled into his phone, "I'm not sending you any money. You figure out how to get home on your own!"

The old man looked at him and nodded, "Yes, it happens all the time."

"But what do they do…the boys? I mean, how…how do they get home?"

"Some are lucky enough to have family who sends money for them to return home, but most do not."

"And what happens to *them*?"

"Well, they end up doing things they would've never thought of. Things that rob them of their dignity and kill their spirit."

"Like what?"

"Like working in brothels, walking the streets."

"Huh?"

The old man leaned forward and looked Tsewang in the eye. "They end up selling their bodies for sex."

"*They do what?*"

"That's right. And what's even sadder is there's never a shortage of men willing to pay—to violate—these boys." He shook his head. "It is an awful truth."

"But…but…"

"But what? I'm not suggesting that is *your* fate. We each have our own journey." He searched Tsewang's eyes. "You said you don't know why you are here, yes?"

Tsewang nodded.

"Well, who knows? You could be here for a purpose that has nothing to do with the man who has sent you here."

"What do you mean?"

The old man leaned back. "What I am saying is you must look for the lesson. Look for the true purpose of each situation. You must not limit your understanding to only that which is visible. Sure, whoever sent you here might've used you for his benefit. But what if you are here for your own benefit, too? For reasons you have yet to consider."

"I'm sorry, sir. I don't understand."

The old man leaned forward and locked eyes with Tsewang. "What I am saying is this: in every situation we are given a chance to move one step closer to our dharma, our life's purpose. And if we have lived a life of good karma, the Gods and our ancestors will help us when these situations arise. They will guide us, protect us, and place people in our lives who will help us along the way. Do you understand?"

"Yes, I think I do."

"Perhaps this situation you are in is simply one of those opportunities." He sat back in his seat. "Tell me, lad, have you lived a life of good karma?"

"I believe I have."

"How do you know?"

"Well, I have never taken anything that is not mine and," he thought of Uddi, "whenever I have been hurtful to someone, I have apologized. Also," he continued, scooting to the edge of his seat, "there are the novices…the boys at Pali Sholing. I…I want to help the children."

"I must say, for someone as young as you, that is a good start."

"Thank you, sir."

"So, now that you are here in India, in this situation, what are you going to do?"

"Do you mean until I return home? I leave in three days."

"And what if you are unable to do that?"

"Do what? Return *home*?"

"Yes. What if no one arrives to take you to the airport?"

"I…I…don't know. Why—"

"Where are you staying?"

"At the hostel next door."

"Um hm, I figured." The old man eased to his feet. "I tell you this, if no one shows up to take you to the airport, let me know. I will be here."

"Will you take me? Oh, no!" Tsewang shrieked, jumping to his feet.

"What is it? They have your passport, right?"

Tsewang nodded, wide-eyed.

"Of course, they do."

"What am I going to do?"

"That is for you to figure out. Maybe they'll return, maybe they won't. In the meantime, think about what I have said to you. And if they do not come for you, let me know."

"And will you…"

"Will I what?" the old man sighed, opening the door.

"Nothing, sir. I'm sorry," Tsewang said, then bowed and wandered onto the chaotic streets of New Delhi.

A'isha

"A'isha! A'isha, please wait."

She recognized the voice with a smirk and turned slowly, shifting her bookbag from one shoulder to the other. "What do you want, Salwa?"

The girl, tall and slender, pushed her thick eyeglasses up the bridge of her nose and hurried toward A'isha, clutching her schoolbooks against her chest. "Thank you for stopping," she panted. "I know…I know it's been a long time since we've talked and—"

"Correction, Salwa. It's been a long time since *you've* talked to me."

"Yes, A'isha. That is true, and I want to apologize. I was wrong."

"Oh, so *now* you want to talk to me, after all this time. Almost two years."

Salwa swept her eyes across the valley below, then raised her face toward the pristine, blue sky.

"You still can't look me in the eye, can you?" A'isha scowled, turning to walk away.

Salwa reached for her arm. "A'isha, please don't leave. I want to speak to you."

"Well, speak. I'm sure you've talked a lot *about* me. Why is it hard for you to talk *to* me?"

"I wasn't a good friend to you. I know that. When…when the rumors about…you know…about…"

"About me and Saira. Go ahead, you can say it."

"And when your father sent you to live with—"

"He didn't *send* me away. He threw me out of his house. But go ahead, continue."

"Yes, when all of that happened, it spread around the village like wildfire and we…we were told to stay away from you because…well, you know…"

"Because of who I am."

"We shouldn't have done that to you. You and I have been friends since we were children, and I want to apologize. It was wrong of me…wrong of us."

"Ha! And what brings about this sudden change of heart?"

"I don't know. I've never been comfortable with any of it. Seeing you shunned…eating your lunch alone…it wasn't right, and I'm sorry."

A'isha huffed. "Let's walk."

They strolled along the ridge in silence, listening to the distant brush of water upon stones.

A'isha inhaled deeply and sighed, "Well, thank you, Salwa. I'm still angry with you, but your apology does mean a lot to me." She shook her head. "I was hurt and lonely so much of the time.

But in a way, I don't regret what I've been through the past two years because it made me a stronger person. I learned how to be my own best friend."

"I understand. I admire you, A'isha. You have the courage I wish I had."

"Yes, but I have paid a price for it. I've lost so much."

"And I have paid a price for not having it."

"Like what?"

Salwa waved her hand. "Oh, it doesn't matter. What good does it do to talk about it."

"It *does* matter—*you* matter. If we don't use our voice to speak our truth, Salwa, someone will create our truths and speak it for us—even if it's something we don't believe."

"You're right, A'isha, but I don't even know what my truth is. I guess I need to figure it out. Maybe one day I will. Anyway, I know you must get home to study for the math exam, and so must I. Senior year is much more difficult. With the exit exams and college applications, I have no time to do anything else."

"You're lucky that's all you have to do. Me? I have my house to tend to *and* the shop…beading abayas, making wreaths. And then I must study for all these exit exams *and* complete college applications. Sometimes, I want to scream."

"That does sound like a lot, but you seem to handle it so well."

"I don't have a choice. Anyway, are you *really* applying to the university?"

"Yes, I am."

"I'm happy for you. I thought you would stay here in Ouirgane like the other girls and be a good Muslim woman, as my father used to say."

Salwa chuckled. "I believe you can be a good Muslim woman and still be educated. Don't you think?"

"Absolutely! In fact, I think you can be a good Muslim woman and honor *all* of who you are."

Their eyes locked. A'isha smiled, and Salwa sighed.

"Yes, I suppose you're right. My father says he'll allow me to go to the university only if I stay in Morocco. Will you stay here, or are you going abroad?"

"I'm applying to both. I'll see where I end up."

Salwa placed her hand on A'isha's arm. "I'm so glad we had a chance to talk."

"So am I."

"And you should know that the other girls feel as I do. We all want to forgive and forget—if that's okay with you."

"But who's forgiving who? And what are we supposed to forget?"

Salwa lowered her eyes, "I don't know."

"Well, I do. I don't know if I can forgive, and I *definitely* won't forget."

"A'isha, I'm just saying it would be nice for you to join us for lunch tomorrow. You don't need to sit off by yourself anymore. I don't know how the adults are treating you, but your friends—"

"*My friends?* I once thought I had friends. And as for the adults, they have been nicer to me than my peers, but that's only because they like my beadwork and wreaths, and I'm the only one in the village who does that type of work. They're just as phony and hypocritical as my peers, but I don't mind. I'm making money!"

"Or maybe they're treating you kindly because they have come to their senses, too."

"Ha! I doubt it."

"People may not like you for who you are, A'isha, but I know they respect and admire you. And anyway, what's more important: to be liked or respected?"

"I have grappled with that question for a long time."

"Me too. Well, I need to get home before my father comes looking for me. I'll see you tomorrow."

"Yes, you will."

A'isha watched her walk down the winding path dotted with clay abodes and wandering roosters. "Don't forget to study," she called out. "The exam is going to be difficult."

Salwa spun around. "Yes, but I know you will get a high score. You always do, the smart girl you are. See you tomorrow!"

***

A'isha spent her senior year doing exactly that: studying for exit exams, sending applications to universities in Morocco and abroad, and tending to the shop—beading abayas and crafting wreaths to sell to al-Majid and the locals. Each month, she would visit Amir's wife to deliver half of the profit from the abayas and chadors she had sold. With her half and the money she made from the sale of her wreaths, she was able to support herself and save as much as she could for "wherever I end up," which she often mumbled after she counted her money, wrapped it in her grandmother's chador, and stashed it in her top dresser drawer.

As rumors spread that she had applied to universities abroad, her customers would enter her shop, peruse her merchandise, then ask, "But how could you even *think* about leaving us? Who will mind Amir's shop? Who will bead the abayas?" To which she would respond with a shrug and a smile.

"Hypocrisy reigns!" she yelled, throwing her fist into the air as she and Nasim leaned against her counter, nibbling on chebakia and other pastries he knew she loved.

"But why do you call it hypocrisy? Have you ever considered that people are sincere when they say they don't want you to leave?"

"Sure, they're sincere. They sincerely want me to stay so I can continue to serve their needs and forget about my own. It's not *me* they care about. They're only looking out for themselves. 'Who's going to bead our abayas?'" she mocked in a high-pitched whine, "'Who's going to make our wreaths?' Sometimes I want to yell, 'Make your own wreaths! I'm out of here!'"

She walked to the door and moved her eyes along the stillness of tarp-covered carts, shuttered shops, a lone rooster, and the blaze of a yawning sun. The men were at the mosque for Jumu'ah Khutbah, Friday prayer, and she was delighted to have spent the day quietly beading abayas until Nasim appeared at her door.

She shoved her hands into her pockets and sighed. "The only people in this world who ever cared for me were my jida and Amir, and now they're gone. Not even my parents cared." She shook her head and turned toward Nasim. "These people don't care about me. They only want to use me for their own good. And they think I'm too stupid to understand that. It enrages me, the hypocrisy of people, the duplicity of their words. How can anyone ever trust the intention of another? Everyone is so inauthentic…so insincere."

Nasim extended his hand to her. "You can trust my intention, A'isha." He walked toward her. "If you stay, I promise I will be good to you. I will take care of you."

"But that's not who I am." She searched his face, partially veiled in the sapphire of an evening gloam. "Nasim, I know how you feel about me; you have told me more than once. But the kind of girl you want–the kind you need–is not who I am."

"I don't care that you like girls or that you always wear overalls. I can deal with that. I love you, A'isha."

"But don't you see? It's not only that. My sexuality is not all of who I am. You want a wife who will stay home and cook and clean and live the way we are told women are supposed to live. But that's not who I am. I want to travel the world. I want to learn about different religions. I want to meet people who are different from me. I want to leave these mountains."

"But you are not being fair, A'isha. The village has accepted you. We all love you. Of course, it took some time, but I see how everyone treats you. You are one of us. If you leave Ouirgane, who will you be?"

"The same person I am now—me. I'm glad everyone has decided to treat me kindly, although they still don't accept me for who I am. For so long, no one even looked at me—not my teachers, my friends…not even you."

"But I have apologized for that."

"I don't need your apology, Nasim, nor anyone else's. I'm glad I went through all that rejection because it made me stronger. I learned how to survive, and I became my own protector. And now that I am preparing to leave, everyone decides they're in love with me. Well, I'm not going to—"

"But who's going to take over the shop? What's going to happen to this place?"

"I don't know, and I don't care. I told my father I'm leaving. It's his shop. If he decides to return and take over, that'll be great. But this place is not my responsibility, and I will not allow anyone to make me think it is. I'm going to follow my dreams."

Nasim moved closer to her, wrapped his arms around her waist, and gently placed his lips on hers. This time, she did not resist. He parted her lips with his own and the warmth of his tongue in her mouth made her moan. She could feel the beat of his heart against her breast, and the rise of his manhood pressed between her thighs. Tightening his arms around her, he looked into her eyes as he led her to the rear of the shop and gently laid her on the roll of black organza, where Nabeel once laid Amir. He unclipped the bib of her overalls and locked his eyes into hers as he slid them off. And on his knees, he embraced her body, first with his gaze, and then with his lips. Softly kissing her neck, breasts, belly, and inner thighs. He touched her…there. Her inner folds pulsated, and her hips gently writhed as she watched him lift his tunic and reveal himself. He held her in his arms as he entered her, tenderly, in a way he hadn't with any other girl. "Uhhhmm," they moaned together, in the stillness of the moonlit room. And he moved more deeply into her, introducing her to a place within, hidden and unknown, expanding her awareness of self, connecting her to it. She dug her nails into his hips as the rhythm of his movement quickened with intensity. And as he deepened his touch, he raised, pressing his palms against the black organza, tossing his head back until they moaned together, in the stillness of the moonlit room.

***

"You should know that I have sent word to your father by way of my butcher in Imlil," Abdullah said, anxiously cutting a slice of khobz. "I told him you might be leaving us in just a few months, and that his shop will be abandoned if he does not return."

"*Really?*" she asked, wide-eyed with a gaping smile. "So, what did he say? Have you heard from him?"

"No, I have not. But I know he received my message." He handed A'isha a cup of tea and continued, "Let's not forget that we are still a few months away from your departure. That's *if* you decide to leave. I mean, things can change, eh?"

"Yes, that is true. But I know one thing that won't change."

"A'isha, have you *really* thought about what you are doing?"

"Of course, I have. I've always said I would leave Ouirgane. Amir knew that."

"Yes, but that was then. We need you to—"

"Abdullah, there is nothing more to discuss." She hopped off the stool. "Thank you for feeding me, but I must get back to the shop. I still have seven more abayas to bead before al-Majid's arrival in a few days."

"Does he know of your plan to leave?"

"No, not yet. The last thing I need is another person to try to make me feel guilty. So please, don't tell him."

"If that is your wish," he sighed.

"Yes, it is. Goodbye. I will see you tomorrow."

She sewed the final bead onto a turquoise chador just before nightfall. Yawning, she turned out the light and slammed the door shut. As she walked home, her mother's face flashed across her mind. She recalled the sadness in her mother's eyes as she spoke about her childhood, her sister's death, her father's affair with Hira, and the pain it had caused her family.

"What nerve!" A'isha growled. "How could that woman agree to shroud my grandmother? What a hypocrite!" She pounded her feet into the earth along the river's edge, and when she approached the path that leads to Hira's home, she stood at the crossroad. She looked uphill at her own home, then down the canopied path toward Hira's home. She decided to give Hira a visit.

Stomping her way under a canopy of trees, she curled and uncurled her fingers, recalling the conversation she once had with Hira. "I didn't *steal* your grandfather away from his family. He made a choice. I'm not responsible for his decision, he is." *Uggh!* A'isha thought. *You did steal my grandfather away from my family!* She paused at the door, panting. As she lifted her fist, she heard her grandmother's voice. *A'isha, you could not have buried me without Hira's help. You needed her, and she was there. In life, you must take the bitter with the sweet, and you must learn how to forgive.* She gasped and spun around. "Grandmother where are you?" she called out, searching, looking beyond the trees. And as she stood at Hira's door, the scent of cinnamon filled the cool evening air. She smiled, then sighed and turned away. Walking beneath the canopy of trees, she whispered, "But how do I do that, my jida? How do I forgive those who have hurt me?"

***

Her teacher walked the aisles of her classroom, distributing the exam. When she approached A'isha, she tossed it onto her desk, glared at her, and said, "You must go to the director's office. She has mail for you."

"May I go now?"

"No, only after you have completed your exam."

You inconsiderate fool, A'isha thought. *Now that you have distracted me with this information, I'll try to do my best with this exam.* She hurried through each question without recalculating her answers and grinned at her teacher as she handed her the test.

"You're finished so soon?" She scowled.

"What can I say? It was easy. May I go now?"

Sitting on a bench outside the office, she bit down on her lip as she opened the first of three envelopes the headmaster had given her. Sweat trickled down her back and her heart pounded as she read the first letter, then placed it on the bench with a smirk.

383

She slid her thumb along the seal of the second envelope, ignoring the sting of its edge against her flesh and the bead of blood it produced. She read the letter, placed it on the bench, then picked it up and read it again. Her smirk grew into a smile, and she slammed it atop the first letter, then she opened the third. Slowly rising to her feet, she grabbed the first two letters, threw her hands into the air, and yelled, "I did it! I did it!" Her classmates snapped their heads up from their exams, listening to her shriek, "I am free!" and bolt out the front door.

She ran down the road, leaving swirls of arid soil in her wake, and did not stop until she arrived at Nasim's shop. She swung open the door and hollered, "I have great news! I have been accepted into three universities!" She jumped up and down and spun around, waving the letters above her head.

Nasim eased off the ladder, brushing carpet fiber off his hands. "Well, are you going to tell me which ones," he snapped, "or do you want me to guess?"

She grabbed him, hugged him tightly, and waited for him to embrace her. She stepped back.

"Are you not happy for me?"

"Should I be?"

Her joy deflated into an anxious guilt, and then resentment. "I shouldn't have come here. This was a mistake. I will leave."

"Maybe you should," he said, turning away and grabbing a stack of prayer rugs.

She ran across the road, entered her shop, and slammed the door shut. Easing onto the roll of black organza, she lowered her face into her palms and wept.

***

As her departure date drew near, she stopped ordering fabric and beads and used her stock to make as many abayas and wreaths as she could.

"This news is bittersweet," Al-Majid sighed. "You leave in just two weeks, you say?"

A'isha nodded.

"Well, I am happy for you, but I'm also sad to see you leave Ouirgane. I have enjoyed doing business with you, A'isha. You are quite the entrepreneur. If you should ever return and open a business of your own, you know where to find me."

"Thank you, sir. I have learned a lot from you."

"As I have from you."

The following week, she arrived at Abdullah's shop with two caged chickens, and with Ali.

"Here they are," she said, placing the cage on the counter. "I know you will take good care of them."

Abdullah tossed his dishcloth into the sink. "Of course, I will," he said, peering at the chickens.

She kneeled and wrapped her arms around Ali's neck. Her eyes filled with tears. "He will be good to you," she whispered. He pressed his cold nose against her neck and released a wilted, "Maaa."

"I will miss you, Ali. You have been my friend and my protector. I will always love you."

She rose to her feet, wiping her tears. "Please take good care of him."

"Of course, A'isha. I promise. And you must return to visit."

"I will, and until I do I will write to you. Please remember to check on my house. And if you place fresh wildflowers at my jida's grave, I will be forever grateful."

"You have my promise." He took her hands into his and smiled. "I am proud of the young woman you have become. You have shown everyone in this village what it means to have integrity, and how to honor your truth. Stay close to Allah, and He will remain close to you. And know that you are never alone. Your jida will always be by your side, and you will always be in my prayers." He reached for a package on the counter. "Here, this is for you." He placed the gift in her hands and wrapped his hands around hers. "It is said that as a tree grows its branches, it never forgets the importance of its roots. May you never forget yours, A'isha."

"Thank you…what is it?"

"It is my personal copy of the Qur'an."

She nodded, unable to speak. Tilting her head, she gazed at him with a faint smile, then hugged him tightly. She knelt and wrapped her arms around Ali and kissed his head one last time, then rose to her feet, crossed the threshold, and closed the door. And as she walked the arid amber road toward her shop, she clutched the Qur'an and absorbed the rhythm of Ouirgane, opening a space for it within her heart. She watched the children run downhill, playing dinifri; and nodded at the men donning pushed-back kufis and dusty tunics, smoking cigarettes, and sitting languidly upon crates at the doorway to their shops. She peered at the women clutching children and cradling babies as they watched her with veiled eyes, muted mouths, and a hidden heart. And she looked into Nasim's darkened room, hoping he had put his absence to an end, so that she may say goodbye.

And in her shop, she walked to each corner, brushing her hand across the counter, touching rolls of fabric, and the black organza. At her workbench, she sat for one last time, moving her eyes about the room. "Be careful, Baba," she could hear herself say, recalling her fear that the nail between his teeth might take him away. And she could hear Amir say, "Hold the bead against the fabric like so." And her love for him tugged at her heart. "Ah, you're a quick study," she could hear al-Majid chuckle, and relived the pride she felt at that moment. "So, when will you make more wreaths?" she could hear her patrons demand, and shook her head at their hypocrisy, then grinned at what she now understood. And she exhaled. Rising to her feet with a blossoming smile, she tugged the chain next to the dangling bulb, then crossed the threshold and closed the door.

Tsewang

"In the name of Mahakala, what am I going to do?" Tsewang begged, grabbing the old man's shoulders, "*What will I do?*"

"I suggest the first thing you do is take your hands off me before I kick you in the nuts."

Tsewang released the old man and plopped into a chair. "Uggh!" he moaned, lowering his head into the crook of his arm. He pounded on the desk.

The old man slammed the door shut and spun around. "Child, you must get a hold of yourself! Raise up your head! Why are you so distraught? Why do you act surprised? I told you this happens all the time, that boys such as yourself are used as mules and abandoned to fend for themselves. What made you think this could not happen to you?" He brushed his hand across his gray hair and waddled toward his desk.

Tsewang lifted his head. "Because he cared for me."

"*Cared for you?* How? What made you think so?"

Tsewang looked beyond the old man, as if he were speaking to the tobacco-stained wall. "Because he took me in when I had no place to go. He fed me. He…he brought my coat. He made sure I would be warm. And he said—"

"He said what?!"

"That I would return home in three days. But I have been here for seven and no one has come for me. The owner wants me out of my room, and I have nowhere to go."

"It serves you right!" the old man yelled, opening a bottle of water. He placed it in front of Tsewang. "Every day I see this happen. When will you kids ever learn? And, trust me," he said, shaking his finger at Tsewang, "I have seen far worse than this."

Tsewang rubbed his eyes with the sleeve of his kasaya and looked at the old man.

"That's right. You should consider yourself lucky that the police haven't come looking for you. So many boys are locked up in prison for doing this sort of thing."

"The *police*?" Tsewang winced.

"Yes, that's right, the police! Have they come looking for you, yet?"

"N-no. What do you mean?"

The man eased into his chair. "If seven days have passed without a knock on your door, then you may be in the clear— abandoned in a foreign country, but still free, I suppose."

Tsewang lifted the bottle of water to his lips and gulped until it was empty.

"A little thirsty, I see. Would you like another?"

"No thank you, sir. Those boys, the ones who have been abandoned here…how do they…where do they live?"

"I told you already. It's not a pretty life. Not the kind you would want for yourself. And from the look of you, you wouldn't survive a minute of it."

"Where are they, those boys?"

"All over, but mostly in the bars and brothels."

"Brothels? What's that?"

"You see, I can tell you're naïve. That kasaya says it all. A brothel is a place people go to for sex, and there are many. Sounds like something you might want to do?"

"In the name of Buddha, I could never do such a thing. I'd be selling my soul."

"Among other parts of you."

"I still have some money. I guess I can ask the owner if he would allow me to stay for another night, until I find my way out. Until I'm able to return to Bhutan."

"Is there anyone back home you can call?"

No," he replied, shaking his head. Then his eyes lit up. He slammed his hand on the desk and jumped to his feet. "Of course, yes! Why hadn't I thought of that?"

"Well, who would that be?"

"I could call Taku—"

"Who?"

"Takum! I could…" He frowned and eased back into the chair. "Well, maybe I can't call him. He works for the same man. He would never put his job in jeopardy for me."

"What about your Rinpoche? Can't you call him?"

He bit down on his lip. "No, I cannot. Maybe if I had apologized to him…"

"Apologized?"

Tsewang sighed, "It's a long story, sir."

The man looked at his watch and stood up. "Well, while you figure out who you can call, I'm going to get some lunch. Later today, I will go next door and speak to the owner of the hostel. He and I are good friends. I'll explain your situation to him. I'm sure he'll give us time to work something out."

"*Really?* You will do that for me?"

"No, I'm telling a joke," he said dryly. "Of course, I'll do that. I know a good kid when I see one, and I want to help you."

Tsewang stood up. "Are you sure, sir? That's what Chimé once said to me."

"Who? Listen, given what has happened to you, I can understand your reluctance to trust me. One of the greatest challenges in life is knowing who to trust." He opened the door. "But it's really quite simple to figure out who is trustworthy, and who is not."

"Is it? How?"

"All you have to do is silence your mind and listen to your heart. I'm sure you learned about that at the monastery. Anyway, I will see you tomorrow."

"Yes, thank you, sir. I will see you tomorrow."

Tsewang spent the day roaming the streets of New Delhi-- wandering alleyways, tiptoeing around human waste, ignoring the calls of men standing in doorways. On the main road, between tilted carts stacked with mangoes and okra, men and women stood before a shrine, chanting and bowing with praying hands; lighting candles and sticks of Nag Champa in devotion to Shiva, while flea-infested donkeys and smoke-spewing scooters squeezed by. Tsewang nudged his way to the front of the crowd and fished a coin from his pocket. He dropped it into the copper canaster, lit a white candle, closed his eyes, and bowed his head.

"My loving Mahakala, Deity of Protection," he said, as waves of gathering believers shoved him about. "I know you are aware of the trouble I am in. I ask that you lead me out of this mess. And if you do, I will return to the monastery, to the life I once lived. Please keep me in your care. Namaste." He opened his eyes, slapped a child's hand out of his pocket, then pried himself away from the crowd.

****

Through the large windowpane that announced in gold lettering, "Silk Suits In One Day," Tsewang cupped his eyes and peered into the old man's shop. A ray of early morning sun stretched across the cluttered room, trapping a tangerine funnel of dust in midair. In a far corner, spools of thread were scattered upon a table adjacent to a black sewing machine with a large, wrought iron foot pedal, and strips of fabric were discarded onto the green linoleum floor. Next to a tall cabinet, crumpled paper and empty water bottles filled a trashcan to the rim, and in the middle of it all, the old man sat with his elbows propped upon his antique oak desk, between stacks of invoices and scraps of paper scattered and scribbled with notes.

Tsewang entered the shop. "Good Morning, sir."

"Good Morning, lad!" the old man said, returning the phone to its cradle. "You're in luck. I spoke to the owner last night, and he has agreed to let you stay in your room. He said you are a quiet, decent resident, and you have caused no trouble at all. But of course, you will have to pay for your stay."

"And how will I do that? I'm already out of money. I haven't eaten in two days."

"I can tell. You have lost quite a bit of weight since we met. You keep that up and the fishermen will snatch you up, toss you into their boat, and use you as an oar. You must eat." He gestured toward the chair. "Sit down."

Tsewang kept his eyes on the old man as he opened a bottle of water and handed it to him.

"So, tell me, is there anyone back home you could call?"

The faces of Tadashi, Dabir, and Kasim flashed across his mind. Shame surged through him and forced his hand onto his mala beads. He shook his head. "No, there is no one I can call."

"Very well. So, here's my suggestion: I can use some help around here. My grandson is returning to the university in a few weeks. You would think he's going to another country. The university is just a bus ride away, but he has told me he does not have time to help me anymore." He removed his eyeglasses and rubbed his eyes. "Anyway, I cannot manage this place on my own."

Tsewang moved to the edge of his seat. "Are you saying I can work for you? *For money*?"

"No, for carrots and a bucket of water. Of course, for money! I make suits for very wealthy people, and when I tell them their garments will be ready by a certain date, they expect me to deliver."

"But I don't know how to sew. How can I help you?"

"I'm not hiring you to sew. *I* will do the sewing. But what I need is someone who will clean up after me. Someone who will take care of the place—open the mail, answer the phone, run errands—that kind of stuff." He swiveled around in his chair. "Look at this place! Not even I want to come in here. And you've seen the bathroom."

"Yes, I have. When can I start?"

"The day is young, how about now?"

Tsewang jumped to his feet. "Yes! Tell me what needs to be done, and I will do it!"

"But don't you want to know how much I will pay you?"

"I'm sure you will be fair with me. But yes, tell me."

The old man laughed. "Oh, so you *do* trust people. Or maybe you are just naïve."

"Certainly, I am naïve. I have proven that to myself. But I have also taken your advice. I have been listening to you with my heart, and it tells me I should give you a chance."

"Ah, you're a quick study!" he smiled, and sipped his water. "So, I am willing to pay for your room, in addition to thirty rupees a week. That should be enough for you to eat and save money to return home. Does that sound fair to you?"

"Yes, it does!" Tsewang gushed, extending his hand the way he had seen Chimé extend his. "It's a deal, sir. Thank you!"

"Very well! The broom is behind that door. Let's get to work."

The man shuffled his way to the rear of the shop and flipped the switch on his sewing machine. Tsewang grinned at the soothing hum of its motor as he swept shavings of fabric and thread into a pile, pausing long enough to touch his mala beads and whisper, "Thank you, Mahakala. Thank you for placing this man on my path."

***

The knock on his door startled him out of his sleep. He sat erect, pulling the sheet under his chin. "Who…who is there?" he called out. *Could the police be looking for me now, after these many weeks?* He listened to the shove and jiggle of a key into the lock and to the doorknob twisting. "Who is there!" he hissed, jumping out of bed and into his kasaya. His hands trembled as he tightened the sash. He tiptoed toward the door. "Chimé? Chimé is that you?"

"No, I believe this is my room," a soft voice whispered. "My key is stuck."

Tsewang eased the door open. Wide-eyed, he asked, "Who are you?" He brushed his hand across the fuzz on his scalp, wishing he had gone to the barber as he had planned.

The young woman raised her head. "My key…it's stuck."

"Oh, allow me to help."

He yanked the key out of the lock and placed it in her palm.

"Thank you. I believe this is my room."

"Only if we are to share it," he smiled.

She glanced at the paper in her sweaty hand. "But it says Room 7."

"Then you are my neighbor, this is Room 8. Allow me to help you with your luggage."

He carried the suitcase to the door next to his. "Here, this is your room."

The young woman eased the key into the lock and whispered, "Please, do not get stuck." It clicked open. "Thank you," she said, taking her luggage. "I apologize for awakening you at this late hour."

"No need to apologize. I'm delighted it was you at my door and not…" He glanced at the staircase. "Anyway, my name is Tsewang. I am from the Kingdom of Bhutan. May I ask, who are you?"

"My name is A'isha. I am from Ouirgane. From the High Atlas Mountains of Morocco."

"Morocco, you say? You have traveled a great distance. What brings you to India?"

"It's a long story," she sighed.

"Yes, I understand," he said, gazing at her, touched by her beauty. "We all have a story to tell; I certainly have my own. Maybe one day you will tell me yours."

"Yes, maybe I will," she blushed, adjusting her hijab.

"And I look forward to hearing all about it. Well, goodnight, A'isha," he bowed with a wide grin. "And welcome to India."

"Thank you, Tsewang," A'isha smiled, and closed her door.

Acknowledgments

Behind **Jagged Edges of Silhouette Trees** is the product of a seven-year commitment to my passion, storytelling. The support and encouragement from the following people helped me bring it to fruition. It is with deep appreciation that I acknowledge: Samir, my guide and teacher during and after my travel across Morocco; Nuwang and Uddi, my guide and driver who introduced me to their beautiful country, the Kingdom of Bhutan; Geeta Tewari, whose editorial assistance was invaluable; my friend, Tira, who steadfastly insisted I was writing a bestseller; my two sisters, Esperanza and Lisa, who served as my almost-unbiased Beta Readers; my father, who has been my lifelong cheerleader; my son, Frankie, whose belief in me means more to me than he will ever know; to my mother and grandmother, whom I can only hope I have made proud; and to the Ancestors, who have cleared the path upon which we walk.

~Stacy